Chosen

Chosen

AN AUTOBIOGRAPHY

Michele Guinness

MONARCH
BOOKS

Published by
Lion Hudson Limited
Wilkinson House, Jordan Hill Business Park
Banbury Road, Oxford OX2 8DR, England

www.lionhudson.com

ISBN: 978-0-8572-1920-6
e-ISBN: 978-0-8572-1921-3

First edition 2008
Second edition 2018

Acknowledgments
Unless otherwise stated, Scripture quotations are taken from the
Holy Bible, New International Version, © 1973, 1978, 1984 by
the International Bible Society. Used by permission of Hodder &
Stoughton Ltd. All rights reserved.
p. 342: Quote from "Death of Flowers" from *Selected Poems* by
Edith Joy Scovell. Used by permission of Carcanet Press Limited.
p. 350: (World excluding USA) Excerpt from "Little Gidding"
from *Four Quartets* by T. S. Eliot. Used by permission of Faber
and Faber Ltd. (USA) Excerpt from "Little Gidding" from FOUR
QUARTETS by T. S. Eliot. Copyright 1942 by T. S. Eliot. Copyright
© renewed 1970 by Esme Valerie Eliot. Reprinted by permission
of Houghton Mifflin Harcourt Publishing Company. All rights
reserved.

A catalogue record for this book is available from the British Library

Printed and bound in the UK, September 2018, LH26

In Memory of Herald Gilbert
And Paul and Jean Guinness

Contents

Acknowledgments

Over the years many wonderful friends have fed and enriched me with the wealth of their wisdom, and may, or may not, be pleased to see it regurgitated here – if they recognize it in this disguise.

A particular thanks to the churches who have had the dubious pleasure of our ministry, and have given us a great deal more than we could ever have given them. I hope I have done your love and encouragement justice.

Thanks to Tony Collins at Monarch for encouraging me to rewrite my autobiography – and taking the risk of publishing it.

Thanks (what else?) to my long-suffering relatives, my mother, late stepfather, brother and sister-in-law for being such wonderful fall guys, and for nourishing me with all that's best in Jewish warmth, wisdom and laughter. I wish my father had been alive to read the book. How he would have enjoyed himself.

Thanks to my children, whose financial needs and hearty appetites made writing necessary – and still do, and who interrupted the muse at regular, two-minute intervals for advice and a cuddle – and still do (though such is their size that I sit on their knees these days). How can I complain about the aggravation, when they also provide such a vital source of inspiration?

And special thanks to that wise critic and partner, my lovely husband, who set me on the trail in search of my Jewish roots, has shared the adventure with me into our more mature years, and complains very little about having the intimate details of his private life made public – all things considered.

Glossary of Hebrew Terms

Festivals

Rosh Hashanah	Jewish New Year (usually in September)
Yom Kippur	The Day of Atonement (a week after the New Year)
Sukkot	The Feast of Booths or Tabernacles (a week after Yom Kippur)
Pesach	The Passover
Purim	The Feast of Esther (March)
Shavuot	Pentecost (The Feast of Weeks)
Hanukkah	The Festival of Lights (December)
Adonai	The Lord – a very holy name for God
Afikomen	Middle piece of three matzos used by leader in Passover service and symbolic of Passover lamb
Bar Mitzvah	Lit. 'blessing of the son', the coming of age of a Jewish boy at thirteen
Bat Mitzvah	Lit. 'blessing of a daughter', the coming of age of a Jewish girl at twelve
Beth Din	The court of rules
Bimah	Raised platform at the front of the synagogue
Charoset	A mixture of apples, wine and walnuts eaten at Passover as a symbol of the mud that held the bricks together in Egypt

Chasid	A very orthodox Jew
Cheder	Hebrew classes
Chollah	The plaited Sabbath loaf
Chuppah	The bridal canopy
Cohanim	The priestly line
Davening	Swaying and praying
Etrog	A citrus fruit held at the feast of Sukkot
Gefilte fish	Chopped fish balls
Goldene Medina	The golden (promised) land
Goyim	Gentiles
Grebens	Fried bits of chicken skin
Haggadah	Lit. 'The telling', the Passover service book
Halachah	Lit. 'The progess or journey', the rules of Judaism passed down by word of mouth that describe the proper path through life
Ha'shem	The 'Name', a common word used when speaking about God
Helzel	Savoury stuffed chicken intestine
Jahrzeit	Annual commemoration of a dead relative
Kaddish	Prayers in memory of the dead
Kiddush	The traditional Friday evening Sabbath prayers
Kiddushim	Marriage, lit. 'holies'
Kneidlach	Matza meal dumplings
Kosher	Prepared according to the dietary rules
Landsleit	A relative

Lulav	Threefold branch waved in synagogue at feast of Sukkot
Ma'erev	Evening prayer
Maccabi	Jewish youth movement
Matzo	Unleavened bread
Minyan	Ten men needed before Jewish prayers can be said publicly
Schmaltz	Chicken fat
Schmatters	Tatters, or cheap clothes
Schochet	The ritual slaughterer
Schul	The synagogue
Seder	Lit. 'The Service', Passover service, usually said in the home
Shabbat	Sabbath
Shema	The prayer said by every Jew morning and evening. Lit. 'Hear'
Sheitel	The wig worn by orthodox Jewish women
Shiva	Seven days of official mourning after a bereavement
Siddur	The Jewish prayer book
Shofar	The ram's horn
Simcha	A party
Tsimmes	A sweet, one-pot stew
Yiddishkeit	A Jewish way of life

Introduction

*I don't think anyone should write their autobiography
until after they're dead.*

Samuel Goldwyn, movie maker

*E*veryone has a story, an autobiography, inside them. To get the chance to write it and share it once is an immense privilege. To do it twice may seem a tad self-indulgent. After all, there are thousands of people still alive, not to mention the ones who are not, who have been far more altruistic, entrepreneurial and successful, have made a far greater contribution to the world and are much more deserving of having their deeds recorded for posterity. I was just little 'Miss Nobody from Nowhere', and still am – a Jewish girl who set off on an adventure that involved being married to a vicar and the Church of England too. Reeling from the shock of it, and from the feeling that the essential person I was would simply be swept away by the powerful force of church culture if I didn't swim for my life, I hung on to who I was. It is that passion for authenticity in the face of expectations and the pressure to conform that has always driven me to record my experiences, in the hope that they may resonate in other lives, stirring up the courage that will make uniqueness a God-given gift to be welcomed, not feared.

I knew when I wrote it, almost thirty years ago, that I had written *Child of the Covenant* too soon, and would one day want to write it again. It's not that the basic facts didn't happen or were inaccurate. It's just that over the years the kaleidoscope kept turning and what seemed important then no longer seems so today, and what I left out then now has immense significance in the light of the way my life has turned out. Distance changes the perspective. I thought I had resolved the culture shock that pursued me through *Promised Land* and *A Little Kosher Seasoning*, that I had become a fully assimilated, totally *kosher* church member, but that was naive. Resolution has come slowly and sometimes painfully, through living with that sense of alienation, embracing it and learning to use it constructively, accepting that being Jewish, and in a foreign environment at that, I'll always be a bit of an objective observer, an outsider, a commentator, what my husband affectionately calls, 'a bump on a log'. For someone with a career in journalism it has actually been immensely useful.

Not only that, but whether I like it or not, thirty-five years is almost two generations, and now, much sooner than I ever imagined, I can set my story in a historical context. The rigid class distinctions of the post-war years that defined my early childhood have vanished. So have the swinging, snogging, scary sixties of my teeny-bop, university era. Now, in the light of rapid advances in technology and communications, and a different world for women, they would seem like quaint timepieces. Anyone under the age of thirty would need some explanation of how we lived in those dim, distant days.

When I reread *Child of the Covenant* I realized it couldn't simply be reprinted, even in an updated form. Hindsight is just too instructive and illuminating a companion. So even though I'm not dead enough yet to follow Sam Goldwyn's excellent advice, I couldn't resist the urge to go back to the writer's equivalent of a drawing board and start the story all over again. So now, if you're sitting comfortably...

Chapter 1

Of Pedigrees, Peers and Poverty

I do love a pedigree. It conveys a sense of history, of continuity, even of immortality. My husband's, presented to me on the occasion of our engagement, is most impressive. He can boast of brewers, bankers and peers of the realm in his family tree – which is both daunting and appealing if there are none in yours – at least, none that you know of.

I could of course say that Abraham the Patriarch was my 'goodness-knows-how-many-great-great-grandfather', but that was an awfully long time ago, and he was a rootless, homeless nomad – the original wandering Jew.

'Where do you come from originally?' people say to me.

'Gateshead,' I tell them.

They look bewildered.

'In the North-East of England?'

'Yes, but when did you arrive from Israel?'

Israel! I didn't even visit Israel until I'd kicked forty. My only knowledge of foreign parts was courtesy of package tours to the Costa del Sol. I want to wave my passport under their noses.

I am the third generation to be born on UK soil. And even if I don't look the classic English rose I'm as British as baked beans on toast. That was the aspiration that sustained my great-grandparents as they fled the cruel pogroms of Eastern Europe, she with her one set of diamond earrings wrapped in an old pair of stockings, hidden among her meagre belongings. They were actually Russian diamonds – marquesite – worth little in financial terms, but the only treasure she had. Securely insinuated into the British middle classes, I am their dream come true – at least, I would have been, had not things turned out rather differently from what they might have expected.

I was twelve years old when my maternal great-grandparents died, within months of each other. It must have been an event of some significance, as my relatives wept, argued and fought a great deal more than usual. It didn't bother me as I hardly knew them. I had seen them regularly enough – around once a fortnight – but their offspring were far too numerous and one child too much like another to warrant individual attention. I'm not sure they even remembered whose child I was.

'Hello, my pet,' great-grandmother would say to me, as she did to all the little people in the family, in a strange Geordie accent with foreign undertones, nipping a slice of my cheek between her bony fingers and squeezing hard until it brought tears to my eyes. It was the only affection I remember – and I could have well done without it.

Visits to their dark, melancholy house in leafy Jesmond, only two miles from the centre of Newcastle, with its extraordinary smell of damp, lavender and fried fish, was always more of an endurance test than a pleasure. In twelve years I never saw any of it other than the dismal oak-panelled hallway and cramped, old-fashioned kitchen. I couldn't imagine them ever going to bed. Great-grandfather never moved from his fireside armchair. His black skullcap perched on his wizened, little polished apple of a head, he would mutter to himself in Hebrew, plunging the piece of lemon in his tea up and down in rhythmical accompaniment to his prayers.

Marion, their ancient, live-in housekeeper-turned-companion, with jowls like a bulldog and hair blanched and yellowed like hay, is bent over the range, stirring some concoction in a huge copper pot. She's been with them since she first went into service – a local girl from Jarrow, but now, by osmosis, almost as Jewish as they are. She heaves herself up, shuffles across the room in pinny and slippers, and without any acknowledgment, deposits her offering on the table, where great-grandmother is having a secretive cackle with one of her many daughters, my glamorous great-aunts.

'Private!' my mother would say to me before I could ask. 'Your great-grandmother's humour has always thrived on the basics of life.' I hadn't a clue what she meant. Not even at the funeral when, oblivious of the range and receptive power of children's ears, my grandmother, chortling as she reminisces with sisters and nieces, reminds them of the time when Aunt Annie, in the very early stages of pregnancy, had sworn their mother to secrecy. It appeared that my great-grandmother had forgotten her promise and announced to a large assembled family gathering, 'Guess who's pregnant?' Her children, all adult with burgeoning families, looked at her in anticipation, and in that moment she remembered she wasn't supposed to say, and redeeming the situation as best she knew how, said, 'I am.'

'You!' they had all responded with horror.

'And what's wrong with me?' she countered tartly, more than a little put out, 'Your father's not away at the front.'

I was fifteen when I finally understood, and it still didn't seem funny – then.

'So eat already,' she would say, taking a large serving spoon to the casserole in front of her, pushing back the unruly wisps of white hair that escaped from her bun.

'But great-grandma, I've already eaten. I'm not hungry.'

'You want to grow into a big girl, don't you?'

'Not too big,' my mother would interject. Her enormous size after she had given birth to me was a family proverb, a warning to all of the dangers of Jewish cooking.

'Eat a bit,' my mother would whisper, 'then put the rest over there.' She pointed to a pile of dirty plates at the end of the table. Marion would follow her gaze, then, sighing and unsmiling, remove them silently to the sink. I never heard her say anything except, 'Mmmmmm' in reply to a question.

It is a sad irony that the young are too young to appreciate their ancestors' history – until it's too late. Buried in that dark, dank house, behind the shrivelled facade of the old pair and their aged carer, were adventures untold, unrecorded, that went with them to the grave. Long after they were gone, when I spent occasional weekends with my grandmother, I was old enough to think of them as people, and wonder.

One night, long after everyone else in the house had gone to bed, I saw Gran, in her negligee and curling pins, creep into the kitchen for a last cigarette. I followed her, and while she sat warming her bony, arthritic hands around a hot cup of tea, quizzed her about her parents.

'They came from Lithuania,' she said, flicking ash into the saucer and watching it disintegrate into the tea slops.

'Where?'

'It's part of Russia now.'

'Why did they come here?'

'They wanted to make a living. Like all Jews, they wanted to live in safety, free from anti-semitism.'

'And they couldn't in Russia?'

'The Tzar wasn't fond of Jews.'

'The Tzar as in *Nicolas and Alexandra*? A baddie?'

'No, just weak. The country was in a financial mess. The poor were starving. A recipe for revolution. The Jews made a useful scapegoat. They always do. The Tzar allowed his Cossack soldiers to ride roughshod over Jewish villages and settlements – *shtetls* as they were called – looting, pillaging, burning and killing as they went. You were lucky to survive, let alone build a future for your children.'

'*Fiddler on the Roof* then?'

Hollywood was my historical guide and instructor in those days.

Gran looked up, but not at me, with an expression of admiration on her face that I had never seen before. What approbation she ever showed was usually reserved for someone much closer to home.

'I was the most beautiful girl in Newcastle,' she would announce, regularly, as we grew up.

'And the most modest,' my sister-in-law would whisper with amusement years later, with the fresh insights that outsiders always bring into a family.

I think my grandmother probably had been rather lovely, with her dainty chin, luminous, china blue eyes and waspish waist. When I was ten I asked her if she would leave me her chiffon party dresses and hooped petticoat in her will. Since she was only fifty-two at the time she found it highly entertaining. The problem was that no one in her orbit – certainly no daughter or granddaughter – could live up to such a paragon of gorgeousness, and it left my rounder mother and me feeling rather inadequate. Even our upright and very proper dentist, she claimed, had been in love with her all his life. His drab and dumpy wife was certainly no competition for my stylish granny, but the thought of it made fillings even more of an ordeal.

I realized, to my surprise, from the way she spoke of him that night, that her father, the skeletal, little old man in the armchair, had been an object of her reverence and love – a real character, a fearless adventurer and charmer. He had set off to South Africa to dig for diamonds – and made enough money to buy a new life. He could have stayed on in South Africa. Many Jews did. But he thought the life too tough for the family he planned to have, and decided on England instead. He arrived without a penny in his pocket. The overcrowded boat offloaded its cargo of immigrants on the Tyne Quay in Newcastle. 'Name?' shouted some customs official. Alexander looked around at his fellow compatriots – all equally bewildered. None of them spoke any English. He presumed his surname was wanted, and gave it, but the official looked blank. Who in Tyneside can spell in Russian? English is hard enough. How many times would he have to repeat it, spell it and what was it worth now anyway? He looked around for inspiration. A man was selling fish from a barrow on the quay. Alexander pointed to a pile of debris left behind by the filleting.

'Fish skin?' the official queried.

He nodded.

'Fishkin, it is then,' agreed the official, relieved to have something intelligible to write in his ledger.

And that, apparently, was how my great-grandfather Fishkin got his name. No child likes having a fishy name in the family. I wished he'd known then what an embarrassment it would be to successive generations.

He set off into his new life with something far more valuable than money in his pocket – a piece of paper that had on it the address of another Jewish family already living in the area – a *landsleit* from the homeland, a distant relative. He was not to know whether they were in any position to offer him assistance – a bed, employment, introductions, a loan, but his luck hadn't run out. It happened to be the address of the local *schochet*, or ritual slaughterer, a man of learning and standing in the small, new community. Here was someone who could teach him English, and provide him with a dowry that would help start a business, for there were several marriageable daughters in the family. From the first it was Kitty who caught his eye, Kitty with her auburn hair and extraordinary violet eyes. But Kitty was the youngest sister, and in those days custom dictated that the elder daughters be married off first.

'So once he had declared his passion, it was only courtesy to marry your great-grandma,' Gran said with a chuckle.

I couldn't conceive of a marriage without love, and said so. It certainly explained the fiery exchanges between them, that I had interpreted as their foreign ways. Whatever Yiddish I learned from them was largely unrepeatable in polite company.

Gran laughed. 'Don't judge on face value. Their quarrels kept their minds alert, fighting gave them something to live for. Besides, they produced eight children and shared a bed to the end. That must say something.'

Gran stubbed out her cigarette and was about to get up.

'And what happened to Kitty?'

She sat back on her chair. 'Kitty was courted by a count. At least, that's what he said he was. The family thought it a great match, but they were deceived. He turned out to be a worthless charlatan. He abandoned her during each of her five pregnancies. She bore him four sons, then died giving birth to a daughter. I vividly remember the day the letter arrived telling us of her death. Father took it with him into his study and laid it on his desk. I crept in a few moments later. He had his head in his hands and was weeping bitterly. I didn't know Mother was behind me. She never forgave him for that.'

His adopted country did not fail my great-grandfather Fishkin. Like many of his kinsmen he made his fortune in the rag trade. The new industrial magnates of Newcastle liked to revolve around the old land-owning gentry of Northumberland – the Percys and Lambtons – with their shooting parties and hunt balls, creating in their wives and daughters a demand for high fashion that parroted London. And before long there was a separate, but equally fashionably exigent, set of Jewish nouveaux riches. Well may the British have allowed the Jews to live in safety and prosper in their country, but it was a long time before they would be allowed to join the upper echelons of society at their golf or tennis clubs. So Jews sniffed at their snobbery and their dress sense, and acquired a taste for show, the more expensive and lavish the better.

On a Saturday evening, when the sun had set and the Sabbath had seen itself out for another week, the doors of the vast mansion Alec Fishkin acquired for his burgeoning family were flung open and Jewish youngsters came from all over the area to eat and dance. After all, he had six daughters to marry off. Festivities always ended at midnight on the dot, when the pianist was issued with the command to 'play God save the king'. One night, my grandmother, too young to attend at that time, was spying through the keyhole. A game of forfeits was underway and a young woman was instructed to kiss the handsomest man in the room. A tall, striking young man stepped forward.

'That's me I believe, since I'm the handsomest man in the room.'

It was young Abe Davis, son of Moshe Davis and Sons, successful furniture manufacturers in Sunderland. Morris, as his workforce affectionately called him, had been a master cabinetmaker with a flair for business and the easy-going ways of a working man. He never forgot his humble origins in Eastern Europe, and always worked alongside the men on the factory floor. It closed for both Christian and Jewish holidays – a bonus as far as the men were concerned. 'Ha'way, Mo,' they called at lunch-break, 'Coming for a pint or two?' And he was always the first to the door. It took four sons to equal his charisma and manage the business, the men, the accounts and the sales, in that order. Being the second son, Abe escaped the responsibility for sales, which was just as well. Being colour blind, the beauties of Dralon velour suites were something of a mystery to him.

Gran drew a breath and pressed her eye as closely to the hole to get as good a look at the upstart as she could.

'He is the best looking man here,' she had to admit. 'I'll have him and bring him down a peg or two.'

She did exactly that, but his philandering was easier to curb than his gambling. She never managed to control his many 'little flutters' on the horses, or prevent the weekly evening at the dogs. The latter was the family's best kept secret – until I revealed all in an essay for my primary school teacher.

'Mother's own experience of marriage made her a stickler about one thing,' Gran confided, on another of our late night encounters in the kitchen. The lateness of the hour, the stillness of the house and a cup of tea that slipped down like treacle always had a strangely liberating effect on her tongue. 'Any marriage could be made to work, whatever the circumstances.'

She paused, the steaming kettle in her hand poised over the teapot, and looked at me as if debating whether she ought to continue or not. Then her face relaxed into a grin.

'You'll never guess what I did on my wedding night?'

I didn't want to hazard a guess.

'I ran away. Well,' she said, taking my silence for ignorance, 'I wasn't having any of that, was I?'

'I thought great-grandma Fishkin was upfront about these things?'

'Oh yes, once she knew that you knew what was what. But she would never have told us the facts of life. It wasn't done.'

She giggled as she poured the water into the pot.

'But she did that night – when she found me on the doorstep.'

'What did she say?'

'She sent me back to Grandpa to get on with it. She told me I was lucky it wasn't an arranged marriage like she'd had.'

'What did you do?'

'What do you think? I had your mother, after all. We always did what she told us. She kept the family together. I still miss her.'

Distractedly, she swirled the tea bags around in the pot with her spoon.

'It's a funny thing – her brothers and sisters were dispersed all over the world – but we never told her when letters came from abroad telling her that one of them had died. We didn't want to upset her. Then one day she described a very vivid dream she had just had. She walked into a room and waiting for her were... and she named every one of her close family we knew were dead. They welcomed her with open arms. She died a few days later. She must be in heaven. She was a good Jew, the best, and a really good woman.'

She poured the steaming liquid into a cup and sipped thoughtfully.

'After she died, when we were sitting *shiva*, Marion came in and asked us whether Miss Weinberg would still get a hot meal every day. "Who's Miss Weinberg?" we all wanted to know. It turned out Miss Weinberg down the road was infirm and bedridden. Mother had taken her a meal every day. That was her Judaism. She lived and breathed it.'

Gran stared wistfully into her cup, as if she were reading the tea leaves.

'I'm not like that. God knows I try. I keep the festivals, I keep the laws... well, most of them,' she said, examining the cigarette she had just taken out of the packet. 'I can't be expected to give these up for twenty-four hours on Sabbath, can I? I keep a strictly *kosher* kitchen, just as she taught me. Have you ever known me mix milk and meat in this house? No, of course not. But somehow, it's not the same. She and Father had a simple faith. They were on familiar terms with the Almighty. They spoke to him like you speak to a friend. But I've never got that close. Life's too complicated. My brother, your uncle Mo, is a clever man. He studies the Torah, the Talmud and other holy Jewish writings, yet he still doesn't help me make sense of it all. Maybe he doesn't think I'm clever enough. Well, none of us ever had their faith and there's an end to it.'

She rinsed her cup and saucer without a word and headed for the door, then stopped and turned around. 'Perhaps,' she said thoughtfully, 'it's something you're given when you specially need it – in all the troubles they had to face. And perhaps now that we've got all this,' she waved vaguely at her spanking new fitted kitchen, 'we don't need it any more. Who knows?'

She shook her head and disappeared. As the door clicked shut behind her the house suddenly seemed very cold and empty.

My father's family were from Latvia. From my perspective there wasn't much of a distinction between Latvia and Lithuania. For those who lived in either country, there was. Latvians were more serious and solid, less mercurial and volatile than their Lithuanian counterparts.

'Ach, she wants to marry a Litvak, a Pole,' Moshe Davis lamented when my mother told her paternal grandfather she wanted to get engaged. And he was an accepting, broad-minded man.

Not all Jews have the Midas touch. My father's family proves it. It wasn't that they didn't aspire to material success or work darn hard to achieve it – but somehow circumstances conspired to thwart them and their dreams always disintegrated in the light of reality.

Over the centuries, whenever the Jews were banished from one country, they would set off for another, and for hundreds of years they kept sailing straight past Britain. The grey-looking land mass with the even greyer skies, sitting beneath a sulphur-yellow pall, didn't seem an attractive proposition – until there was nowhere else in Europe to go.

The really lucky ones acquired a red ticket to the United States. My father's relatives thought they were destined for this *Goldene Medina*, the turn-of-the-century equivalent of a promised or golden land, flowing with milk and honey and money. Throughout the years of oppression, when Jews were not allowed to enter the professions or earn a reasonable living, the vision of a skyline dominated by the mighty Statue of Liberty had sustained them through the bleak, waking moments. But their luck and their ticket ran out at the Newcastle docks. Like many Jews they were tricked into life in the damp and dismal UK.

With my paternal great-grandparents came their four sons, including great-uncle Isaac who worked on the railways in track maintenance and was too deaf to hear the train coming that robbed him of his glorious future. And great-uncle Mark, who went gold prospecting in South Africa, found nothing and lost everything he started out with – except his debts. There were two other brothers and two sisters, including my grandmother Rose. The parents couldn't settle in such a dreary country, and went back to Latvia, leaving their daughters to clean and keep house for their four elder brothers.

Back in Eastern Europe, well into middle age, the parents had two more daughters who grew up hearing all about the elder brothers and sisters in Britain they had never met. Poverty and persecution continued unabated and the old couple decided to try to emigrate again – this time, to the United States. They chose to sail on a ship which docked en route in Southampton, so that the two younger girls could meet their brothers and sisters for the first time, and so that they themselves could see their beloved children, possibly for one last time.

My grandmother and her brothers were beside themselves with excitement at the thought of seeing their parents again and meeting their two younger sisters. For weeks they spoke and thought of nothing else as they saved up the precious pennies and planned the great adventure, a journey that would take them from one end of the country to the other.

At last the great day came and they sat on Southampton quay in a fever of anticipation. A dot appeared on the horizon and materialized slowly into a ship, coming ever closer. Suddenly it stopped and weighed anchor. They waited and watched, but it didn't move. Frantic, they hunted round for someone to ask and were informed that due to unfavourable tides and an outbreak of measles onboard, the boat would not now be docking after all.

For several hours they continued to sit on the quay, straining their eyes to catch the tiniest glimpse of someone vaguely resembling a person. They didn't even have a pair of binoculars to help them out. And they were still watching, when, at last, the ship pulled away and disappeared into the distant horizon.

My grandmother Rose's life seemed destined to be blighted by disappointment. It was many years after her death that we finally received a letter from great-aunt Regina in Philadelphia, one of the younger sisters. She was seventy and felt the time had come to make that trip across the Atlantic to meet up with her family at last. We all congregated at my cousin's house in Manchester to await the arrival of the dear little old lady, imagining, I suppose a hillbilly granny with bun and brogues. Nothing prepared us for the vision that walked in through the front door. Aunt Regina was a wrinkled, rather wild-looking woman with waist-length blond hair, in leather boots and a leather skirt which barely covered her bottom. My father choked on his brandy, then managed to pull himself together enough to go and give his aunt a kiss. I couldn't reconcile the woman standing before me now, with bright, bead-like eyes and a huge American, dazzling-white smile, as the sister of my slow, black-clad, bent little grandmother.

Rose had already met and fallen in love with her future husband before she left Latvia for the UK, but both sets of parents thought it an unsuitable match for her, because he was an out-of-work mercenary soldier after the Franco-Prussian war, and for him, because she had been left with a limp after a childhood fall. But Michael Gelbart pursued her to Britain, changed his surname to the anglicized Gilbert, married his Rose, set up the first charabanc business in Middlesbrough, and did very well – until his partner made off with all the profits. Fate didn't smile; it positively leered at grandfather Michael, who was a gracious, gentle man with pale, short-sighted eyes, fluffy fair hair and moustache, and a large cleft in the middle of his chin. Rose could be decidedly shrewish, and he was no match for her once she had set her heart on something. Sadly, her wilfulness was rarely balanced with wisdom.

Their eldest child, my aunt Ida, was one of the most gloriously generous, loving and eccentric people I have ever met. She always wore purple, her favourite colour, from head to toenail – shoes, stockings, suit, gloves, handbag, lipstick and eyeshadow. In buying shoes, she could out-Imelda Mrs Marcos, long before the world knew of the obsession of the first lady of the Philippines. If she liked a pair of shoes, aunt

Ida bought them in triplicate, one in purple, one in black for funerals, and one in gold for evenings. I once asked her if I could borrow a pair of gloves for a special occasion. I imagined a neat little pile of three or four pairs, squeezed into the corner of a drawer as mine were. Big mistake. She opened her wardrobe door and began to heave at an enormous sack that wouldn't budge until we both pulled. Taking a deep breath she turned it upside down and tipped a vast, rainbow-coloured mound of gloves onto the carpet.

'Help yourself, darling,' she panted, 'if you can find a matching pair.'

Money meant nothing to her, as long as she had it to spend. Only Ida could stew best sirloin steak, but then cooking was not her strong point. She never could follow a recipe, convinced that if you doubled certain ingredients, it must make the result doubly nice. She was never deterred by the fact that many of her offerings ended up in the dustbin. A friend once told her that rice pudding was extra creamy if you added an egg. So she broke one onto her next concoction and was surprised, when her pudding emerged from the oven, to find it had a poached egg on top.

The joy of my life was a shopping trip with her to Newcastle. As she had no children of her own, she loved nothing more than to spoil her only teenage niece. It was like having a fairy godmother – albeit a purple version with permed hair flattened to her head, a make-up mask covering a poor complexion, pencilled-in eyebrows, and a painful, wonky disc limp. Every shop assistant knew her. How was the back today? 'Fair to middling' was the best it ever was. Laden with jeans, smocks and miniskirts, whatever I wanted – which was heaven for a child whose mother's idea of teenage clothes bypassed anything vaguely trendy – we trundled into Tilley's for afternoon tea to the musical accompaniment of an all-female string quartet, or into the Eldon Grill, where Ida was always joined by the miserable, tight-lipped manager for a moaning session on their fate at the hands of heartless men.

Despite her warm heart and sense of fun, she was not a happy woman, and not just because of the pain of not having children. Uncle Jack, the husband who provided the wherewithal for her lavish generosity, was as mean as she was extravagant, a surly man who never showed anyone any affection, and only snorted with amusement at his own snide remarks.

'Why on earth did she marry him?' I asked my father, after one of our weekly Sunday afternoon visits. Their bickering and sniping had been worse than usual. Resentment crackled in the air around us, and aunt Ida had doubled the number of fancy cakes – delivered in a huge box from Smythe's the bakers every week – that she normally put on my plate. All that jam and icing had left me feeling decidedly queasy. 'Did she ever love him once?'

'She thought so. She was infatuated at least.'

I had never made a distinction between love and infatuation before. It was a revelation. 'But did he love her then?'

My father put down the medical journal that was his statutory Sunday evening read, and shook his head sadly.

'I don't think so. Jack came from a poor family in Leeds. But he had aspirations. He'd scraped his way financially through medical school, but needed money to set himself up in General Practice. In those days, the only solution was to find a girl with a decent dowry.'

'But you told me grandpa Michael had no money.'

'He didn't – and that was the tragedy of it all.'

My aunt had apparently been a happy, popular girl, great fun if not overly pretty, whiling away endless hours with countless boyfriends in Pasito's ice cream parlour on the front in Redcar. One day she fell hopelessly in love – but with a mere barrow boy, and not good enough for ambitious grandmother Rose, who had set her heart on a doctor for Ida. A doctor spelt security, status and acceptance into the unattainable echelons of the British middle classes. On the rebound, Ida met Jack Phillips, a redheaded Charlie Chaplin of a man, with a dapper little moustache, Leeds Jewish accent, and no social graces. But he was a doctor. Rose would have him at any price. And price there was.

Several weeks before the wedding Ida stood outside her father's study door, ear to the keyhole, and heard Jack demand more money from his future father-in-law, or the marriage was off.

'Ida,' her father said to her, 'Don't have him. He doesn't love you.'

But she and Rose wept and begged and pleaded, and Michael conceded.

A few weeks after the wedding, Michael's partner disappeared with the business profits. Jack complained he might not get his money, but my grandfather begged and borrowed every penny; then, to pay off his debts, went back to the only trade he had learnt back in Latvia – tailoring. He worked all day, and sometimes all night, and almost as soon as every debt was paid, had a massive stroke that left him speechless and paralysed down one side. He was only fifty-five, and he died two years later.

In the fullness of time Ida made an unsuccessful attempt at revenge. When she died her will revealed that she had left their luxury apartment in Newcastle, which was in her name, as Jewish tradition dictates, to my father, not to Jack. But Jack threatened to contest the will. He would say she was mentally imbalanced. My mother would have fought him tooth and nail through the courts. My father could not bear to have Ida's name defamed. How would it look in the papers – two Jewish doctors fighting over money? Like his father before him, he conceded, and handed over the flat. Most of my father's values were based on his father's – honour, dignity, courtesy, peacekeeping at any price.

'You would have loved my father,' he used to say to us. 'I wish he could have seen you three children.'

Rose was another matter. 'An old witch,' my mother called her. Nothing mattered to her except her son. And no one was good enough for him.

My father had been a gift, the unexpected, longed-for son, born when Ida was eight. They called him Herald, and no one ever knew where that extraordinary name had come from.

'It was based on the Hebrew name Hesh,' my father used to say to his Jewish friends. 'They couldn't have called me Harold, like most sensible parents, because then my Hebrew name would have been Hash.' To his non-Jewish friends, he said, 'I was born on December 23rd. Outside the house carol singers were giving us a loud rendering of "Hark the Herald Angels". At least I wasn't called Hark or Angel.'

Why no one ever asked Rose, I had no idea. But by the time I knew her she was already a frail, wizened old lady with a pudding basin cut of thinning white hair, eyes like raisins in a sponge cake and a tongue as sharp as her hooked nose. Aged before her time by arthritis and disappointment, she needed care by the time she was sixty. She wanted to live with her son – but my parents had three children, so Rose had no choice but to move in with her daughter and son-in-law. She may well have got her way with Ida's marriage – but now she really lived to regret it. Jack never made her welcome. She never went into his sitting room. She sat, instead, in her self-imposed imprisonment in one room of their large house.

'They think I don't know that they fry bacon. And he eats it after he *davens* every morning, puts his phylacteries on and prays – the hypocrite! Well, I may not be what I once was, but I still have a nose.'

'Smoked beef, Mother,' my father would try to reassure her.

Nothing made her smile any more, not even my clowning, dressed up in her best Sabbath hats with their long, drooping, birds-of-paradise feathers. The world had turned sour on her.

'How could you do this to my son?' she screamed, when my mother announced she was pregnant with my sister, Nicky. 'Two children are expensive enough.'

'It takes two to make a baby, remember?' my mother retorted. 'And besides, we thought you'd like another grandchild.'

My father would make excuses for her – the hard and lonely life she had endured after Michael's premature death – but even he had no idea of the lengths to which her unforgiving nature had driven her.

Long before my parents' marriage, some time shortly before the Second World War, a disagreement arose between her and Michael's family in France, probably a minor tiff which grew into epic proportions in Rose's eyes. From that moment on she intercepted and destroyed every letter they wrote to her husband. My grandfather was deeply saddened by their silence, but gradually, as the years went by, when his letters were never acknowledged, resigned himself to the fact that they must have perished at the hands of the Nazis.

He used to tell my father repeatedly how aggrieved he was that the only family he possessed had died in the Holocaust.

My father, too, lamented his lack of family on his father's side. It wasn't until after his death that we received a letter from cousins in France. They had indeed been in grave danger during the Nazi occupation, but had managed to flee to the Alps where a small community of Italians, unsympathetic to Mussolini, had hidden them for several years. They had tried to reinstate the correspondence with their cousin Michael once the war was over, and couldn't understand why he had never replied to their letters. In the end, they had simply given up.

What would my father have thought of his mother's actions? We would never know. One snowy afternoon I overheard her telling Dad that she had dreamed of Michael, and that he had told her he was coming for her.

'Don't be ridiculous, Mother,' my father had replied.

But she died three days later – on Christmas Day. I always thought she must have had a revelation – like great-grandma Fishkin – and couldn't understand why my father was so upset, until I was old enough to understand about the empty bottle of tablets by the bedside.

As for my parents' romance – strange how we can never imagine our parents' falling in love – but mine both assured me that they did so I'll have to take their word for it.

They were at a Jewish wedding, which is a very good hunting ground for unattached males, as every Jew knows. Dad was thirty, back from the war where he had served with distinction in the Royal Army Medical Corps in North Africa with the Desert Rats, running a field hospital where he met the German General, Rommel. One morning, the staff had awoken to discover their hospital was no longer in British hands. The Germans had advanced half a mile in the night and taken it.

'I observe the Geneva Convention,' Rommel had said to my father, bowing.

'So do I,' my father replied.

'Then,' Rommel said, 'I can rely on you to ensure the German wounded have the same quality of care as your own men?'

My father assured him that they would, but was relieved nonetheless when he awoke two weeks later to find that Rommel's troops had vanished, and that he was no longer a German prisoner of war.

On one occasion the advancing British army discovered that as part of their booty they had managed to acquire the entire contents – human and otherwise – of a brothel. My father ordered a strictly no-touch policy for the men as the women prisoners were riddled with sexual infection, but also had to add several hundred packets of sanitary protection to his medical and drugs supplies list – to the bewilderment of the administrators at base.

Many years later, when I lived in Coventry, I met one of his men, sent, I gathered, on a dangerous mission to liberate a bottle of malt whisky identified within enemy lines. Having recovered the bottle, Ron thought he deserved a small swig. After all, no one would notice. And then he needed another to sustain him for the journey back. And then another on the way, and so on, until, like Pooh with the honey pot he took as a present for Eeyore, there was nothing left in the bottle when he finally arrived back at base.

'Ron!' my father expostulated, when he saw what remained of the whisky he'd been anticipating for so long. As an officer and a gentleman, it was all he could bring himself to say.

From North Africa he joined in the liberation of Italy, where the young women had apparently thrown flowers and a great deal more at the feet of their deliverers. It was a long time before I understood why my mother found this information so entertaining, and why it was always accompanied by knowing winks at my father, whose face betrayed only the slightest, reluctant hint of complicity and amusement. Here was something he did not want his children to understand.

By 1946 he had very much had his fling. He was in the process of buying a medical practice with his commission and had reached that stage where he thought it might be nice to have someone to run the vast practice house and warm his underwear in the morning as both his mother and then his batman had done. He had rarely dated Jewish girls, but marriage was different. It had to be Kosher. His mother insisted. So here he was at a wedding, dancing a suave little 'Military Two Step', when a lady's heel from behind lodged itself in his trouser turn-up and dragged both him and the lady in question to the floor. She was furious. He was charmed. With such an introduction what else could a chivalrous gentleman do, but say a polite farewell to his dancing partner, and ensure that his victim received the due care and attention she deserved?

My mother was seventeen and very green. She had never been courted by a real man. Her former boyfriends – all familiar members of the Sunderland Jewish community with whom she had grown up – were mere boys by comparison. Along came my father, all five foot three of him, and bowled her over with his charm and worldliness. And he was a doctor. Only one cloud darkened her glorious horizon: he appeared to have little interest in Judaism.

'But, Darling, I've fought in a war. I've treated the dying. I've seen suffering you can't even imagine. How can there be a God?'

'Don't talk like that. You can't really mean it.'

'Oh, but I do. "Do unto others as you'd have them do unto you" – that's the only Judaism I want. But don't worry. You can keep whatever traditions you choose.'

My mother refused to dwell on the subject. What did it matter? Her mother had just presented her with a baby brother. At seventeen, marriage was a more glamorous proposition than staying at home to babysit. She wanted to make a Jewish home, cook Jewish food, and in the end, had no doubt that she would create the perfect Jewish man out of her intended. That was her destiny, her calling in life – to inspire in the next generation the faith of her ancestors.

Chapter 2

The Docta's Bairns

I was born in Gateshead in a little mining village called Felling, notable only for its male voice choir. Gateshead was a fairly dismal, depressed little town in those difficult days of post-war rationing and belt-tightening, and Felling was about as dreary as it came. Ration cards were barely in the bin when the north-east coal house doors started to close, and as one pit after another whirred to a halt, the queues lengthened outside the employment exchange, the dole offices and the doctor's surgery.

This was where my father had bought his medical practice. It was all he could afford. Some budding Jewish doctors were given financial help by their parents, who had already scrimped, scrounged and starved to get their offspring into a well-established profession that would confer automatic security and respect, and enable them to make a contribution to the society of their adoption. But with no father to support him through college, my father had few resources left, and was thrilled with the potential of the vast old stone house he had acquired.

It wasn't exactly what my grandparents had in mind for their daughter. Empty for some time, each of its seventeen rooms was in a state of disrepair; it wasn't at all like their smart semi in Sunderland next door to football star and manager, Don Revie. They surveyed the general dilapidation, swallowed their horror, and tried to kindle some enthusiasm in my mother, who had given way to hysterics at first sight. It was a beginning, wasn't it? Everyone has to start somewhere, and standing in solitary splendour on the top of a hill, looking down on a rabbit warren of cobbled streets and smoking, higgledy-piggledy miners' cottages, it did have a certain charm and dignity, even if the vast wheel of the local pit shaft loomed large in every window at the front of the house.

Gran supervised a total redecoration, ordered carpets, curtains and furniture, interviewed maids and a gardener. There was already a housekeeper in residence, a formidable woman, 'just like Mrs Danvers in *Rebecca*', my mother whispered. She was terrified of her.

'Nonsense,' Gran snapped, 'You'll soon get used to managing the staff.'

'But not the rats,' she wept.

A tunnel, said to provide access directly to the River Tyne, had been dug directly into our cellar – for contraband, for supplies in war? No one knew, and though it had been blocked off, the vermin had found a way through.

'Rats never bother humans,' my father reassured her.

One day his surgery was brought to a standstill by a blood-curdling shriek. Patients in the waiting room froze in terror. My mother rushed into the examination room, oblivious to any state of undress some poor soul might be in and screamed at my father, 'A rat, a rat, there's a rat in the oven. And,' she added as an injured afterthought, 'it's licked all the custard out of the custard tart I was making for tea.'

'Can't you see I'm busy?' my father whispered loudly, taking her by the arm and ushering her out as quickly as possible. 'All this fuss for a little mouse.'

But he followed her into the kitchen all the same, and nonchalantly opened the oven door.

'You see,' he said, then peered in. 'Good grief, it is a rat,' he exclaimed, slamming it shut in a hurry, 'And a big one at that – about the size of a cat.'

They switched on the gas and waited fifteen minutes, but when he gingerly opened the oven door again, the rat had vanished.

From then on the rat-catcher made a courteous, quiet visit once a month and took away whatever he found in our cellar in his big, black suitcase. The rats never worried me. Their scuffling and scratching beneath the floorboards at night could be a bit annoying when I was trying to get to sleep, but it never stopped me hunting in our cellar for the secret tunnel to the Tyne.

On her twenty-first birthday, my mother sat in a nursing home bed, enveloped in cards and flowers, a tiny, dark, curly-headed baby on her lap and a heavy infection within, lamenting, in a fevered haze, the golden days of her vanished youth. The food was terrible, the infection was the final straw. She wasn't paying for that! She could have picked up a germ in one of the larger, public hospitals – for free. So she swept up her belongings, including the tiny, chuckle-headed bundle that was me, and took them to the place where a Jewish Mama reigns supreme – home, except that motherhood didn't bring the serenity promised in the women's magazines of the time. She was too young to be so tied. She hadn't lived.

Felling provided most of the local collieries with manpower, and the manpower was afflicted with every lung disease known to miners. When they were out of work, poverty destroyed what bodily functions coal dust hadn't.

There was no such thing as an appointment system in those days. In good weather and foul, patient queues snaked from the waiting room down the street. My father disappeared into the surgery early in the morning, and worked until late evening, interrupting his house calls every day to come home for lunch, which he expected to have placed on the table in front of him. This he washed down with a large glass of Tizer, delivered fortnightly by the crate, even though all fizzy pop, which he loved, made him burp for most of the afternoon.

If my mother complained about a leak in the loo or problems with the staff, he would dismiss it with a, 'Can't you see I'm having a very busy day, dear? Spare me the minor details of life.' He didn't intend to demean my mother's work, but he didn't rate it either. In those days, the male was provider, his kept woman a mere adjunct to his status and importance. As a daughter, it was the only thing I resented about him, and forgave him, as he genuinely cared about every bent and bronchial figure who came to the surgery door, coughing as if his rib cage was about to split. The women came in slippers, pushing prams and bearing gifts of tinned salmon – gold at a time of post-war rationing – to say thank you. He delivered their babies at home, and they called the girls Michele.

'That's a pretty name you've called your little girl, Doctor. Where does it come from?'

'Michele Morgan, the Hollywood film star,' he told them.

Pointless to explain the Jewish tradition of calling a new baby after a deceased relative, to keep their memory alive in the family, or to say that it was French for Michael, the name of his beloved father, who had died too young.

My Hebrew name was Malchah Golda, after great-grandma Fishkin's pious mother, so devout that after her death her body was laid in the synagogue for twenty-four hours, a rare token of respect, especially for a woman. Though in her lifetime she would never have understood the path I have taken, I like to think that she does now, and that I walk in her footsteps, after a lapse of several more secular generations.

Despite the kindness and friendliness of the local people, my mother missed the Sunderland Jewish crowd, the social life with its parties and dances. Though 'Mrs Danvers' had long been dismissed, there were two live-in maids and a char with chaffed and reddened hands who did all the hard cleaning work. Bedding was tied up in a large sheet, labelled and handed to the laundry van that called every week. Clothes were washed by hand, then wrung through a hand-operated mangle outside that was usually frozen solid in the winter. It was years before we acquired one of the first spin dryers. It had a life of its own and used to dance from one side of the kitchen to the other unless someone sat on it.

With nothing else to do with her time, or justify her existence, my mother devoted herself to the environment – her environment – making the house as perfect as it could be. No picture was ever crooked, no ornament out of place, no book or magazine left out, no armchair or settee out of the official indents made by the castors on the carpet, every curtain fold measured to the last quarter of an inch. Not a fly on the wall would have had the gall to mess up her world. And, in the heavily regulated 1950s, even the baby fed, slept and wee-wee'ed to order.

She was not the only one of her generation of Jewish women to succumb to obsessive behaviour in her home. It appears to be a cultural and professional hazard handed on from mother to daughter. There might just as well be a ceremony for Jewish baby girls, a ritual on the eighth day, when, just as the baby boys lose part of their anatomy, the girls are presented with an addendum: a feather duster.

'You've heard it said,' quips comedienne Rita Rudner, 'that neurotics build castles in the air and psychotics live in them? My mother cleans them.'

Whenever it was in use, aunt Ida would stand outside her toilet with a duster in her hand, waiting for it to be vacated so that she could polish the seat. She once stippled it with gold paint. And the light switches to match. Her friends and relatives giggled about it behind her back, and then got merrily on with their own little peculiarities.

A certain Jewish cookbook, instruction manual for many a Jewish bride, suggested that the Jewish home should run as smoothly as a Swiss clock. It was to be swept, dusted, scrubbed and polished daily, as of course were the children, so that the man of the house could return home from work to order, serenity and his favourite meal piping hot on the table. Order and food every Jewish man got in abundance, but serenity was another matter. Peace was his only if he did as he was told, and sat in one armchair, its back covered in a lace antimacassar to mop up any rogue scalp oils that might leave grease on the moquette.

The growth of Zionism meant there was always fundraising to be done, but it didn't appeal to my mother. Instead she became pregnant again and seventeen months after I was born, my brother, Michael, the much longed-for son, appeared. My birth had cost my father a fiver. Like most Jewish men, he had desperately wanted a boy to carry on the family name, and had bet £5 each way on it with his father-in-law. So when the formidable nursing sister, in starched-white uniform, crinkled her way into the hospital waiting room to tell the expectant father he could stop pacing the floor because he had a lovely daughter, Dad asked her, 'Are you saying it is a girl or you only think it's a girl?'

'Doctor,' she said disparagingly, for those were the days when a senior nurse could reduce even a competent medical man into blancmange with one twitch of her winged hat, 'we do have ways of knowing these things.'

Now, as well as discovering the surprising joys of having a daughter, my father had his son.

I adored my father. Bedtime was his time. He always popped upstairs between patients to tuck us in and say goodnight.

'What shall we have tonight then, kids?'

'Anything, Dad, but "Oh Yes, We Have No Bananas".'

'Dash it, I've forgotten my ukelele.'

He fancied himself as a belated successor to George Formby, but we were always glad to be spared the banana song, even if it meant we had to have, 'When I'm Cleaning Windows'.

'Just tell us a story, then.'

He made up the most wonderful stories. On other occasions he sang, 'Your Tiny Hand is Frozen' from *La Boheme*. I knew few nursery rhymes, but could manage an aria or two from Puccini or Verdi. Sadly, my mother's loud abuse whenever he started to sing hid from us just how good a tenor voice he really had.

My brother Michael and I were inseparable companions in that vast house. Hand in hand we rushed down the endless dark corridors pursued by ghosts, hobgoblins and wicked witches. Behind every curtain, in every cupboard, at the crook of every staircase was a hidden world, peopled with imaginary beings. Occasionally we came across my mother on hands and knees, straightening the curtains we had ruffled, irritated with the unknown forces that kept thwarting her efforts at perfection.

At all costs, father must not be disturbed, not at breakfast when he opened his post, warming his legs in front of the dining room fire, not at coffee-time when he and his partners smoked their pipes in his study. At lunchtime he went out on visits, at teatime he was back in the surgery, so we normally ate in the draughty kitchen with the nanny and maids around a long pine table. The atmosphere greatly depended on the mood of the adults present, how often one of the bells in the box on the wall above our heads summoned them to my mother and how well they related to one another. They certainly never gave us the time of day. Some meals were eaten in oppressive, stony silence. Others were accompanied by the blare of the BBC Light Programme. One thing was sure – the domestic staff never stayed the same for long. Few could attain my mother's exceptionally high standards and the turnover was rapid. No sooner did I become attached to one of them than she disappeared from my orbit. It was very unsettling.

Friday night, the Sabbath, was the pivot of the entire week. It was the only time we ate with our parents and had them to ourselves. Nothing was allowed to interfere with this family time, no night-clubbing, dancing or dinner parties, not even the big Rotary dos that took over their lives when my father became founder President of the new Felling Rotary Club.

An open fire blazed in the dining room hearth. The heavy velvet curtains, shut tight, severed us from all connection with the world outside. No television tonight, nothing but profound silence, broken only by the ticking of the clock and the occasional spit and crackle of an exploding piece of coal in the grate. Bathed and scrubbed, Michael and I would sit in silence, reading, waiting for Dad to appear.

From time to time, Mum would rush in, look anxiously at the clock, and grumble.

'Where is he? He knows what night it is,' as if he had deliberately encouraged his patients to find extra ailments, just to spite her. Then she would rush out again to see to the potatoes. Minutes later she would be back to check the table, set for a banquet. She scrutinized the silver, her eyes darting from one piece to another.

'Lizzie always misses that patch right there, just under the handle.' Out of her pocket would come the inevitable duster, so that she could put our charwoman's lapse right.

Usually she lit the candles before my father arrived.

'They should be lit at sundown,' she explained.

'Then why can't we leave school early on Fridays, like other Jewish children?' we moaned.

Our non-Jewish classmates couldn't understand why some of us did, and some of us didn't.

'Because it's not necessary,' she snapped. 'We're not that religious.'

We had learned not to argue almost as soon as we could speak. There was never any rationale behind many of the decisions – none that we could see, at any rate. For her, being Jewish was a matter of feeling, not reason.

She picked up the box of matches and lit each of the two candles, muttering to herself in Hebrew. As the flames sprang to life, casting strange shadows on the wall and giving the room a magical glow, she paused, transfixed, a look of something almost resembling piety smoothing out her fine features and skin for just a moment. That stillness was so unlike her usual self that Michael and I never failed to be fascinated by it. We supposed she was praying, but never really knew.

'What are you saying?' Michael once dared to ask.

'Trying to pray.'

'What about?'

'Never you mind.'

Small wonder that my childish mind associated the prayer at the lighting of the Sabbath candles with making a wish when you blew out all the candles on a birthday cake.

'You're supposed to do a kind of wave now,' I once said to her.

'Who to?'

'Not to anyone. You beckon, welcoming in *Shabbat* as if it were an important visitor, a bride or a queen.'

At Hebrew classes they had shown the girls how to make the appropriate sweeping motions over the flames and I had been terribly impressed.

'Then you hide your face in your hands, ask God to send me a good husband, and when you open your eyes, hey presto, all is light and the Sabbath has come.'

'All this waving sounds a bit surplus to me,' she said. 'And besides, you're perfectly capable of finding yourself a husband one day. As long as he's Jewish.'

Perhaps, if she had known then how things would turn out, she might have prayed harder.

Some time after seven, the surgery door would slam shut. There was a pause as my father took off his white coat and threw it onto a peg. Then he rushed into the room, donned his skullcap and searched for the Sabbath service in the prayer book.

'Is the food spoilt?'

'Is it ever? Isn't it always *gefilte* fish on *Shabbas*?'

'I wonder who started that tradition? Do you suppose

Moses' wife inflicted cold fried fish balls on him every Friday evening?'

Dad lifted the lid of a tureen and peered inside. 'And salad!'

'Now don't grumble. You'll start the children off. I've made it with the dressing you like.'

Made with ascetic acid and sugar I later discovered, not oil, in those days before international cuisine. Small wonder that in later life my father succumbed to tooth rot, the consequences of being an antacid junkie.

'I don't like salad eith...'

Michael was silenced by one of my mother's terrible stares.

'*Vy'erev vy'voker yom hashishi* ...and it was evening and it was morning, the first day...' I loved the lilting, familiar sound of *Kiddush*, the Sabbath prayers. It was a tradition my father took seriously, and one of the few pieces of Hebrew he could read with any fluency because he knew it by heart. I was familiar with every inflexion of his voice and could whisper the words quietly with him, but I had only the vaguest notion of what they meant. Any attempt my father made at reading the translation simultaneously for our benefit, or out of courtesy for any non-Jewish guests, was interrupted by my mother after the first line with a, 'stop messing about', or an, 'oh, get on with it.' The gist was that God had made the world in six days and rested on the seventh and that was why we had weekends. Which all seemed eminently sensible. If only we didn't have to spend all of it visiting relatives. But then maybe my mother's younger brother, Martin, only four years older than I was, would take us up to the attic to play the latest Del Shannon or Bobby Vee. That too was always interrupted from below with the command, 'Martin, play us some Jim Reeves', but Martin was one of the few people in the world who had no qualms about defying my mother. Or maybe Aunt Ida would let me rummage through her jewellery and make-up boxes. Or even better, maybe it would be one of those marvellous Saturdays when Mum was too busy to visit the family, and Dad would take us down to the seafront at Whitley Bay to eat fish and chips smothered in ketchup, then buy us huge ice cream 99s.

Almost before the final prayer had left my father's lips, my mother had returned from the kitchen with a tureen of potatoes.

'Amen,' he said wearily, closing his *Siddur*, 'Perhaps one week I'll manage to finish?' He lifted the large silver goblet, thanked God for the wine in it and passed it round so that we could each take a sip. Then he broke off the end of the *chollah*, the plaited Sabbath loaf, sweeter than any bread we ate during the rest of the week, and gave us all a piece. It was a mysterious ritual I never fully understood, but never questioned either – not then.

'Good *Shabbas*.'

'*Shabbat shalom*.'

Everyone hugged everyone else, although we had all been together for some time. Usually, my father's partners turned up at the end of surgery to say goodnight and get their Sabbath kisses.

When the Sabbath was over, on Saturday evenings my parents always went out together. My mother loved dancing and Dad, who was equally gregarious, was happy to indulge her fancy for nightclubs and parties. Her sumptuous wardrobe of diaphanous chiffons and glittering sequins transformed her into a fairy princess, especially since her normal attire was a nylon pinny. We loved seeing her in all her splendour when Michael and I were summoned to the lounge, a room we never normally saw, and, standing lumpishly in our dressing gowns, were instructed to say hello to the guests having their pre-dinner-dance drinks.

The Blue Parrot, my parents' favourite haunt, hosted a renowned cabaret, popular with visiting celebrities and locals alike. Once, Michael and I were summoned downstairs, bleary-eyed, in the small hours of the morning to meet the entire cast of *Emergency Ward Ten* – the 1960s precursor to *Casualty* and *ER*. I was too dazed to enjoy it, too overawed to say anything sensible. How we admired my pretty, vivacious mother on occasions like that. But when a cuddle and a soft cosy lap was called for, the home helps would have to do.

I should have liked a friend. But since I went to school across the river in Newcastle, all my school friends lived a long way away. Michael was all very well, but he was a boy. We drove our trikes to the end of the long drive and stared out through the wrought iron gates at the queue of patients at the waiting room door – a huddle of faceless grey figures, a hotchpotch of anoraks, flat caps and dotted head-squares, who never acknowledged our existence. I never knew whether it was because we were 'the docta's bairns', or whether they sensed we were somehow different because we were Jews.

Mum was always telling us that Jews were different from other people. Sometimes she referred to them as Christians. At other times, when she wanted to be slightly derogatory, she called them *goyim* – a Hebrew word for Gentiles.

'The goyim don't dress like we do. They don't cook the way we do. They don't eat like we do.'

Our secluded little world was completely cut off from the one beyond the six-foot stone walls surrounding our garden.

'Shall we go exploring?' I suggested to Michael one morning, when there was nothing of any interest to see through the gate. I must have been about eight at the time. I didn't intend to run away. I just wanted to see what was out there.

'No,' Michael shook his head vehemently. 'We'll get into trouble.'

'But out of the car window, I've seen a park with some swings and a slide. It's not far away.'

I tried the gate and it opened. No one was around. We ran as fast as we could, revelling in this new sensation of freedom. My only fear was that I couldn't remember with any degree of accuracy where the park was. I was never blessed with a sense of direction. But after we had been running for what seemed an age, and were just beginning to gasp for breath, a brightly painted children's playground miraculously appeared like a mirage. Why had no one ever taken us there before? Such was my exhilaration that I did not notice the two cars that suddenly converged upon us with a screech of brakes. A firm hand on the back of my neck whisked me through the air and deposited me on a car seat. Two minutes later we were once again safely back behind the six-foot walls – in fact, in my father's study receiving a ceremonial spanking with his slipper. Never again did Michael allow himself to be carried along by my insatiable curiosity.

One Boxing Day the pair of us was invited to the home of one of our maids. It was a damp, chilly afternoon and I slid my hand in hers and huddled close as the iron gates clanged shut behind us and we set off on our adventure down the hill. In the foggy haze of that afternoon each street seemed much like another, row upon row of terraced cottages, and nowhere any sign of a garden, or even a tree. We suddenly came to a stop outside a bottle green door. No one here had a key, let alone a gate. She turned the knob and pushed, and as the door opened, it was as if I was being given the chance to go inside one of those musical boxes that hide a tiny magic world behind their lacquered veneer. Here was the brightest, cosiest little room I had ever seen, with roaring coal fire, and a vast Christmas tree in the corner, shimmering with countless coloured baubles. We huddled around the fire, pulled crackers and ate mince pies.

'One day I'm going to have a home like this,' I told myself, as we went back out into the fog and trudged back up the hill to the Christmas-less house at the top.

The real highlight of our lives was our fortnight's summer holiday in Blackpool. We stayed at the Norbreck Hydro which seemed the height of sophistication and probably was in those dreary post-war years, with its pageboys in uniform and jewel-filled glass cabinets lining the entrance hall, its murals on the walls around the swimming pool and long, plant-lined sun lounge facing the sea, its palm court orchestra by day and dance bands by night. I can still taste the home-made oxtail soup, served from silver tureens by waitresses in black dresses with frilly aprons in the huge, pillared dining room with its garishly patterned red carpet. My father was as excited as a little boy. He adored the hotel, that epitome of all that was quintessentially English, the culmination of all his aspirations. It was the only place where my mother was completely relaxed. She had, I gather, on her first visit, delivered a volley of complaints to the manager, David Quinlan, who was wise enough to invite my parents to be his guests at dinner. They became very close friends, and my parents were subsequently treated like royalty.

For children, the long summer days on Blackpool's golden beach, the hours of play in the swimming pool and well-equipped nursery, the film shows, endless ice cream and relaxed and happy parents all amounted to a taste of heaven. I was lulled into a contented, exhausted sleep every night by the wheeling of the gulls and the regular click-clacking of the trams as they rattled their way up and down the prom. We lived for that fortnight.

As I grew older and watched my mother float down the vast, impressive staircase to dinner in one of her shimmering evening dresses, I told myself that one day, when I was the grown up, I would like to make an entrance like that. Over twenty years later I did – in shocking pink satin pyjama suit admittedly, not evening dress. But then this was the early eighties, and times had changed. My first book was launched at a booksellers' convention in that very hotel, fallen on harder times, no thanks to package holidays abroad, but still glittering in my memory. Halfway down to what was once the grand ballroom, the sense of déjà vu, like an electric shock, stopped me in my tracks. It was an extraordinary moment of realization – that there is an order and planning and symmetry to our lives, that dreams can and sometimes do come true – in ways better than we ever dare imagine. For with the fulfilment of some very conscious wishes, had come the fulfilment of unconscious wishes – longings I didn't even know I had – for acceptance, redemption, wholeness, joy and hope.

I told the gathered throng below the story of how my mother once went out onto the fire escape in her negligee to hang up the children's washing when the door had slammed shut behind her, and since there was a huge drop at the bottom, had no alternative but to climb back up, knocking on every window she passed. Eventually she found one open a few inches at the bottom, heaved it up with relief, and saw, to her horror, a man sitting on the toilet.

'Madam,' he said, with great presence of mind, 'would you mind waiting until I'm finished?'

He was as good as his word, reopened the window, let her through and locked the door after her.

'Who was he?' David Quinlan had asked, wiping his brow with his handkerchief in mock anxiety, unable to disguise his amusement.

'Don't be silly,' my grandfather interjected, 'She wouldn't recognize him with his trousers on.'

I don't imagine any of the delegates at that booksellers' convention were able to use the facilities without looking over their shoulders at the window behind them.

Had I known it, I could have also leant out of the window on our car journey there and back, pointed to a house on the A6 in Lancaster as we passed through, and said, 'I will live there one day.' As it was a private house and not a vicarage in those days, it wouldn't have unduly disturbed my parents' peace of mind.

When I was nine years old everything changed. We moved away from the constant ringing of the telephone and doorbell of the practice house into a large semi in what was regarded as the posh part of Gateshead. My sister, Nicky, was born. Relatives intimated she was a little surprise, but my parents insisted she was planned. They intended providing her with a companion, but she screamed her way through the nights for almost two years and was condemned to grow up alone.

Those were the days when central heating was regarded as a luxury for wimps. In our front room, that was only ever used when we had visitors, we had one of the latest electric fires. Behind the bars was a rotating light that reflected a sequence of rainbow colours onto the back, a cycle that managed to induce a hypnotic, though deadly boring trance in all of our guests. Generally, the house was freezing. I scratched the ice off the inside of the bedroom windows when I got up in the morning, then dressed in a hurry, virtually stuck to a two-bar electric fire. When leather mini shifts were in fashion and Aunt Ida bought me a cheaper, imitation plastic version, I stood so close I melted the front of it, smoothing out its 'leather-effect' crinkles.

Despite only having four bedrooms, my mother insisted on a live-in maid, or 'home help' as they came to be known in an increasingly class-conscious Britain. On nights off she arrived home in the small hours of the morning so rolling drunk it took her several attempts to get up the stairs. I used to count her slow, uncertain progress, wait for the inevitable crash as she fell back down, and start counting again as she steadied herself and headed for the top. It was my own revised version of Snakes and Ladders.

Michael and I were left much more to our own devices. We went to school on the bus, did endless 'messages' for my mother, to-ing and fro-ing to the high street shops, and played in the street with other children. And with my father. There were constant complaints from the neighbours about the proximity of our cricket ball to their windows. One of them rang the police. 'Tell the doctor, then' the police said to her. My father was a police surgeon, and a great favourite with the local constabulary – though he was half their height – turning up with amenability and courtesy several times a night to test the alcohol levels of drunken drivers in those pre-breathalyser days.

'That's the trouble,' the neighbour declared in exasperation, 'The doctor's playing with his children.'

The police reported it to my father with glee.

For this tiny glimpse of normality there was a price to pay – Hebrew classes. We had never really mixed with Jewish children and it worried my mother. She rang the rabbi in Newcastle who said he would be delighted for us to join his *cheder* – or Hebrew school.

'Two hours every Sunday morning,' Michael groaned. 'Do we have to?'

'It does seem a bit much,' my father said mildly.

'Oh, you, if it depended on you a right pair of little *goyim* we'd have.'

Like most Jews she resorted to Yiddish when roused. That her children should grow up like non-Jews with no ability to read Hebrew was the worst threat she could hold over my father's head. She had given up on him by now. He kept the traditions that suited him, like Sabbath, because it created a sense of family cohesion, but being a Jew was never allowed to interfere with his professionalism as a doctor, or his leisure. My parents had countless arguments over his Saturday morning surgery and season ticket to Newcastle United.

'You would rather I give up medicine for lingerie, would you?'

This was a dig at one of her cousins who had married into a very orthodox family and been prevailed upon to give up medical studies for a partnership in the family business. It was usually enough to silence my mother. But there was a time to put her foot down – and that time had just arrived.

'Michael will be *Bar Mitzvah*-ed in five years. You may not mind us looking fools in front of the entire Jewish community – but I do. I may not be as good a Jew as I would have liked to have been – but my children will be.'

That very Sunday morning she straightened Michael's tie, patted the bow on the back of my dress and deposited us on the synagogue steps looking like two china dolls in a glass cabinet. We were ushered by the rabbi's two daughters into a large, airy hall filled with small groups of children, whose chatter died away as two little strangers appeared in their midst.

'Name? Date of birth?' demanded the darker, more ferocious-looking one of the two, with the hairy arms, recalling my attention.

I was disappointed. I had hoped the kinder-looking, prettier sister with the red hair was going to be our teacher.

'Do you know your alphabet?'

A stupid question, I thought, at our age of course we do. I looked at Michael. He didn't move, just stood there looking at them with those enormous blue eyes of his. I nodded for both of us.

'Then read me this.'

A large book was pushed under my nose filled with the strangest hieroglyphics I had ever seen. I looked up helplessly.

'So you don't recognize Hebrew?'

'Ah well,' she sighed, softening a little, 'I don't know what parents are coming to these days. I suppose we had better start at the beginning. You'll stay in my class, the bottom class, though the other children are much younger than you two. Turn the book round the other way. We read from right to left.'

Aleph, bet, gimel, daled... After one lesson I could string two or three consonants together with a couple of vowels, after two lessons I could manage a Hebrew word, after five or six lessons a short sentence.

'When do they teach you what it all means?' I whispered to a fellow student. His friendly little face became a total blank. So eventually I summoned up enough courage to ask the teacher.

'Well, my little one, do you want to run before you can walk – or talk? As long as you can read your prayer book that's all that matters. Hebrew is God's own language. He can understand it, even if you can't.'

I thought of how my mother hated going to the synagogue because my father always let her down. She would watch him from upstairs in the women's gallery laughing and joking with his friends, fumbling his way through his prayer book and digging them in the ribs when he couldn't work out where the service was up to. The women knew that virtually every other woman could barely translate a word of what they were reading, but at least they read Hebrew well enough not to lose the place. When a man did so, it was ignominy. He was the spiritual leader in the home. But not my father. He never even attempted to hide his unfamiliarity with it all, and that riled my mother even more. A decent show of piety would have kept her happy, but Dad was no hypocrite. She lived in dread of the day the rabbi would bestow the great honour on him of inviting him up onto the *bimah*, the raised platform, to read a portion of the Law from the silver-encased scrolls. But I always had the sneaking suspicion that should that happen, Dad would rise to the occasion as he always did. He simply enjoyed annoying her.

'You two had better be good pupils,' she snapped, whenever we complained that Hebrew classes were boring, 'or you'll end up like your father.'

We waited until she was out of earshot.

'Didn't you ever go to *cheder*, Dad?' It was like asking him why he'd never gone to school.

'Your grandmother thought I did,' he said with a grin, 'but there was more fun to be had on the beach at Redcar with a football and our ukuleles. And if I caught your Aunt Ida in Pasito's with a boy, she would buy my silence.'

The beach at Redcar! 'I should be so lucky,' I grumbled, as I huddled closer to the miserable paraffin heater in the synagogue kitchen in a vain attempt to feel my extremities, watching the steam rise from my sodden mackintosh. I had graduated to a more senior Hebrew school in the archaic synagogue building round the corner from my high school. That's where being a studious pupil had got me – Mr Rosenberg's class, one hour three times a week in the evenings, and two hours on Sunday mornings. Torture! His lessons started at five. School finished at three thirty. An hour and a half to kill – it seemed like forever for a twelve-year-old. A dedicated scholar, I tried to do my homework – almost impossible in the damp, unheated building, after a run in the pouring rain, with feet squelching in my shoes, stomach grinding with hunger pangs and terminal numbness setting in.

Five o'clock at last. Prayer drill. Boys line up facing Israel, girls sit quietly at their desks. The boys are learning to be men. One day in their homes, after *Bar Mitzvah*, they will wind phylacteries around their arms and forehead morning and evening and recite the ancient prayers. Dad never has. Uncle Jack does – swaying and muttering, as if he were on ball bearings. It's called *davening*. Can swaying help praying? And then he has the bacon breakfast that rules out any answers from God, according to my mother. I wonder why God doesn't listen to women. I could *daven* as well as any boy. Well, maybe not as well as the rabbi's son. He's really fast. Always the first to shut his prayer book, kiss it and return to his desk.

'Sir?' asks Peter, an outsized boy, who looks as if he has to be squeezed into his short trousers every morning, since he balloons out of every possible exit, 'Are you sure Israel's

in this direction?' He stares at graffiti on the wall until he's
cross-eyed. No response.

'A pity,' Peter never knows when to stop, 'because if it was
in the other direction we could all face the window.'

A sudden crack like gunshot fills the air. Peter gasps and
rubs the side of his face where Mr Rosenberg has just slapped
him. But within seconds he's smiling again, a huge piece of
pink bubble gum revolving around his mouth like smalls in
a washing machine. Mr Rosenberg has just caught sight of
it, but after a few seconds of indecision, does nothing. Either
he's mesmerized, or seeing the tie flung over one shoulder
and the skullcap now hanging limply over one ear, decides
not to take on what is obviously a hopeless case.

'Continue praying,' he snaps and goes back to his seat.

Before Peter turns back to the wall, his eyes catch mine.
He rolls them to the ceiling and starts to make a strange
gobbling sound, then, with his back to me, begins to rock
backwards and forwards. The pages of his prayer book
flick over at unbelievable speed. Two minutes later, a world
record in praying, since *ma'erev* normally takes around
fifteen minutes for a fast reader, he stops and swaggers back
to his seat.

'Not bad, eh?' he says, looking round at me, and the other
girls. 'I too can pray like a rabbi's son.'

'Open your books at page 72 and we will begin our
translation. The children of Israel, if you remember, are
wandering around the desert.'

'Not still, Sir. They were doing that last week. In fact,
they were doing that last year.' With a self-congratulatory
smile, Alan, whose ears stick out horizontally from his head
and serve as hinges for his school cap, looks round for our
approval. He was always in trouble. I lost count of the times

that grin that stretched the whole breadth of his face would be wiped off by one of Mr Rosenberg's violent swipes. The cocky little lad would then break out in the most nerve-grating howls, and embarrassed by his lack of control, and even more by the terrible din, Mr Rosenberg would be forced to cover him in kisses.

'Ugh,' he whispered to me one day, wiping his face with the corner of his sleeve, 'I think I prefer his slaps.'

Mr Rosenberg was reputed to be one of the most learned Jewish scholars in the north-east. If he was, it was wasted on us. With his grey hair and beard we thought he must be one of the oldest men alive – and he was about forty-five at the time. Everything about him was bird-like – his little beak of a nose, his balding round head, the goatee beard resting on a puffed-up little chest, beady black eyes peering at you through bottle-bottom spectacles that periodically slipped down his nose and were lifted by a facial contortion that made you wonder if he held you in utter disdain, or had just had a whiff of a rather nasty smell.

'Malchah, continue translating.' Mr Rosenberg insisted on calling us by our Hebrew names, which I always found disconcerting.

'Boys, listen to Malchah. Her translation is always faultless.'

'Little squirt,' murmured Peter, to my immense satisfaction. Only I knew that I couldn't really translate a single word. Mr Rosenberg read it at the beginning of the class, and having an excellent memory for languages, I simply learned it, parrot-fashion.

The boredom of the exercise was excruciating. Any avenue of escape was worth a try.

'Please, Sir, can I be excused?'

'You, Malchah? Well, I am surprised. But of course.'

I ran upstairs, savouring every minute of freedom, dawdling as long as I dared, then ambled nonchalantly back into the classroom.

'And the blessing?'

Mr Rosenberg's words halted me in my track back to my desk.

'The blessing, Sir?'

'Yes, the blessing for when you've been to the... you know where. You may come to the front of the class and say it for us all.'

In Judaism there is a blessing for every occasion – a journey, a visit, brushing your teeth, combing your hair, fruit from the ground, fruit from a tree, presuming you knew which came from where, and Mr Rosenberg ensured we knew them all. But up to that moment, this particular one had escaped my notice. And at that moment, it seemed to me to be the longest in the prayer book. 'From earth you came, to earth you return.' Yuk, I didn't much like the sound of that. One thing was sure – I decided that day that there had to be cleverer ways of escaping translation practice.

'Please, Sir, tell us a Bible story.'

'Please, Sir, why don't Jews mix milk and meat?'

'Please, Sir, why do Jewish boys have to have that little operation... you know, the one that leaves us with less than the other...'

'Please, Sir, who was Jesus Christ?'

The room went deadly silent. Everyone was staring at me. That question was manifestly not on the list of acceptable distractions.

'P-p-please, Sir, it's just that the girls at school said that I had killed him, so I just wanted to know who he was.'

Mr Rosenberg swelled to twice his normal size before my very eyes. Was that steam coming out of his ears? I thought he was going to burst.

'Never,' he hissed, 'let me hear that name on the lips of a Jewish girl.'

I sat down. Mr Rosenberg cleared his throat, shrank back to his usual shape and the class continued in an uncomfortable sort of way.

I had an unquenchable thirst for matters of theology, and continued to afflict the poor man with my endless questions.

'Why must we always say a blessing for everything?'

'To remember our constant devotion to God.'

'How do we please God?'

'You learn Torah – the first five books of Moses, the laws of our people and you keep them.'

'Five books – but we've barely started the first one,' Alan interjected, waiting for the laughter. He was always butting in. Now I had to regain Mr Rosenberg's attention.

'What happens after you die?'

'Malchah, you worry too much about these things – for a girl.'

The problem was I don't think he was able to distinguish genuine soul-searching from the distraction techniques we all resorted to in every lesson. Either that, or he couldn't believe a child could want or need debate on such profound issues. So I never received a satisfactory answer.

One day he asked me to stay behind after class. Nervously I approached his desk.

'Malchah,' he said, wrinkling his nose up so that he could peer at me more closely through his spectacles, 'I have a great privilege for you. Since your translation is so faultless, since you have such a desire to learn, you shall be the first girl to study for my Torah Diploma.'

'Oh, thank you, Sir,' I muttered, and backed out of the room. What else could I say? What had I let myself in for?

In the event, I discovered that the Diploma consisted of a written rather than a verbal examination of the translation we had already done. While the rest of the class continued to appal Mr Rosenberg with their ignorance, I was sent into the next room with the rabbi's son to transcribe onto paper the words recorded on the tape in my head. Within twenty minutes I marched back into the classroom and proudly handed in my work. Mr Rosenberg scanned it, making the occasional, unintelligible grunt. Then he stopped, raised the paper for closer inspection and gasped, 'Malchah, what have you done?'

I peered at my paper over his shoulder. What had I done?

'There,' he whispered in horror, 'look there.'

I followed the long, bony finger and read, 'God. It says God.'

'I know what it says. Please do not add to your shame by letting that word pass your lips. Only in earnest prayer do we use the name of the Blessed One, holy be he.'

'Ah,' I said, 'now I understand. That's why, when we do translation, we say *Ha'shem*, the Name, rather than...'

'Of course,' Mr Rosenberg snapped, interrupting me before I could abuse the word *Adonai*, or Lord. 'Nor can we write it in full.'

I watched him take a tiny penknife out of his jacket pocket, and cut a square out of the paper all around the letter 'o' in the middle of my 'God'.

'In future you will write G dash D. Do you understand?'

I understood *what* I was to do, but not *why*. As if God cared! How pointless. But despite my aberration, I got my Diploma and it cost my parents around £50 – a great deal of money in those days. There were no congratulations.

Somehow Mum discovered that Mr Rosenberg lived in the middle of the ultra orthodox enclave in Gateshead on our way home, and offered him a lift, courtesy of my father, from the Sunday morning classes. Michael and I were not exactly pleased. If it wasn't bad enough having him in the car, Dad kept up a constant banter on all subjects from religion to politics. We could tell from Mr Rosenberg's uncomfortable shuffle, and the fixed smile on his face, that he didn't quite share Dad's sense of humour but couldn't be rude because he was getting a lift. He must have seen that my father wasn't a religious Jew, but I hoped he wouldn't see just how bad he really was. Sometimes, I thought my father set out to shock him deliberately and was almost under the back seat with embarrassment when we drove up to Mr Rosenberg's gate.

One day his wife was waiting to meet him. I was staggered.

'Oh, Mum,' I said when we arrived home, 'you should see Mr Rosenberg's wife. She's young and pretty and dainty, and has lovely red hair.'

Mum smiled. 'She may do, I suppose.'

'What do you mean, may do?'

'Her hair won't be her own. She wears a *sheitel* – a wig. When orthodox women marry they shave off their hair and keep their heads covered for the rest of their lives.'

Mum looked at my horror-stricken face and laughed. 'And her marriage will have been arranged for her. A learned man's considered a good catch among the ultra orthodox. Now aren't you glad you have parents like us?'

Had I ever had any pretensions at orthodoxy they vanished in that moment. God could ask too much.

With immense relief I graduated from Hebrew classes at thirteen with my expensive Diploma and almost no understanding of the philosophy of Judaism whatsoever. My brother was not so lucky. He had a *Bar Mitzvah* coming to him – the most important moment of his life, when, in the eyes of the entire Jewish community, he would prove he was a man. This feat was achieved by standing before parents, grandparents, aunts, uncles, cousins twice and twenty times removed, to sing a portion of the Law. No pressure – but it would be word perfect.

One to one Hebrew drilling was the only concession to his having any importance on the occasion at all. My mother rushed around like a virago for months, arranging caterers for a Sabbath luncheon, choosing menus and finding a band for the Sunday afternoon tea dance, desperately trying to kindle some interest in my father, who only reacted when he saw the estimates.

'What am I, Rothschild? We have two daughters to see married, and you want 200 at a *Bar Mitzvah* party? Where do you find so many relatives? Just as well Hitler put paid to most of mine, eh?'

'So we have mine instead.'

The volley continued, week in, week out, but from the beginning there was only one assured victor.

'The seating plan's all wrong,' she moaned. 'We can't have uncle Jack and uncle Myer at the same table. They haven't been speaking for years.'

'So move one of them to table twenty.'

'That's the table for the divorced and married-outs. We can't do that. And by the way, there's a bill in the post from Books Fashion House. You have a wife and two daughters to clothe, and since the Books family is related, at least we get a discount.'

Mum liked to keep her money in the family and the family was only too happy to keep it there too. From the moment we walked through the dress shop door, half a dozen harpies swooped on us both and carried my mother off to the model gowns department. I was left to wander around on my own, and spent a long while fingering the rows of gorgeous satin, silk, and lace dresses – but not for a fourteen-year-old. And then I saw it – the dress of my dreams. It was a dainty, pretty creation in royal blue chiffon with a frilled square neckline and large, puff sleeves, very much like the dress worn by Walt Disney's Snow White. I had never worn frills before. Mum liked to hide my puppy fat bulges in what she referred to as 'something tailored' – usually beige and ugly. Lovingly, I took the dress down from the rail, got it on as quickly as I could, then rushed to find my mother who, clad only in bra and corset, was shouting instructions to the entire department.

'Da, daa,' I shouted desperately, as I twirled in front of her. 'Isn't this fantastic?'

She stopped mid-sentence and quickly looked me up and down.

'It's a bit revealing, isn't it?'

'Not really. It's just that I'm high busted.'

'She has got a lovely figure for her age,' said one of the harpies, suddenly aware of a sale in another direction.

'You mean she's got a big bust? Well you ought to know. It's your side of the family she gets it from. No, I can't have her looking like a barmaid.'

I argued, I begged, I pleaded. My happiness depended, in those pre-aunt Ida shopping spree days, on having that dress, not some boring outfit that made me feel the awkward and unattractive teenager I thought I was. Fortunately, Gran took my side. And eventually, with decisions enough about her own wardrobe, Mum conceded – on condition that a 'dickie' was cut off from the hem and sewn across the offending cleavage. By the time we went home, leaving garments strewn from one end of the shop to the other, everyone was exhausted, but happy.

As the great day approached, presents began to arrive: five writing cases, seven alarm clocks, nine fountain pens. They all had to be displayed for the guests, without Aunt Sadie noticing that her present was an inferior version of Auntie Hilda's. In our more modest house, space provided something of a challenge. But for a *Bar Mitzvah* all things are possible – even if there was barely room for Michael to get into bed at night. The official photographer, the arranger of plastic flowers, relations, waitresses, caterers with vast tureens of chopped liver and chopped herring which they mixed by hand, all fought their way into every available corner. Michael and I stood and goggled. We had never seen anyone elbow-deep in chopped liver before. I couldn't bring myself to eat any of it at the buffet.

Great-aunt Rae took me by the chin, and submitting my face to close scrutiny, said, 'Greatly improved' – one of the best backhanded compliments I have ever had. 'What a big girl you're getting, so like her mummy,' chirped the rest, a refrain I heard so many times I was tempted to join in. '*Soon* there'll be a boyfriend, and then, please God, a wedding. That will be the next family *simcha*.'

And under my breath I added, 'But first my O levels and A levels and university, please God.'

'She's time enough,' my father answered to my relief, thinking of his bank balance. Besides, I knew he intended me to go into medicine.

Michael, scrubbed and cropped, in a suit for the first time, wore an expression of disbelief, as if it were all happening to someone else. Like a wooden soldier he stuck out his arm to greet his guests, escorted his mother out onto the dance floor and read his after dinner speech.

'I would like to thank my wonderful parents for all they have done for me.'

They had written it. Nevertheless, like every Jewish parent Mum lapped up the applause.

I felt sick inside – but why on earth should I? There were relatives here I hadn't seen for years, some from Israel I had never met before. My generous-hearted Aunt Marie, as wide as she was tall, in stilettos and false eyelashes and flirting unashamedly with every male in her orbit, had said in front of my father, to his immense pride, that I was known in my family for being loving and kind. Yet still I couldn't enter into the occasion. What was it all for, the effort, the expense? Michael would be the same tomorrow as he was today. There were some things about our religion I couldn't grasp. No one else seemed to feel as I did, so something must be wrong with me. I put it out of my mind, too frightened to delve any deeper.

Chapter 3

Lessons in the Jewish Way of Life

*J*ewish daughters learn all they really need to know, not from Hebrew classes, but from their mothers. And what does a Jewish daughter need to know? How to get herself a good catch, that's what.

'Your father's not a wealthy man,' my mother would say with a regretful shake of her head. 'There's not much of a dowry for you. You'll just have to get by on your cooking.'

If all her hard work and effort had been properly rewarded I should have netted a Rothschild at the very least. By the time I was fifteen there was nothing I didn't know about keeping a *kosher* kitchen.

'Stand here and watch... stir this, beat that. How many times have you salted the meat? Do it again – until there is no hint of blood in the rinsing water... Make the Yorkshire puddings – with water, not milk... No, we can't have a cheese sauce. How many times must I tell you, we can't mix meat and dairy.'

In interpreting the law that said, 'Thou shalt not boil a kid in its mother's milk,' my mother never went to the lengths of some of her friends – separate dishes for milk and meat, separate sinks to wash them in, separate tea towels, even

73

separate dishwashers when they became available. But she wouldn't serve the two together at a meal. No pastas for us – unless we went to an Italian restaurant. Fortunately, Dad was a meat-and-two-veg man. And that meat always came from a *kosher* butcher.

'Why bother?' my father murmured, whenever she complained about the price of *kosher* meat. 'There's only one way to slit an animal's throat humanely and let the blood drain out – whether it's the Jewish or the British way. It's all the same. All you're getting for your money is an expensive blessing.'

Yet Mum persisted in the belief that every Jewish man would only know true inner peace when he was sure his wife kept a strictly *kosher* kitchen. It was a law – on an equal par with a variety of unwritten rules that carried the same weight, like eating cold fried fish on Friday evenings. That tradition probably began with the command not to work on Sabbath. And since, on Friday evenings, our washing was always hung up to dry on a rack hanging across the kitchen ceiling, it was just as inevitable that Michael and I would go to school on Monday mornings smelling like fried fish. In later years, I can't think it did much for us in the romance stakes.

Sabbath also meant chicken – a versatile creature appearing in a dozen different disguises over a 24-hour period. The Friday morning ritual began with a crackling and spitting pan on the cooker, as my mother rendered down the chopped-up fat she removed from the bird's rear orifice, then threw in any extraneous skin, cut into small pieces. Fried in the liquefying substance, the pieces of skin were removed when well-browned, drained on kitchen paper and served up, as a special aperitif called *grebens*. We fought over the crunchy, crispy, greasy morsels, my brother and sister and I. They were much tastier than potato crisps – probably an early precursor to the barbecue chicken variety.

Mum strained the remainder of the liquid fat into a large jam jar which solidified in the fridge and she used to make a stuffing, boiled in a piece of the chicken's intestine, known as *helzel*. Or it contributed to her delicious chopped liver pâté, or *kneidlach*, matza meal dumplings. In fact, virtually every favourite Jewish delicacy was made with chicken fat or *schmaltz*, which not only gave Jewish cuisine its distinctive flavour, but also lent a colourful new Yiddish word for an excess of sentimentality, to the American language. It also, no doubt, warmed our arteries, providing them with the kind of cosy, furry lining which helped many a Jewish man, including my poor father, on his premature way into the next life.

No tiny bit of the chicken was wasted. My father's favourite Friday night hors d'oeuvre was the boiled heart, stomach and neck. He slurped and squelched his way through this particular delicacy, reserved especially for him, after it had contributed towards the production of that indispensable feature of Jewish life – chicken soup.

Dad was highly amused to read in the *British Medical Journal* one day that scientists had discovered what the Jews had known for centuries – that chicken soup is the best and only cure for the common cold, not to mention virtually every other affliction to ail humankind. He insisted on telling us over the meal table, that research had shown that chicken soup released any infected mucus blocking the higher nasal passages. It drained the sinuses, cleared the head, and allowed for a speedy, and presumably tasty, recovery.

There's an old Jewish tale that a man collapses and dies at a large function. A little old Jewish lady pushes her way to the front of the throng and shouts, 'Give 'im some chicken soup.'

'Madam,' says the young doctor in the throes of attempted resuscitation, 'chicken soup won't help.'

'Ah,' replies the old Mama, knowingly, 'But it won't hurt either.'

The chicken soup-making ritual was precise. My mother would bind a leek, a parsnip and a carrot into a bundle and put them into the pressure cooker with the fowl, which was immersed head-first in a grossly indecent-looking pose – its last act of defiance. After a few moments the mixture would begin to bubble and brew and my job was to skim off the filthy scum which rose to the surface. How I ever managed to eat it later will forever remain one of life's little mysteries. But we did, chasing with our soup spoons the *kneidlach* or dumplings that bobbed up and down like unexploded sea missiles in our bowls.

The actual chicken reappeared at Sabbath lunch on Saturday, cold and in pieces, lacking a little 'je ne sais quoi', which was presumably in the soup. It was irrelevant that in the affluent sixties Jews no longer needed to live so frugally. The tradition of the soup which looked like dirty dishwater and tasted better than fine old whisky had been far too long established.

Yiddishkeit, not Judaism, that was what really mattered to my mother and her friends. You could be as ignorant about your religion as you wanted to be, reject whatever ritual you found too tiresome, never attend synagogue, as long as you had that elusive, indescribable feel for a Jewish way of life. Tradition was more important than piety. All that was incumbent on a Jewish mother was to pass on to her daughters the art of Jewish homemaking, handed down for generations. This was the key to the stability of the Jewish family and the survival of the race.

'Ah, but there's something very special about Jewish family life.' It is a chorus in a romantic Gentile ode to Jewish values, repeated so often I began to convince myself that non-Jews must know something I didn't. True, the Jewish home weaves such a web around its occupants that they are bound to it by thousands of taut emotional threads. One tiny tug is all it takes to pull in the prey. How? Our home was not exactly average, but nor was it untypical. 'We don't do that, we're Jewish,' was almost a daily mantra. I didn't want to be different. I wanted to be like my friends, except that somehow, being Jewish did make me feel special. That was home's secret, that was what it gave me – a sense of destiny, the feeling that it was a privilege to be Jewish and not just an embarrassing genetic defect. After all, if Hitler had had his way, or the Tzar for that matter, or any of the many other master practitioners of anti-semitism down through the centuries, I wouldn't have existed at all. I was one of a chosen people, chosen by whom and for what I had no idea, but that wasn't the point. We had our own festivals and celebrations which none of my school friends really understood, a secret bond between all Jews, linking us inextricably to one another.

The only festival I envied my non-Jewish friends was Christmas. They didn't really celebrate any others as far as I could see. By comparison with a Jewish festival, handing out a few chocolate eggs at Easter hardly constituted a celebration. But fantasizing about the mysterious world hidden behind the closed curtains of every non-Jewish home, I thought Christmas must be the most joyous occasion imaginable, with happy families nestling cosily around an open fire sharing undreamed of delights wrapped in crêpe paper and topped with satin bows, eating melt-in-the-mouth mince pies, and listening to familiar carols singing softly in harmony around a baby grand piano, while fairy lights twinkled on a sweet-scented fir tree. It was a vision that owed more to Charles Dickens than reality. I knew nothing of the near murders which ensued when Mother-in-law took over the kitchen, Granny left her hearing aid at home, Billy rode his new bike over the baby and Daphne announced she'd become a vegetarian. It would have amazed, even shocked me had I known then that many non-Jews lived in dread of this major event in the Christian calendar, submitted to it with stoic resignation and endured it in an uncomfortable, stomach-stretched, semi-inebriated state.

I would have loved a tree, dripping with tinsel, and fairy lights twinkling around the front door. Mum bought a turkey, since technically, Christmas was a bank holiday, but it just wasn't the same without crackers or decorations or presents to be unwrapped. But then, virtually the entire world had Christmas. And there were always the parties and a tree at school. So our festivals were unique, and therefore more magical after all.

It was just that Michael, Nicky and I were at a great disadvantage when it came to understanding what they all meant. Mr Rosenberg reckoned that parents would make the necessary explanations, but our mother never could remember which was which, or why she was doing what when.

'What's this one about, Mum?' we asked her one December, as she lit her *hannukiah*, the nine-branched candelabra used at *Hanukkah*, the festival of lights.

'Er...' she said vaguely, checking that each of the tiny candles was absolutely vertical, so that no wax would drip on the brass and ruin the display, 'Something to do with the Temple?'

'Yes?' we prompted.

'Somebody's oil lasted eight days?'

'Whose?'

'How should I know, I wasn't there.'

'Does Judas Maccabeus ring a bell?'

'Who?'

'The Jewish hero who drove the Syrian army out of the Temple.'

I had actually heard the full story at school.

'*Hanukkah* is all about Judas Maccabeus' heroic victory when he drove out the wicked King Antiochus Epiphanes of Syria, who had sacrificed a pig on the altar. The Jews went to rededicate the Temple, but only had enough holy oil to light the sacred flame for one day. The miracle was that it lasted eight days – until more could be found.'

'Well, whoever it was,' she muttered, watching the wax defy her and drip all over the candelabra anyway, 'I wish he'd never started this business, because now we have to do it every year.'

Mum regarded most of the major Jewish holy days as an affliction to be endured. She carried out her traditions as if the appeasement of God's wrath depended on it – not because it gave her any spiritual comfort or joy. The arrival of September filled her with dismay.

'Three Jewish holidays, three in four weeks, and I haven't started to think, cook or clean.'

Rosh Hashanah, the New Year or Feast of Trumpets, is the first, which means the Jewish New Year actually begins in the seventh month of the Jewish calendar. Jews are always late for everything – except their own funerals, which, as a throwback to their fridge-less, desert days, have to take place within twenty-four hours if possible, and are arranged almost as the about-to-be deceased draws their last breath. It's a major distraction for the grieving relatives during those final moments. 'If he goes in the next hour or so, they'll be able to fit him in tomorrow before the Sabbath.' They're late for parties and late for meetings. They even walk into the synagogue anything up to two hours after the service has started, sometimes just in time for the final prayer. 'Jewish time' is officially half an hour later than the stated time. But celebrating a new year seven months late could seem a step too far.

It's not as illogical as it sounds. Although the Jewish year officially starts with the Passover, the birth of the nation, its deliverance from captivity, its receiving of the Law and the beginning of its special relationship with God, *Rosh Hashanah* is supposed to mark the anniversary of creation, when time began and human beings first became subject to the ticking of a vast universal clock. And even if God didn't bring the world into being some time in September, why should it not, like the Queen, have an official birthday? And since seven is a holy number, the seventh month might be highly appropriate.

For Christians a new year is a new year, and begins where it should begin, in the first month. The only problem with that is that very little begins in January because it has already started – in September. That's when thousands of bleary-eyed children, satchels bulging with first-day paraphernalia, make their way back to the great portals of education; when an advancing army of tousled-haired juvenility in regulation denim and oversized jerseys head back to academia; when the teaching profession reluctantly collects its books and bags from the corners where they have lain for six weeks, and heads sadly for the car, ruminating wistfully on those halcyon days in Brittany, Betws-y-Coed, Mull and Majorca. It is the new academic year. Real life begins again.

The Jewish New Year was an important enough occasion to merit a new outfit, or 'rigout' as my mother called it, as if, like a yacht, a woman was unequipped for the high sea of Jewish society without the tackle of matching shoes, gloves, hat and bag. Dressed up in miniature-adult finery, the children would sit in the synagogue waiting with great anticipation for the weird sound of the ram's horn. Producing any sound on the *shofar* is no mean achievement, but I didn't appreciate the fact then. I wondered why it seemed to take such an effort, and, as the rabbi turned damson and the veins in his temples swelled, conjured up a vivid, nightmare scenario where, like a balloon, he finally exploded, spraying bits of brain across the synagogue.

A long, loud blast on the *shofar* was supposed to rouse the snoozing congregation to reflection on past failure and future potential, but we were all so focused on willing a note out of the instrument, there was little time for meditation. One New Year not a note emerged. The synagogue was filled instead with the sound of an old man snoring. He had passed into unconsciousness some time during the fifth attempt, and the rest of the men were too engrossed in their own chatter to poke him in the ribs. Upstairs in the gallery, his wife waved frantically, trying to attract the attention of her sons and nephews, the feathers of her New Year hat fluttering with the effort, as she gesticulated in the direction of the sleeping figure of her husband, slumped in his seat below.

'What? What's she trying to say?' the men in her life mouthed back at her. By which time most of the congregation understood, even if they didn't.

The rabbi, irritated by the distraction, and even more by the waywardness of the instrument, steadied his hat, summoned every ounce of dignity he possessed, drew his breath, and blew. Out came a shrill, cracked little squeak. The respectful silence was suddenly broken by the raucous laughter of a child who manifestly couldn't hold it in any longer. I was relieved it wasn't me. The rabbi removed the ram's horn from his mouth and fixed the young renegade with a look so terrible that I feared he would turn to stone. Oh the shame for his parents. No New Year pocket money for him. Finally the rabbi managed to hold a note, and with relief, the adults all sang the familiar, accompanying words – *Tekija, teruah*, roughly translated, 'wakey, wakey' – a little too lustily, by way of moral encouragement, while we children giggled uncontrollably.

Played properly, the *shofar* sounds like the bellowing of a rhinoceros trying to attract a mate from another herd twenty miles away. It is supposed to herald the arrival of the sovereign of the universe. God is absolute monarch over all he has made, and the congregation, not to mention the entire neighbourhood, should be reduced to trembling.

The *shofar* has always had happy associations. In the early days of the Jewish people, it was used as a kind of bush telegraph sending messages across the miles, such as, 'Down tools, lads, the Sabbath's almost here.' In fact it was probably the Hebrew equivalent of the shop floor manager's whistle. Except of course, like everything else in Judaism, it also has its own symbolic significance, derived from the story of Abraham and Isaac. God tested his servant to the limit when he asked him to sacrifice his only child – his every dream, his future and the future of his people. But Abraham was prepared to submit to the King of the Universe, and give him what he loved most in the world. It was then that God provided a ram, caught in a thicket, as a substitute. The ram's horn has been used on important occasions ever after, and Jewish sheep have been giving hedges a wide berth.

As the *shofar* curves, say the Jewish people, we, like Abraham, must bend to the will of the Almighty. And he, the 'All-Merciful', will take account of how vulnerable we are. A lamb that is shorn at the end of summer and throughout the autumn, until the new wool grows, is at the mercy of the climate. With no natural protection, an early cold snap could kill it. So its horn symbolizes how, at the beginning of every new year, our future hangs in the balance. But as we move out into uncharted waters, we have a constant guide and protector.

The old chasidic sage, Levi Isaac of Berdichev, once told the story of a king who was lost in a forest. Eventually a wise old peasant found him and escorted him safely home. The king was so grateful that he gave the peasant a key job in his government. Several years later the official made an unwise decision and was forced to give account before the king. He arrived wearing the ragged old clothes he had worn the first time they met. The king remembered that meeting, and forgave him. As the *shofar* reminds God of his people's good beginning, said Rabbi Levi Isaac – the sacrifice of Abraham, their commitment at Sinai to accept his kingship – so he will remember the noble intentions with which we set out on the journey of faith, forgive our failure to live up to them and help us fulfil them in the year ahead.

Rosh Hashanah is a chance to look forward with excitement and expectation. Families eat pieces of apple dipped in honey, and pray for a sweet new year. We ate carrots, lots of them, in a stew called *tzimmis*, because of their sweetness, and, since the Hebrew word for carrot means, 'to increase', they represented abundant blessing. It was definitely preferable to eating a fish head, as some Jews do, in the hope that we may be 'the head and not the tail', the front and not the rear end, of God's handiwork.

My mother never quite entered the spirit of the occasion. Her annual *Rosh Hashanah* refrain was always, 'Please God, may next year not be as bad as the last.'

'You said that last year, and it was,' we remind her.

Then she cheers up and says, 'At least it can't get any worse.'

From the eve of *Rosh Hashanah* to *Yom Kippur*, the Day of Atonement, are 'The ten days of awe' – ten days for dealing with all the unfinished business of the past year, for quiet reflection on lessons to be learned, for mending broken relationships, for giving charity, for tying up any remaining loose ends and for remembering the dead.

For us, as for many Jewish families, that involved an annual, dreaded pilgrimage to a variety of cemeteries. Mike and I were left waiting in the car outside together for what seemed an eternity. On one occasion, on the back window ledge the dear little lad found the walking stick my father had confiscated from a Nazi officer during the war. Within its leather sheath was a sharp and lethal sword, and he spent the next half hour brandishing it round and round the car, almost decapitating me in the process. I was terrified. But when the adults emerged, serious and blinking, I was told to stop telling tales.

'What did you do, Dad?'

'Said a prayer.'

We had driven fifty miles to Teeside, dragged the local rabbi away from his fireside chair on a Sunday afternoon, had hung round for what seemed an eternity on a biting autumnal day and I had almost been beheaded. For a prayer?

'Couldn't you have said it at home?'

'No, I needed to be here.'

No explanation. There never was. That was something I could never accept.

Later, in my teens, I accompanied my parents. Everyone stood around looking sheepish. No flowers are left on Jewish graves. A stone is the preferred symbol of remembrance – but they can be hard to find in the well-picked-over gravel and neat little paths. My mother read and reread the inscriptions on the slabs as if they might have changed since last year.

'Did we use the right wording, do you think?'

'Too late to change them now', said the matter-of-fact doctor.

'Have they been dead that long, God rest their souls? Where do the years go?'

'I still miss them.'

As she passed the graves of my great grandparents, renowned for their incompatibility in life, my mother would muse on their probable incompatibility in death.

'Can you hear anything? She's probably giving him hell. Funny they should lie together so peacefully when they did nothing but row in this life.'

'Happy New Year', say the *Rosh Hashanah* greeting cards, 'And well over the Fast', they add ominously, as if the Day of Atonement was a two-week feat of endurance, rather than a twenty-four hour inconvenience for the stomach. It is in fact the most solemn occasion in the Jewish calendar. For every adult over the age of thirteen it is a total fast, not only from food (listen out for the interesting orchestration of gut and wind instruments), from washing and bathing (have your air freshener handy throughout the day), shaving (the men in the synagogue look like a gathering of escaped convicts in bowler hats), sex (no one can check up on you) and wearing leather (thank heavens for plastic).

Once I was twelve, no sip of water was to pass my lips from sundown to sundown. It is a day for confessing one's sins to God, but at that age I found it hard to know what my sins were, so I went to the synagogue for light relief instead. The service takes all day so there is no time to eat anyway.

'Who do you think will be the first to faint and be carried out this year, Mike?'

'Peter – again.'

'He does it just to show off.'

'All right, then, let's have a bet on it.'

We waited with ghoulish anticipation for the first victim of hunger to crumble into a heap. It was almost always a man. We women had a bird's eye view from the upstairs gallery. By about three o'clock in the afternoon, Gran, a tiny bird of a woman, used to whisper that she was gasping for a cuppa, or better still, a ciggy or a whisky, but she stood stalwartly in her pew in the gallery, prayer book in hand, watching with undisguised disdain as some six-foot giant below, overcome by hunger pangs and the heat, crumpled in a heap and was manhandled out into the fresh air.

The service then resumed with even more chatter, shuffling, yawning, stretching and tummy rumbling. My favourite moment came late in the afternoon. The chatter and the play of children stopped, and an awed hush descended on the congregation. Downstairs, the *cohanim* – the men who were members of the priestly line descended from the tribe of Levi – covered their heads with their prayer shawls, and began to sway in harmony, chanting a blessing on the people. No one was supposed to look, but I never could resist a peep, fascinated by the haunting sound and uncanny sight of wave upon waves of the shimmering white and silver sea beneath me. This is the moment when the minister utters the Tetragrammaton, JHWH, or Jehovah, the holy and mystical name of God, who alone has the power to forgive sins. The slate is wiped clean. God's great Book of Judgment, supposedly opened at *Rosh Hashanah*, in which is inscribed all the deeds of humankind, is shut for another year.

From that moment on the women's gallery began to empty. One mother after another was lured away to her kitchen, overpowered by thoughts of roast chicken, chopped herring, luscious desserts and all the ritual preparations for breaking the fast. Food always tasted marvellous on that night. It was amazing how much you could put away once your tummy had been cajoled into coping with the onslaught by a glass of milk and soda water. What would be on the menu tonight? The drooling anticipation became almost unbearable until the prayer books slammed shut in unison with an almighty crack, and the synagogue emptied in record time. Why linger to chat this evening when there would be food on the table?

Sukkot, the Feast of Booths or Tabernacles, was the last of the autumn festivals, and suffered in our home as a result. Sad, because it is the most joyous and the most fun of the three, but it was difficult to take any more time off school – especially at the beginning of an academic year. It certainly appeared to be more meaningful than the Christian harvest festival, celebrated annually at school on a Wednesday morning in early October. I was always the only girl in my class without four apples on a piece of purple card, wrapped in cling film, or four cans of baked beans in a cardboard box, sitting on her desk. At the sound of the bell, the girls gathered their treasures to their ever-expanding chests, marched into the Assembly Hall, and sang, 'We plough the fields and scatter', only they hadn't. Their parents had purchased the necessary at the local grocers or fruiterers, and by the time they were deposited on the school stage all that remained was a large pile of bruised and battered produce.

Sukkot, meaning Tabernacles or Booths, is much more than a harvest festival. 'You shall live in booths for seven days, so that future generations will know that I made the people of Israel live in booths when I brought them out of the land of Egypt.' It commemorates the forty years my ancestors spent wandering around the Sinai Peninsula – no small achievement, considering the fact that the Egyptians couldn't hold out three days when they found themselves trapped there in 1967 during the Six-Day War. 'I gave you food, drink and clothing', God reminds his people, just in case their gratitude has worn a little thin with time. 'Even your shoes didn't wear out.' On such rough, stony terrain, that was a major miracle. A bad time in the history of Jewish cobblers.

When I was a child my brother and I desperately wanted to spend a week in a *sukkah*, a sort of makeshift tree house at ground level, made out of planks, branches, twigs, bits of carpet, and any other spare materials that are to hand. *Sukkot* was supposed to be a celebration of nature, a special moment when human beings, overawed by the great canopy of the night sky, are stripped of the conceit of considering themselves masters of the universe.

'Dad, build us a tabernacle in the garden.'

'A what?'

'Well a booth – a kind of wooden shed will do. All Jews are supposed to have one.'

Michael and I envisaged moving into it for the eight days of the festival, with sleeping bags and pyjamas. Despite the autumnal chill, I thought it must be terribly romantic to sleep out beneath the stars, just as my ancestors had done – a sort of glorified camping holiday, in the back garden.

'Your father, build a shed! Are you crazy? He can't even change a plug.'

We looked from Mum to Dad hopefully, willing him to defy her words, but he didn't. With a father who didn't know one end of a screwdriver from another, and a mother who couldn't sew a button on, it was a non-starter. Inventiveness, creative genius, had hardly been bestowed in any noticeable quantity on my family, and even if it had, how could my mother keep a tabernacle clean? Or the house, if we were tramping in and out all day and night?

We would have to be satisfied with the *mega-sukkah* at the synagogue, though a communal booth just wasn't the same. Unfortunately for us, Tabernacles did not necessitate an end to Hebrew classes. The only difference was that for light relief we were spared an hour of regimented translation work, and marched out into a large canopied contraption, leaning for safety against the synagogue wall. Branches and twigs above us dangled plastic grapes that threatened to throttle us if we didn't watch our step. Mr Rosenberg, his little chest puffed out until he was as round and plump as a well-fed robin, presented each of us with a glass of lemonade and a plain biscuit.

We sat in rows on wooden benches while he beamed at us all over his beard with festive tolerance, waiting for the appropriate blessing. It was more like a leer.

'Which one is it?' we hissed at each other. 'What's the blessing for? Biscuits or lemonade?'

'Try the one for lemons.'

'There are probably no lemons in it.'

'Does a lemon grow in the ground or on a tree?'

And woe betide us if we got the wrong one. There was no law preventing a child from standing in the corner of a *sukkah*.

It was all supposed to be a huge treat, but ungrateful wretches that we were, unused to such rabbinic benevolence, and used to gorging ourselves on a great deal more than plain, sweet biscuits, we kept our eyes on the lemonade in our plastic beakers for as long as we could, its fizz tickling our noses, then someone ruined the performance by looking up and grinning, and we all tried to hide our helpless giggling behind the plastic greenery. The boys burped lemonade loudly all the way back to the classroom.

Few of my classmates had a *sukkah* at home either. The Jewish community in which I was raised was prosperous and comfortable. They had no desire to remind themselves of the hard living conditions, either of their forefathers in the wilderness, or of their parents who had fled the pogroms of Eastern Europe. They wanted to forget that they had once been poor immigrants, thankful for a roof over their heads and the means of earning a meagre living. Perhaps it was a pity, for when wealth abounds, there's a value in remembering our humble origins, in being grateful for what we have and sensitive to our fragile existence. Material possessions are flimsy, shaky and temporary, and living in a *sukkah* for a few days is a symbolic placing of oneself beneath the permanence of divine protection and care.

I suppose I could hardly blame my parents and their friends for their reluctance. The rules governing the construction of booths are extraordinarily complex. The roof must be made of material grown from the earth, not mined, it must be cut down, not connected to the ground, and not subject to any ritual impurity. It would have made matters considerably easier if there had been a do-it-yourself *sukkah* kit on sale, a sort of glorified wendy-house, which could be erected and taken down every year, like a fake Christmas tree.

Mum only insisted we attend synagogue for major festivals, and since she rarely came with us, that seemed grossly unfair. But one festival was too good to miss – *Purim*, the Feast of Esther, sometime during the month of March. The synagogue was always noisy, with people coming and going and kissing their relatives as they came and went, but the rabbi only ever stopped the service when he could no longer hear himself. He would rest his elbows on the pulpit and, tapping his foot with a look of mock weariness on his face, fix the evil eye on the women's gallery, from whence, it must be said, most of the noise ensued. It could take up to two minutes for the realization to dawn that the service had ground to a halt, and then a penitent, but very temporary silence would descend. But at *Purim*, the more noise the better. As the rabbi recounted the famous story of Esther – in English fortunately – we cheered loudly for Esther and her Uncle Mordecai, then booed and hissed with all our might at every mention of the name of Haman. Some children waved rattles or even bounced on whoopee cushions.

Hebrew classes inflicted *Purim* plays on our parents – a sort of nativity play, with children playing bloodthirsty soldiers, not benign little angels. Like every other girl, my dream was to play the part of Queen Esther. But the tubby little figure I squeezed into a school tunic every day thwarted my aspirations to stardom. Instead I was cast as

the inevitable Persian soldier – a walk-on extra – and being
small, wrestled with the visor of an oversized helmet which
kept falling over my eyes, so that I couldn't see to make
a decent entrance or exit and kept falling over my sword,
which trailed along the ground. Still, it made up for the years
I had never been allowed in the school nativity play, however
appropriate it might have been for me to play the part of that
Jewish girl, Mary.

Of all the festivals, Passover made the others pale into
insignificance. Eight days without bread, cake, biscuits,
or corn flakes. Eight days craving the things you never
normally ate anyway and of Gran complaining of chronic
constipation. I cannot think why I loved Passover at all,
except that the first two Seder, or 'service' nights, made up
for the sacrifices the rest of the time. On those two nights
the whole family gathered to celebrate the deliverance of our
people from slavery in Egypt three thousand years ago.

Every year followed an invariable pattern. That was part
of the fun. You knew exactly what was coming.

'We can't start, we can't start,' panted Gran, as she
opened the front door. She was back in the kitchen before
we were in. 'The meringue isn't risen and Martin's still in
the bath.'

The bungalow resounded with a bass voice singing scales,
and the occasional loud splash.

'He would be, of course,' my mother exploded. 'You get
out of there and quick,' she yelled as we passed the door.

'All right, sister dearest,' came the reply, mimicking her
voice exactly, but the singing and splashing continued.

'And stop the racket.'

'Just getting into voice for the occasion. *Chad gad ya... ha,
ha, ha.*'

Michael and I giggled. The song about the kid sold for two farthings was a sort of Jewish 'Ten Green Bottles' and the climax of the second half of tonight's performance.

Mum shrugged and headed for the nearest armchair.

'Teenagers! Let me sit down. What a week! I'm worn out.'

She flopped into the armchair next to Grandpa. There wasn't a visit when the luminous green of my grandmother's suite didn't seem out of sorts with the sapphire carpet and gold curtains. But Grandpa insisted the three-piece suite was blue. He refused to take it back to the workshop, so what could Gran do? A furniture manufacturer would never admit he was colour blind.

He was hunched as ever, over the two-bar electric fire, trying to achieve what his circulation no longer could and rub some warmth and feeling back into his hands.

'Uh-huh,' he said. That and, 'What time do you plan to go home?' was all he ever said, but it was sympathy enough for his daughter.

'The price of Passover food this year. And no one has everything you want. I went to Cohen's for cheese, Steinberg's for chocolate and Bloom's for orange squash.'

Fired by the thought of the huge cardboard box in our hallway, packed to the brim with jars, packets, tins and bottles, Michael piped up, 'I thought you could eat anything as long as it didn't have yeast or anything in it that would make it rise.'

'Right,' I said knowingly, 'we can't eat leaven.'

Mike was silent for a moment or two, then asked, 'Does cheese have leaven in it? Does squash, or chocolate or jam?'

Dad looked at us over the top of the evening newspaper.

'No, they don't. But at Passover you can only eat food that has the special "kosher for Passover" label.'

'What difference does that make?' Mike asked incredulously.

'A great deal,' replied my father, 'it doubles the price.'

Dad had very little time for the *Beth Din*'s system of sanctioning *kosher* food. The *Beth Din*, or 'Court of Rules', was based in Finchley. Dad called it the 'Death Bin'. 'They'd sanction anything – if you paid them enough.'

'Now, Herald,' Gran remonstrated, arriving to check the table one last time, 'you know we do things properly in this family. I've always expected it of my daughter.'

My father disappeared behind his newspaper.

'And, incidentally,' she added, looking at my mother, 'you have soaked the glassware, haven't you?'

'Yes, Mam.'

'And changed over to the Passover set of crockery?'

'Yes, Mam.'

'And checked the house for breadcrumbs?'

'Why do you think I'm so exhausted?'

Mike and I caught each other's eye and smiled. We knew that no glassware or crockery had been touched – but that the housework had been done to perfection. One tradition we dispensed with in our home was the father's torchlight search for any leaven which might have escaped the spring cleaning. Dad regarded it as a futile exercise since no self-respecting breadcrumb would ever dare defy the daily help's vacuum cleaner, or my mother's meticulous inspection of her work.

'Good evening one and all.' Martin appeared, all six foot of him, ruddy and polished and ready for the fray. 'A kiss from the nieces and nephew and then we'll begin.'

'You took your time,' my mother scowled, resenting the way her handsome younger brother always took control of events. Useless to expect any support in her grousing, for in

Gran's eyes Martin could do no wrong. He was son, husband, friend and her entire world.

We made our way to the table. The cloth had been bleached a dazzling white, and starched until it crinkled when we moved up against it. The best silver had been polished to perfection, and I could see a rather odd, distended reflection of myself every time I held up my wine goblet, which shimmered in the candle light. The wine was poured into the goblets, and looked like a mass of ruby jewels. The scent of it was heady. An embroidered coverlet, draped over three pieces of unleavened bread, added a startling dash of scarlet and emerald.

'What's that for?' I asked, pointing at an egg with a badly burned shell, lying on the dish of Passover symbols in the middle of the table. We were so used to seeing these peculiarities every year that it took some time before we really looked at them and realized we hadn't a clue what they were there for. Even if an explanation had once been given we always forgot it in the intervening twelve months.

'It symbolizes the Temple of old which was destroyed in AD 70 and has never been rebuilt. Some rabbis think an egg also speaks of hope and new life,' explained Martin. He was a fount of all knowledge and the only one who would ever explain anything. He was going to be a journalist and travel the world, he said, when he finished university. Four years his junior, I held him in awe rather than sisterly affection – though it's hard to remember now, in the light of what was to come.

'And what's that bone next to it for?'

'The shank bone represents the Passover lambs slaughtered in the Temple to grant us access to God. And, of course, the lambs whose blood was daubed on the doorposts of the homes of the children of Israel, so that the Angel of Death would know not to pay a visit there.'

'And this?' I held up a piece of parsley.

'That reminds us of the hyssop that your ancestors used to smear on the blood.'

'Yuk. And...'

'Oh do be quiet and wait,' my mother snapped. 'Where are the *haggadahs*?' She looked on the sideboard for the service books, but Martin was already handing them out.

'Don't give me that one.' Gran handed it back. 'I had it last year and the print's too small.' Her glasses were so smeared with food, it would be a wonder if she saw anything. 'Who has mine? It has a wine stain on page 52.'

'I don't want this one,' I moaned. In fact, it was revolting. The pages were so congealed with old food I couldn't turn them. I gave it back and demanded another.

'I want the one with the colour pictures of the plagues.'

'Little ghoul,' Martin said, cuffing Michael across the ear.

'Damn, I've forgotten my reading glasses.' Dad fumbled in his pockets.

'Will someone please start,' Mum demanded, 'before I go barmy.'

'All right then, Michael, off you go,' said Martin. 'Ask the four questions.'

'Which four?'

He knew very well which four. This was his moment of glory, when everyone's attention is focused on the youngest male child, whose questions form the basis of the whole service.

'Any four you like,' Martin grinned.

We opened our *haggadahs*, the appropriate opening blessings were made, then Michael read the four questions. Why is this night different from all other nights and why do we eat unleavened bread? Why do we eat bitter herbs instead of the usual vegetables? Why do we dip our food in the dish twice? Why do we eat leaning on our sides?

'Why do you ask the same questions every year,' Martin joked, 'because you always get the same answers?'

Grandpa began to read in Hebrew the long, learned, rabbinic response from the haggadah. The word *haggadah* means 'the telling', because it tells the story of our flight from Egypt, but I don't remember the four questions ever really being answered. He got slower and slower until his words were strung together in one loud snore. I used to think the cushions Gran put on his chair, there to symbolize the pretence that we were leaning, were really to prop him up and keep him awake.

'For goodness sake take over,' Gran shouted at Martin, 'or we'll be here all night.'

'Not yet, he's not quite asleep.'

'Ooooh, look,' Mike exclaimed, holding up his full-colour pop-up *haggadah*. 'Look at this picture of the Egyptian soldiers in the Red Sea. If I pull this tab, the waters roll over them and they all get drowned.'

'Gruesome little beggar, isn't he?' Martin said, staring at the picture with fascination.

There was another loud snore from the top of the table and then Martin began to sing – in perfect Hebrew. I could hear Mr Rosenberg's voice.

'Your uncle Martin, how he sings, what pronunciation, what diction, what delivery. Such beauty. He sings like a true *chasid*, like one of the most orthodox.'

His singing was impressive. Gran watched him, one moment with adoration, the next with aggravation as he stopped mid-flow to discuss the latest progress of Newcastle United with my father.

'Continue,' she snapped, and when he did, she continued to deliver her own piece of gossip to my mother. 'So, seemingly, Auntie Gertie...' I couldn't make out the rest of the whisper.

'What a terrible time we had in Egypt,' Grandpa suddenly exclaimed. Everyone looked up in surprise. 'Oy, such things we had to endure. Making bricks all day.'

For a moment I was convinced that he had actually been there.

Martin was whispering a joke into my father's ear, one of those adult jokes I presumed from the way his hand was cupped over his mouth, and Dad started giggling like a naughty schoolboy. He caught the full glare of Gran's ferocious eye, cleared his throat, and began murmuring, 'And we were slaves in Egypt. And the Egyptians oppressed us...'

'Herald,' Gran said, with an air of injured dignity, 'You aren't by any chance reading the English translation, are you? You know we don't do that in this house. We're Orthodox, not Reform or even Liberal, God forbid.'

I knew my father had started attending the new Reform Synagogue in Newcastle from time to time to see what it was like. Their services were half in English and they only kept the most basic of Jewish traditions. It appealed to his modernizing spirit. He had tried to hide his interest, but nothing in the Jewish community could ever be concealed for long – not from a mother-in-law.

'Dreadful wine,' my mother interjected, 'Whoever trod on this lot forgot to wash his feet first.'

'Well, drink up your second cup, sister dear, because there's a treat in store.'

It was time for the bitter herbs. Grandpa came to again with a grunt, saw everyone staring at the Passover dish and responded to his cue. He picked up the large horseradish root, shaved off miniature matchsticks and passed them round. I kept passing mine on until I ended up with a piece small enough to swallow in one gulp.

'You're supposed to be able to taste it,' Gran said, peering at the tiny speck on my palm, 'and it isn't meant to taste nice. It's to remind you of the bitterness endured by your ancestors.'

'As if we need reminding,' my mother muttered, quietly enough for my father not to hear. I suspected she had Grandma Rose in mind.

We dipped our horseradish into a bowl of brown mess called *charoset*. How was it possible that ingredients so delicious on their own – ground walnuts and apples, cinnamon, sugar and wine – could taste so vile when combined? Or was it force of suggestion? *Charoset* represented the mortar the Israelites used to mould their bricks into palaces, and that was exactly how it tasted.

Then came the sandwich of horseradish and *charoset* together, stuck between two pieces of *matzo* or unleavened bread. This represented an actual brick. No wonder Grandpa behaved as if the exodus had happened last year.

Only one more endurance test before the meal – a bowl of hard-boiled egg slices floating in salt water, the eyes and tears of my ancestors. I couldn't bear egg in any form and had to concentrate hard on keeping it down.

Life without yeast was definitely bearable. The meal was enormous – chopped herring pâté, chicken soup, roast chicken, *tzimmes*, then fruit, meringues, and traditional coconut haystacks and cinnamon cookies. To refuse any part of it was a personal insult of mammoth proportions.

'What do you mean you're full?' my grandmother would ask, in a voice I had learned to dread.

The word 'full' did not exist in Gran's vocabulary. It was never even a remote possibility – extraordinary for such a tiny woman who was anything but the conventional, well-rounded Jewish granny.

'I've stood here all day making coconut haystacks for you. They're your favourite.'

I usually responded with a weak smile of assent and forced down another unwanted mouthful, while my mother, sitting opposite, would lament my loss of a waistline.

'Can you never say "no"? You'll be lucky to get a man at all.'

I was caught, painfully, between two contradictory forces. But it was the Mama's Mama who always won. That was how things were in a matriarchal society. My poor father, who had given up any attempt at protest about anything within minutes of his engagement to my mother, ended the evening in the bathroom, swallowing half a bottle of antacid.

Fortunately Gran was a wonderful cook and baker. No one else's festival *tzimmis* was as tasty as hers. Her fluffy Passover meringues melted on the tongue. Her *Hanukkah* doughnuts spoilt the supermarket variety for us forever. Her spicy, New Year noodle pudding filled her entire bungalow with the enticing smell of cinnamon, honey and apples and filled the stomach so thoroughly that it rendered most of her guests unconscious. Each occasion had its own special food, and because we knew what to expect, my brother, sister and I looked forward to it with mouth-watering anticipation.

And we ate until we could hardly get up from the table. But whenever we suggested that Gran try eating some of the food she had so lovingly prepared she always declined.

'I'm absolutely packed,' she always said, and went on waiting on us. I made a mental note to try the word 'packed', instead of 'full', but she simply thought I was being facetious and ignored me.

It was years later, after she died, weighing a mere thirty-five kilos, that the staff in the nursing home asked my mother when she first realized that her mother was anorexic. We were shocked. It had never occurred to us that she was, but she had apparently lived on nothing but Woodbines and double whiskies for years. This, at least, explained why, in later life, she so often wobbled her way around her bungalow, complaining that her legs were not what they used to be. Succumbing to the pressure to stay slim, she sublimated the pleasure she derived from food into feeding others.

Throughout the meal, we never took our eyes off Grandpa. Sometime during the dessert he drew out the middle of three pieces of *matzo* under the coverlet and broke it in half. One half was the *afikomen* (the Alfie Cohen, my father called it), symbol of the Passover lamb. He would now have to hide it for us children to find and sell back to him. We watched him with unblinking concentration.

'Have you hidden it yet?'

'Have you seen me get up?'

We had to think. 'Yes... no... yes.'

Like a magician he always managed to elude our determined observation.

'Well it's gone.'

'I hope it's not going to be like last year,' I said self-righteously, 'when you forgot where you'd put it until Mum sat on it. A fat lot of good it was then.'

We jumped up from our chairs and tore round the bungalow, searching behind every curtain, in every drawer. Martin watched us in bored amusement.

'Got it,' shouted Michael.

'Decoy,' Grandpa replied, and produced five identical pieces from different corners of the room.

'Come on, Grandpa, this is the real one.' Michael wasn't going to give in that easily. 'Fifteen shillings split three ways between the two of us and the baby.'

'I don't want it this year.'

'You have to want it.'

'What for?'

'Because it's... it's a tradition.'

Eventually Mum intervened and negotiated a reasonable deal.

'At last,' Martin said, as the meal was cleared away by Ella, my gran's cringing shadow of a cleaner, who had come in specially for the occasion, 'because there's something I want you to hear.'

While the grown-ups had a coffee and a smoke, Martin took us upstairs into the loft, his own magic world. He put a vinyl record on the Dansette.

'Listen,' he commanded, and closed his eyes.

I heard a sound that was familiar but completely new. Martin had introduced us to Buddy Holly, Elvis Presley and Cliff Richard, but this was different. This was a sound that filled every space under the rafters, pounded in the guts and left you desperate to hear more.

'They're called The Beatles. Like 'em, eh? They're going to be big.'

And then, too soon, we were summoned down for the second half. Grandpa took the *afikomen*, broke it, blessed it and passed a piece to each of us. No more food would touch our lips tonight. Then he lifted the third cup of wine, the cup of blessing, and we all drank. Gran went to the front door to wait for the coming of Elijah. Would he come this year for his own, special goblet of wine and to tell us the Messiah was coming? No sound and no sign. Except the year Gran gave a sudden, heart-stopping, strangled cry, but it was only

Ella who had crept up silently behind her in her felt hat and tweed coat, and whispered, 'Goodnight, Mrs Davis.' Every year we were disappointed by Elijah's reticence to appear – except for my father who drank his cup of wine for him in his absence. It did occur to me that if he came, he wouldn't be able to stand after he had been to his first street, but I imagined that like Father Christmas, he would have ways and means of overcoming such difficulties.

Gran loved to recount the story of how, when she was a girl, her mother once opened the front door for Elijah, and to her shock, found a tramp standing on the path outside.

'You're not Elijah by any chance?' Great-grandmother Fishkin asked the bundle of rags and tatters. The beard, at least, looked authentic. Once she had established that he didn't know who Elijah was, there was no goblet of wine for him. But she fed him all the same.

As Gran stood at the door and Grandpa prayed for God's anger to come upon the wicked nations who didn't keep his commandments we drank the fourth cup, at which point Dad managed to launch his goblet across the table. Mesmerized, we all watched the steadily expanding red pool on the table, until Gran arrived back, took one look, and rushed out for a cloth.

'Herald, you get the laundry bill this year.'

'But Mam,' my mother said, rising to his defence, 'he didn't stand a chance. We've knocked the goblets over so many times their stems are all bent, and they don't stand up straight any more.'

'And whose fault is that?'

'Well,' Mum continued, taking a calculated risk, 'It was you who knocked the wine over last year, if you remember.'

Gran paused. 'Martin, get singing.'

'And a happy *Pesach* to all,' he grinned. 'It isn't a real Passover until someone spills the wine.'

He began to sing the traditional folk songs, faster and faster, until Michael and I gave up altogether. Gran sang different tunes, the ones she sang as a girl. Dad, the only other person present with a decent voice, couldn't follow the Hebrew. The racket rose to a crescendo during 'The Kid Sold for Two Farthings', which we all knew off by heart. Then suddenly it was all over and the books slammed shut for another year.

'Next year in Jerusalem.'

'And please God, may British Airways reduce the fare.'

Chapter 4

A Very Anglican Education

*M*y secular education was courtesy of the Church of England. There was no Jewish day school then, and even if there had been, my parents would have automatically dismissed it as, 'too narrow'. They wanted their children to mix easily and excel in the country of their birth, and that meant attending good private schools with reputations for academic success. If this was provided by the Church of England, in my case the Newcastle upon Tyne Church High School, then so be it.

I was only three years old when I made the first of what must have been thousands of half-hour trips from poorer Gateshead to the posher part of Newcastle. I was the baby of the nursery class. We lay down, wrapped ourselves in a blanket and had a one-hour sleep after lunch. I was driven to and fro either by my mother, or more often by Albert, the jovial local postman, who had been an admiral's batman during the war, and after it was over, had taken a shine to my rather impractical father who exuded the quiet authority of the senior ranking officer he had been. Albert looked after 'the docta' as if he were General Monty himself. Gardening, chauffeuring, boot-cleaning and general maintenance, there was nothing he wouldn't do for my father, and he had an entire day to do it in once the late, mid-morning post was delivered. Ideally, he would have liked to have exchanged his postman's uniform for that of a chauffeur, but my father convinced him that in these days of the new National Health Service, it wouldn't do a great deal for the doctor's image – not in a mining town.

I loved having Albert collect me from school. He was as comfortable and dependable as his old tweed jacket and flat cap, and inexhaustibly good-natured. Occasionally, he would insist it was time to pay 'the old folks' a visit, and take me to see my great-grandparents, with whom he was a great favourite – though how they ever understood each other's Yiddish and Geordie dialects was beyond me. Every journey ended with him singing loudly, 'I don't care if the sun don't shine, I get my loving in the evening time', while I added the statutory, 'with my Albert', to the amusement of big Nelly, his wife, in thick overcoat and even thicker hairnet, amply filling the back seat of the car.

He was a real knight errant, rushing over to get me whenever the school said I was unwell, once from the Christmas party when watching Mary Chivers masticate a meat paste sandwich with her mouth wide open had made me feel sick. But he really came into his own on those frightening days when fog rose up from the River Tyne like a vast wad of lemon-coloured roof insulation, so dense that it enveloped every street light and muffled every sound, burying all the familiar landmarks. He would make my mother drive, while he sat beside her like a guide dog, quietly directing her along invisible roads. Or if it was so bad that you couldn't see the hand you held up in front of you, he got out and walked in front of the car, tapping reassuringly on the bonnet as we went. The six-mile journey home might take anything up to three hours.

As I grew older I was enthralled by his stories of the war.

'Your Dad won it on land, and I won it on the sea,' he said proudly, though his war seemed to have been spent escorting glamorous Hollywood movie stars to and fro across the Atlantic.

'Don't believe a word of it,' my parents laughed, until the Admiral himself, on a visit to friends in a stately home in Northumberland, came to see his old retainer in his little council house in Felling. None of the stories had even been embellished. They were all true.

When I was eight I came face to face with discrimination. Miss Towns, the form teacher, tall and ungainly, bicycled daily into school in sensible lace-up shoes, thick camel coat tied lumpily round her middle, and a pink felt hat perched on her head. With her bulging, glassy eyes and thick, pale, slimy lips she reminded me of a fish, and she was as sour as pickled herring, one of a generation of women whose prospective husbands lay buried beneath a gravestone marked, 'unknown soldier'. Nothing I did was good enough for Miss Towns. Nothing I had to say was worth hearing. She made no attempt to disguise her antipathy, and the class scented sport. That was the year I was splashed with muddy water from one of the puddles in the playground for killing Jesus. Perhaps that explained why Miss Towns disliked me, I told myself. Perhaps I deserved it. But since I had only the vaguest idea who Jesus was, and no recollection of killing anyone, it was an impossible accusation to counter.

One day Janet Brown bit her own hand so hard she drew blood and left tooth-marks in the skin – they were mine, she told Miss Towns. None of my protestations were to any effect. I had proven, Miss Towns announced to the class, that I was a vixen as well as a liar. I was to sit in the corner for the entire afternoon, and no one was to speak to me for a week.

I cried all the way home, but told Albert not to tell my parents what had happened. After all, Miss Towns was the teacher. I must surely be as horrible as she said I was, and I didn't want them to find out. But Albert was incensed.

'No one treats my girlfriend like that,' he said, patting my knee reassuringly.

'Anti-semitic bitch,' said my father from his armchair, when Albert repeated my sorry tale.

'So what are you going to do, Docta?' he asked. 'That's no way to treat the poor bairn.'

'Leave it to me,' announced my mother, 'These teachers get too big for their boots. I had one like that. I always wanted to give her a piece of my mind.'

That was what I feared, but the next morning, heavily pregnant and as wide as she was tall, she marched into school, head high, and demanded a meeting with the headteacher. Miss Towns was summoned from the classroom, and as she left the room, every head turned in my direction. She arrived back some fifteen minutes later, unusually cowed, never once catching my eye, and from that moment on I had no further problems.

I have no idea what passed between the three women. Mum claimed she had, 'wiped the floor with the horrible woman', which meant that she had delivered her 'piece of her mind' as loudly and clearly as only my mother could. Looking back, I suspect she threatened to remove me from the school and inform the rest of the Jewish community that the reason was anti-semitism. So it was money that spoke the loudest and clearest that morning. But whether Shirley

Towns was really anti-semitic, or whether, like some teachers she simply had irrational preferences and pariahs that she couldn't keep to herself, no one would ever know.

By the time I went up to the senior school, the fashion in the Jewish community was to send their daughters to the Roman Catholic School called *La Sagesse*, known locally as 'La Sausages'. Their parents presumed another minority religious group would have more sympathy for Jews, but my parents were horrified by dark and gloomy convents with morose religious paintings on the walls and melancholy statues of the Virgin in every alcove. And the girls were taught by nuns. My mum had never met a nun, except courtesy of Hollywood, and suspected their powers of persuasion, if Audrey Hepburn or Deborah Kerr were anything to go by. Perhaps there was a hint of déjà vu, but she didn't want her daughter, destined to make the right kind of match, opting for the wrong sort of veil. Besides, as a girl, Mum had attended the Sunderland Church High School – and survived – though there had been three other Jewish girls in her class.

As she laid out my clothes for my first morning in the senior school, checking to see that everything was adequately labelled, she told me she had had a form teacher who used to say, 'In recent years the Jewish people have demonstrated an exceptional brilliance. It is of the utmost disappointment to me that I happen to have four exceptions in my class.'

'Why? Didn't you work hard?'

'What was the point?' she muttered, patting the pile of winceyette underwear, 'Are you sure you'll be warm enough without a liberty bodice?'

I threw her a look of disdain.

'You don't need to pass exams to get married and have babies, do you? Still, times have changed. You will have chances I never had.'

If the Sunderland Church High School did little for my mother academically, it appeared nonetheless to have accommodated her ethnic origins. Anti-semitism was the terror of the Jewish community in the years immediately after the Holocaust. The tiniest hint or rumour of it in any establishment or organization would ensure it was blackballed by an increasingly prosperous microcosm of local society. Yet anti-semitism, though unwitting, was often endemic. At a time when immigration on a massive scale was only just beginning, British institutions had very set ideas about what constituted being quintessentially and acceptably British. But on the Jews' rather arbitrary scale of what constituted prejudice, the Church of England fared quite well.

'The Church of England is very tolerant,' my mother said reassuringly. 'They understand about Jews.'

That first morning I arrived in my new classroom with her words resounding in my head. 'If they get onto anything religious, say you're Jewish and opt out.' The assembly bell rang. The classroom emptied and I was left sitting alone at my new desk, a rickety old thing, covered in graffiti carvings and black ink stains. It was the only one left when the other girls had finished choosing theirs. I was never very assertive – then. At least it gave me something to read. 'Natribus sitribus on the deskalorum, deskibus collapsibus and Nattress on the florum'. Mrs Nattress, I had discovered would be introducing us to the joys of Latin.

I presumed I must be the only Jewish girl in my class.

My new form teacher went on marking the register, cleared away her papers, picked up her handbag, and got up, registering my presence with an unpleasant start.

'Why haven't you gone with the others?'

'I'm... Jewish.'

'Well don't just sit there. Jewish prayers, third classroom down the corridor on the left.' Her gaze followed me across the room and out of the door.

Jewish prayers! I couldn't imagine what they were. I wandered down the long, dimly lit corridor, peering into every classroom, looking for something vaguely like Jewish girls praying. The idea seemed a bit indecent. Jewish girls never prayed. The men did it on our behalf.

Finally, I came across a small group of girls sitting together at a few desks at the very front of an empty classroom and decided they looked Jewish enough. I struggled with the doorknob, and five faces turned to stare at me through the glass.

'Turn it the other way,' the Prefect shouted. She was apparently in command, sitting on top of a desk facing the others.

'Come in, don't be frightened.'

'Let's have a look at you. All right, who do you know and who are you related to?'

'Shut up, Marilyn, and let her sit down,' said the Prefect, smiling. She nodded towards the chair just beneath the desk on which she was perched. I sank into it. 'I'm Judith. Have you brought your prayer book?' she asked kindly.

'No, no one said I needed to.'

'Then bring one tomorrow.'

I made a mental note to ask my mother where my ivory-bound bridesmaid's present was.

'We're bound to be cousins; I'm related to everyone,' Marilyn whispered over my shoulder. The other three girls said nothing and kept their heads down. One of them was twisting her prayer book round and round on the desk.

'Sharon!' She jumped at the Prefect's voice. 'Your turn to read.'

'Er... I was hoping you wouldn't ask me. What shall I read?'

'Something from the morning service, I suppose.'

Nervously, Sharon flicked through several pages of Hebrew.

'It's very long,' she gulped.

'Not all of it,' Judith said impatiently.

'Where shall I start?'

'Anywhere you like,' the Prefect finally snapped with exasperation. 'It's all the same.'

'Page eight, Sharon,' Marilyn chuckled, 'the paragraph that thanks God we're neither Gentiles nor women.'

Sharon began to read in faltering Hebrew. It was painful. I sighed with relief. At least when my turn came I could read more fluently than that. Judith yawned and Marilyn giggled.

'Something funny, Marilyn?'

'Just passing thoughts,' she said, her head on one side, weighing up the older girl like a baby bird waiting for food. 'Want to know who I was with last night?' She rolled her chewing gum under her tongue and held it there. 'Danny Greenstone. He took me to Grey's Club.'

'I don't believe it. He's so tight he never takes anyone to Grey's Club.'

'Hmmm,' Marilyn agreed, maximizing her advantage, 'He says his cousin has a thing for you.'

She stretched out a black-stockinged leg to one side of the desk. Her tights were full of holes and the circles of white flesh they revealed were ringed with red nail polish. I thought she must be the kind of girl my father referred to with some disdain as 'fast'. Black hosiery and nightclubs did not pass parental guidelines in our house.

'He hardly knows me,' Judith said dismissively. 'Er, Sharon, keep reading, here comes the teacher on duty. We'll have to at least look as if we're praying like Christians.'

Sharon droned on in an expressionless voice for a few minutes. None of us dared look up. Heavy footsteps moved slowly past the door.

'Amen,' shouted Marilyn, rudely interrupting Sharon's efforts. She slammed her prayer book shut, kissed it and tossed it onto the desk. I caught a momentary expression of hurt on Sharon's face and felt sorry for her.

'Well his mother told my aunt Phyllis who told my mother that at Lisa's wedding he had especially asked who you were.'

'Come on, girls, the hall doors are open, time for the notices.'

The Prefect jumped up in a fluster and rushed into the assembly hall.

'Where do we go now?' I asked Sharon, disappointed that the fascinating conversation I had witnessed had come to such an abrupt end.

'Just follow the latecomers and Muslims.'

'Do they have Muslim prayers?'

'Of course not. There are only two of them. They do their homework.'

As we marched into the silent assembly hall and lined up at the front beneath the stony stare of headmistress and staff, who manifestly couldn't distinguish between miscreants and Jews, I wondered why we were called on to perform such a charade. Was it the same in other church schools? I only knew it made me feel horribly conspicuous when I would far rather have just been like everyone else.

It didn't help that being a Jew in the autumn school term is a bit like being a human boomerang. Along with the stresses of a hostile new environment, scratchy new uniform, new desk, and new timetable, I now had to tell a new form teacher that I needed two days off almost immediately for the Jewish New Year. I would be back for a week, then off for the Day of Atonement, back for a few days, then off for the beginning of Tabernacles, back for a week, then off for the end of Tabernacles.

'Hecky thump,' shouted one of the class, 'What do you have to do to become a Jew?'

She was silenced with a glower, though I wasn't exactly at the receiving end of grace and favour either.

'I suppose so, if you must,' the form teacher said grudgingly, with barely a glance at me.

The request appeared to have irritated her. I wanted to say, 'I didn't choose to be the class "Jack-in-the-box", popping up just enough to make sure you don't forget my existence. I'd really rather not have to catch up on work when I've barely started it. But it's one of the penalties of being the chosen people – whatever that means.'

Just my luck, there was a *kosher* meals service organized by several well-meaning ladies at the synagogue around the corner where I went for Hebrew classes. They had persuaded my mother that I ought to be eating *kosher* with the other Jewish children in the area, but it only compounded my sense of separation and isolation. I was the only Church High girl in a sea of 'La Sausage'-goers, so tramped there on my own, ate alone and had no chance to meet up with school friends in my lunch break. The food was appalling. The day they served us fried eggs on mashed potato – and that for a small fortune – Mum relented. I could have school dinners.

The boundaries for a Jewish girl in an Anglican school were clearly defined. No religious education, no act of worship, no singing any of those dirge-like Christian hymns, no kneeling the way 'they' do, and no praying in English. God, apparently, objected to being addressed in any language other than his native ancient Hebrew. I became terribly confused. Every year, at Prize Giving, the entire school sang together on a raised stage for the dubious pleasure of friends and relatives. One year, one of the songs was a setting of a psalm. I excused myself from practices. I wasn't allowed to sing those kinds of songs, I said self-righteously to the music teacher. She never questioned my reasoning and I went back to my classroom, and got on with my homework.

'Why aren't you at singing practice?'

The Deputy Headmistress poked her head around the classroom door, perturbed to see the solitary figure bent studiously over her desk.

'I'm not allowed to sing hymns,' I said.

'But it's a psalm,' she explained gently.

'Yes, but...' was all I could stammer. I didn't know how to explain that sung like that, with English words to churchy-sounding music, it seemed vaguely indecent. I knew somehow that my mother would never approve of me singing that sort of song in public.

To my relief, the teacher shook her head and left the room, a look of amused disbelief on her face.

It was years later my mother told me that when they were children, she and a cousin had once won sixpence each for singing 'Jesus Wants Me For a Sunbeam' at a Salvation Army beach mission on the front at Roker. Their parents, who only realized what had happened when the winners were announced on the tannoy system, slunk home with their hats pulled down over their eyes, in case any of the Jewish community happened to be taking a seaside stroll that day.

On the whole, apart from the one or two hiccups, I fitted in quite well at school and was happy there. The creaking floorboards and wooden steps were worn and polished by the relentless tramping of generations of schoolgirl shoes, the pale green gloss corridor walls were decorated with official school photographs – generations of smiling and scowling girls, now mothers or grandmothers or long since dead and buried. We were simply raw material in a huge machine, whose cogs turned out Tyneside's young ladies on its production line. We wore an unusual and unflattering combination of bottle green tunics and Wedgewood blue blouses, brown socks and mackintoshes tied like sacks in the middle that did nothing for a figure struggling with puppy fat. Our compulsory felt pudding-basin hats shrank in the rain, so we tied them on with a tickly piece of elastic under the chin, and whipped them off when we saw the boys from the grammar school in the distance.

Non-Jewish boys, they were my mother's continual nightmare. What if I should meet one, like one, and horrors, want to marry one? That was marginally worse than getting pregnant out of wedlock, though why the latter happened and how it could be prevented wasn't very clear to me – not until I was fourteen when our home help, bored with the ironing, took pity on me and relishing every minute of my shocked innocence, explained the facts of life in basic, gruesome detail.

'Well the Queen certainly doesn't do that,' I responded haughtily.

She laughed so much she left the iron too long on my father's nylon underpants, and burnt a hole in a significant place.

'You're of an age now,' my mother said to me when I was fifteen, 'when you must understand that you can no longer go to your school friends' parties.'

'But why not?'

'Because they're starting to invite boys, that's why.'

'What's wrong with boys?'

'Nothing – as long as they're the right sort for you – the *kosher* sort.'

'But I'm not planning to get married yet.' I thought I was so overweight and plain that it was highly unlikely that any boy would ever fancy me anyway.

'And,' my mother said with finality, 'You know what happens to a Jewish girl who marries out? She never sees her family again. Cut off without a penny.'

I rarely had time to socialize with my school friends anyway. On Saturday mornings there was the weekend shopping to do. My mother's brain worked in strictly chronological fashion and I could be hanging around waiting for an hour before it reached shopping time. Resentment simmered and flared.

'I thought we weren't supposed to shop on the Sabbath,' I muttered as she chewed the end of the old pencil she kept in her overall pocket.

'We're not,' she said distractedly.

'But you won't let me be in the school play or hockey team because practices are on Saturdays.'

'That's different.'

Different? How was it different from my father going to a match on Saturday afternoons because he had recently been appointed medical officer to Gateshead Football Club, a very fourth division team that was eventually relegated out of league football altogether, such was my father's positive influence? How different from our going to my grandparents in Sunderland by car on a Saturday afternoon when travel was expressly forbidden? Different because it only spoiled my life, not theirs. I often sulked all the way to Gran's, staring out of the car window, sullenly refusing to enter into the conversation. In downtown Gateshead, renowned for its Jewish orthodoxy and its *Yeshivah*, a theological college for rabbis, we passed small groups of bearded men in long frock coats and shiny black hats, out for their Sabbath afternoon stroll.

'See where fanaticism gets you?' my mother said, jerking her head in their direction, then, turning to me, 'I can't be like that, but certain standards I must maintain.'

'I wish they would realize this is twentieth-century Britain, not eighteenth-century Poland,' my father muttered. 'No wonder there's anti-semitism, when they attract attention to themselves like that. At least I fought for this country.'

'We know. Doesn't Albert polish your medals every week?'

We drew up at my grandmother's door, and as I got out, Mum noticed the patchwork bag in my hand.

'You haven't brought your knitting, have you? On the Sabbath. What will Gran say? She'll think I don't know how to bring you up.'

'How else am I going to pass the time?' I asked, clutching the bag defiantly as I went into the house. Since Martin was in London studying sociology there was little to relieve the monotony.

The noise of the Saturday sports commentary filled the house. Grandpa was slouched in his favourite armchair in front of the television, snoring loudly.

'Wait until the horse racing comes on,' Gran grumbled, 'that'll wake him up.'

'Had a little flutter again, has he?'

'A flutter? That's what you call it? Well you know your father.'

'I thought we weren't allowed to watch television on the Sabbath,' I said self-righteously.

'We're not allowed to gamble either,' Gran retorted, 'but it's never stopped your grandfather.'

'Listen who's talking, with her cigarette hanging out of her mouth,' Mum laughed.

Gran shrugged and drew a lung full of nicotine just as Cyril and Pearl passed the huge bay window on their Sabbath constitutional, and waved. Cyril and Pearl were very orthodox. They even had their house wired so that the lights and heating would come on automatically on the Sabbath. It saved having to pay a neighbour to do it. Gran was about to wave back when she remembered the cigarette in her hand, looked around for somewhere to put it, and stuffed it into the nearest plant pot. Grandpa stirred and groaned.

'No wonder I can never grow tomatoes.'

The Jewish law was a complete mystery to me. How did anyone decide what to keep and what not to keep? Did children grow out of it when they became adults? After all, if you were rich enough like Cyril and Pearl there were obviously ways of getting round it. And if you weren't, did it really matter? Most of the Jews I knew broke the law with impunity, ate at non-kosher restaurants and went to the synagogue when they felt like it – and there was no thunderbolt from heaven. When it came to driving on the Sabbath, even the local rabbi had given up and told the congregation they could park outside the synagogue instead of several streets away since everyone knew everyone else had come by car anyway. What sort of a God really cared about such trivial details? Supposing I tried to keep all the laws I knew, would I ever fully succeed, and if I did, would I feel any closer to this glorified and heavenly version of my old *cheder* teacher, Mr Rosenberg, with his odd and arbitrary list of statutory requirements? I suspected I wouldn't. And my life would be even more miserable.

I remember once going to the synagogue with the express idea of finding God. It simply wasn't enough to believe that this mysterious being in the sky had created me and made me Jewish. I wanted to know whether that was the sum total of his interest and responsibility. I thought that the religious atmosphere might help him come out from behind the silver-encased scrolls, or wherever he hid himself, and communicate with me. I closed my eyes like the Christians when they prayed, and concentrated hard. Rachelle, next to me, dug me in the ribs. She was pointing beneath us.

'Have you seen Anthony Green recently? Take a look then. Much improved. I could quite fancy him.'

Behind me, someone said loudly, 'Have you seen Audrey Zellick's hat? It looks like a flying saucer. Why must she wear such ridiculous creations? They do nothing for her.'

I tried to shut out the chatter, the gossip, the growing hullabaloo as the morning wore on. 'You beyond the ceiling, beyond the sky or wherever you skulk, can you hear me?' The prayer books slammed shut, were kissed, put away in the space under the seats, and I went home disappointed.

It was just that life seemed so meaningless at times. I was sixteen, studying frantically for GCE O-levels, so that I could do A-levels, so that I could go to university, so that I could get a good job, so that I could earn good money, to eat, work, eat, work and die. What if you died before you ever had the chance to find out why you were alive? That would be a waste.

'Mum?' I asked, as I watched her straighten the candlesticks on the sideboard for around the sixth time that day. 'What's life all about?'

'Well,' she said, delicately manoeuvring one candlestick a quarter of a centimetre to the left with the tip of her index finger, 'You meet a nice Jewish boy, get married, have a nice home, children, cars...'

'And what then?'

'When?'

'When you get all that, what then?'

Distracted at last by the question, she looked up at me and thought for a moment. Manifestly, nothing came to mind.

'What more do you want?' she announced with exasperation. 'You and your questions. Why can't you just accept things as I did?'

Mother's greatest ambition was to see me married under the *chuppah*, the canopy of flowers erected in the synagogue for every bride and groom, representing the nomadic and rootless destiny of the Jewish people, condemned to wander indefinitely around the desert. With this end in mind, and to provide me with a little 'safe' social life, I was packed off to *Maccabi*, the Jewish Youth Club, dressed for the kill. The trouble was that everyone else's daughter was on a similar mission. When I had managed to bag my first rabbit I took him proudly home.

'What did you say his name was?' The interrogation began the moment the front door closed. 'It rings a bell. Wait a minute. I know who his father is – underwear business. No good. You can do better than knickers.'

I tried again.

'Family's too orthodox. Do you want to have to shave your hair off and wear a wig forever after? Besides, they won't even have a cup of tea in my house, in case I'm not strictly *kosher*. It's insulting.'

And again.

'Mother's only half Jewish.'

When I eventually dragged home a satisfactory conquest, a budding accountant with little conversation, everyone was delighted except me. By that time I had been round most of the boys and fallen out with all the girls, so there was little more fun to be had. I remember entire evenings in the 'Ladies' when every girl wept streams of mascara into the washbasins because she couldn't ensnare the man she wanted – more out of frustration than genuine heartbreak.

There were discos and there were parties. At the discos the music was so loud no intelligent conversation was possible – probably just as well since it wasn't likely in any event. The 'parties' involved pairing off for some lengthy, very public snogging. In fact they were simply an opportunity for a giant saliva exchange, the boys looking more and more smug the longer they managed to sustain mouth to mouth contact.

'What do you get when you kiss a girl? You get enough germs to catch pneumonia.'

The Carpenters certainly knew how to capture the mood of the age. Nowadays the body fluids in question would be rather different, the transfer of germs potentially more lethal, but on many occasions there must be a similar sense of fulfilling a social and cultural obligation with little real pleasure, and the vague sense of disappointment and dissatisfaction that goes with it.

I spent my life looking forward to the next event, then hating it because it never lived up to my fantasy. The real fun was in the getting ready – the long, luxurious bathtime soak, the meticulous work with back comb and lacquer, the master stroke with eyeliner brush and lipstick, and the silky feel of new tights. The work of art complete, you make an entry in a haze of *Coty L'Aimant* or some other cheap smelly, look furtively round to see who has noticed, then fade into a corner when it's obvious that no one has. Same people, same music, same small talk. Why on earth did I bother?

Sitting on the smoky upper deck of the bus for that dreary half-hour journey to and from school every day, wiping a hole in the condensation on the window and watching the water trickle down in rivulets of tears, often seemed to reflect how I felt inside.

There were tensions at home. Unhappy with her lot and desperate for an outside interest, my mother had opened a pram shop in Crook, a small Durham mining town. But even her fine business head couldn't come up with profits when the coal-house doors clanged shut for the last time, leaving the locals little money to spend on posh prams. Her need to tidy, order and control her world became even more pronounced. The home help finished work at 6pm, which meant that even in our late teens Mike and I were bathed and ready for bed before her shift ended, so that the bathroom could be cleaned. Visitors raised their eyebrows when they found us in our dressing gowns and asked if we were unwell. We began to sense that our existence wasn't quite normal, but no one understood Obsessional Compulsive Disorder in those days. And even if they had, my father the doctor would have been too ashamed to admit that anyone in his family needed that kind of medical help. Mental health was tightly wrapped in stigma, and tidied away.

Consultants filled him with awe. He grovelled embarrassingly at Sports Days whenever he bumped into Chris Philpot, cardiovascular specialist and father of one of my school friends, and was delighted when I was invited to a party at Judy's house. It was one of the deadliest events I had ever been to, spoilt by her mother's constant whining about having a migraine and her refusal to let us have any music on. The great consultant employed all his powers of reasoning, then walked out, slamming the door behind him. Judy looked embarrassed. The atmosphere was all too familiar. Perhaps our home wasn't so unique.

I didn't want what I saw – the miserable existence of my mother's generation of women, materialistic, middle class and meaningless. Symbol of their husbands' success, they were strictly ornamental, and reduced to using every manipulative wile in their armoury to win attention and prove their usefulness. Small wonder their emotional health suffered. But the prospect of marriage to a Jewish man offered me little alternative. Dad claimed he wanted me to be a doctor, but referred to his female colleagues as 'horses'. What was the point of studying all those years to give up my career for a man, or have them all call me a horse?

There has to be more to life than that, I repeated to myself on the bus every day, looking out on the dismal, treeless landscape of docks and riverside industry that lined my journey home. *But what is it and where do I find it? If you are out there God, give me a chance to live before I die.*

Chapter 5

The Forbidden Books

Ros was the daughter of missionary parents and we had absolutely nothing in common. She had long pigtails, owlish National Health spectacles and a full skirt that flapped around her sensible shoes, while my hemline had halted just on the right side of school rules. Although she was in my class, I had politely ignored her for years, and when I didn't, I was anything but polite. She knew nothing of the cosmic battles that raged between the followers of Elvis and the followers of Cliff, between the supporters of Newcastle United and the supporters of Sunderland Football Club. In fact she cared little for pop music or football.

I'm not sure what it was about her that caught my attention, or why I began to notice her at all. Perhaps it was the look of gentle pity in her eyes whenever I teased her or laughed at her for not being the with-it little teeny-bopper I reckoned myself to be. There was never any reproach or snappy reply, no embarrassment or discomfort. She took it all with a quiet dignity that told me that nothing I could say to her was of any real consequence. The truth was I knew she was right. I was empty-headed and unsatisfied. She had an inner confidence that made her stand out from everyone else.

Curious, I tried to put it into words one day.

'Ros?'

'Mmmmmm?'

We were in the cloakroom, struggling into our hockey boots. Her ample form was bent over, bottom facing me. She looked round, straightened up and panted slightly. 'I do hate this awful game.'

'I've noticed. You tend to run in the opposite direction when you see the ball coming.'

I was a fast little left wing. It annoyed me when someone let the team down. She grinned sheepishly. I tucked my knee under my chin, and instinctively, she moved over to the wooden bench and sat down beside me. Our heads were enclosed in the green mackintoshes that hung down from the pegs above us.

'The new French teacher goes to church with you, doesn't she?'

'She goes to the same church, yes'.

'She seems a happy sort of person.'

'She is. Extraordinary when you think she nurses an invalid father – alone.'

I struggled to put my thoughts into words.

'So what makes you both so... happy?'

'Being Christians.'

I laughed out loud.

'How can that make any difference? This is a Christian school but many people here seem a great deal more miserable than the Jews. And anyway, you've no choice in the matter. You're born a Christian or born a Jew.'

That was the end of the argument, as far as I was concerned, until Ros lobbed a grenade at me.

'You just don't understand,' she explained carefully. 'You can't be born a Christian. It's a choice people have to make.'

Now she wasn't making any sense at all. I stared at her, and after a while, demanded aggressively, 'So what is one, then?'

'You could come to my church and find out,' she said quietly.

I snorted. The idea of it – me going to a church, for everyone to stare at me as if I'd missed the synagogue. 'No thanks,' I said, grabbed my hockey stick and rushed out onto the playing field.

I had never been inside a church for an actual service, and in the end, curiosity got the better of me and I decided to try it – just the once, I told myself – to see what some of my school friends got up to.

I was late. It couldn't be helped. As usual on a Sunday night, the home-help's half day off, I had to bath Nicky before I went out. I could hardly say, 'Sorry, not tonight, Mum, I'll be late for church.' She wouldn't have let me out at all. So I simply told her I had to be at *Maccabi* early. She raised an eyebrow, which probably reflected annoyance at being left to clean the bath, rather than suspicion of my movements. Fortunately both the church and the youth club were across the water in Newcastle, round the corner from each other, and they met on Sunday nights. I could go on to the club afterwards. That way no lies were told.

The only problem was that the dress code for *Maccabi* was strictly disco. I put on a tiny glitzy number that barely covered my backside, ringed my eyes with black kohl á la Dusty Springfield, applied such copious false lashes I could hardly open my eyes, painted on white lipstick, and finished the creation with my bright red Mary Quant PVC mini mac and matching, wide-brimmed hat.

A small library was thrust into my hands as I walked hesitatingly through the door. 'Thank you, but what do I do with these? I'll slip into the nearest pew and pretend I'm not here.' But the back pews are taken, so I continue to tiptoe on my stilettos towards the front, click-clack, aware of a sea of staring eyes following my ever-decreasingly confident progress down the aisle. No pork sausage could have felt more out of place at a *Bar Mitzvah*.

Finally, an empty pew receives me and swallows me up. I arrange my books in a neat pile on the ledge in front of me, like everyone else. The silence is unnerving after the general hullabaloo of the synagogue. I can hear my own breathing. This place is so alien. It smells of beeswax, age and decay. It's gloomy. No satin and velvet, crimson and gold. There is more Tyne fog in here than down at the docks. Dead saints glower at me from grimy, stained glass windows. I have the strange sensation that the living are watching me too, but when I look up, can't catch anyone actually looking in my direction. The distant droning sound from the front comes to an abrupt halt. There is a long pause while everyone shuffles expectantly. Now what? They're all on their feet, chanting something from one of the books. 'And Make Thy Chosen People Joyful'. The chosen people! Why are they singing about us, the Jews? We're a great deal more joyful than they are. I've seen more joy at a Jewish funeral. I can't find the place. I have two choices – to pretend or look helpless. Before I can decide, the book eludes my fumbling and falls to the hard, stone floor with a thud that echoes around the building. A hundred pairs of eyes follow my scrabbling beneath the pew, either because the mac is crinkling loudly as only plastic can, or because it isn't covering my bare necessities. When I finally emerge, everyone else has disappeared. They're kneeling. I have never knelt in my life, but decide I ought to show respect and have a go. How much more is there of this? How long before I can simply melt away? Never has *Maccabi* seemed so attractive. I was out of my seat the moment the service ended, but found my exit blocked by a group of school friends.

'Coming for coffee?'

'No, I'm going to the Jewish Youth Club round the corner. Just popped in on my way there actually.'

'Five minutes?'

How could I refuse? They led me round to the church hall, to a cold, dingy little building with bare floorboards, peeling paintwork and the worst mug of coffee I have ever tasted. Somehow, they managed to persuade me to stay for the youth meeting, and surprisingly, I managed to enjoy it enough not to worry too much about my unsuitable attire. There were slides about missionary work in Africa. Not a geography lesson, please, I said to myself at first, when a map appeared on the screen. I cared little for the world outside my tiny orbit. Yet despite myself, I was profoundly challenged by the pictures of poverty, and amazed that anyone should be willing to give up hair dryer and shopping to do something about it.

'I'd better go,' I whispered to Ros urgently, as I came to with a start and realized I'd spent almost the entire evening at the wrong club.

'Want to come hiking with us on Saturday?' Ros asked as she escorted me to the door. 'The vicar's a fanatic.'

'Me, hike?' I asked incredulously. 'My family never walks across the street if we can take the car.'

But later, at *Maccabi*, lined up at the mirror in the Ladies with comb, lipstick and lacquer, listening to the usual empty small talk, I thought, what the heck, why not try something new?

'Can I go for a hike on Saturday?'

'Where's the thermometer?' my mother asked my father. 'She's evidently not well. She who fears her hair will frizz if anyone near her so much as sneezes. Since when have you walked further than to the bus stop?'

'Some of the girls from school are going.'

'It's the Sabbath.'

I played a trump card. 'Walking is actually allowed on the Sabbath.'

'Oh, let her go,' my father said mildly over the top of the *Readers' Digest*. 'What harm can it do?'

'I'll need old trousers.'

'You haven't got old trousers.'

'Well, something that doesn't matter if it gets dirty.'

'Clothes are not meant to get dirty. I don't buy you clothes to ruin.'

I turned up looking dressed for a *Bar Mitzvah*. There were no suitable shoes in my wardrobe. But at least I was there. There hadn't been a minute in the preceding six days when I hadn't feared that Mum would find an excuse to keep me at home, and felt sick before I ever had a chance to experience the vicar's mini-bus driving. Within three-quarters of an hour we were in the heart of Northumberland, slung our picnics over our shoulders and set off.

Fortunately, it was a glorious, balmy, breeze-caressing day. At every turn of the path the view was more exquisite than the last. All this was so nearby, virtually on my doorstep, and I had never seen it before – not like this at any rate. An outing had always been a drive to a café down at the coast. I loved the moody North Sea – gentle, silky, foam-tipped aquamarine, or churning, turbulent, gunmetal grey. But the countryside had only ever been a view from the car window en route to somewhere else. It felt so different outside the car.

On a mountain top, where the luscious green hills rolled away and melted into the distant horizon, I stood completely still, revelling in this new sensation of complete and utter well-being, with the wind in my hair and sun on my back, aware of the gentle bleating of sheep, of birdsong and the buzzing of bees that seemed to create a music that was healing to my soul. I hadn't known how much, consummate townie as I was, I really yearned for this restorative space and peace. As I gazed at the 'new' world spread out at my feet, an extraordinary patchwork of precision and beauty, I wondered whether anyone could believe it was simply a random act of nature.

We found an idyllic spot for a picnic beside a little brook that could be crossed by stepping stones. Inevitably, given my footwear, I fell in and had to borrow the French teacher's spare pair that was several sizes too big. I laughed as I never had before, and became aware, with a start, that someone curled up inside me who had been asleep for a very long time, seemed to be stirring. It was deeply unsettling. I sensed that just beyond the grasp of my understanding was the kind of life I had always imagined and wanted. But if I pursued it, what of the other life, the only one I had been brought up to expect?

For several months I lived a schizoid Sunday, caught between two very different worlds. First I went to the youth fellowship at the church, though not the church itself, and then I hitched up my skirt, plastered on the makeup, and tottered round to the Jewish Youth Club. Gradually, the world I was supposed to belong to drew me less and less, and attendance became an irritating necessity enforced upon me by my distaste for lying, while the new world, alien and strange as it was, had an irresistible attraction.

'Have you ever actually read the New Testament?' Ros asked me one day.

'You're joking,' I said to her.

'Well you believe in the Old Testament, don't you?'

Memories of endless translation practice came flooding back – the children of Israel, forever stuck in the wilderness. Believe it? I barely knew it. But I didn't want to explain all that to her. So instead I accepted the study notes she gave me.

'John's Gospel,' she said, as if she were recommending a Latin textbook. 'Best place to start.'

That night I went in search of my old school Bible. My mother had been informed by the school that it was a statutory requirement for the Old Testament lessons I was expected to attend. We had gone to WH Smith's in Newcastle and in a voice that resounded through the shop she had demanded to know if they had any Bibles, 'without the end bit'.

'We're Jewish, you see,' she explained loudly, 'we don't believe in it.'

I wanted to disappear beneath the counter.

There were of course no New Testament-less Bibles, so the full version came home with us and ended up on a bookshelf, as Religious Education at the Church High School turned out to be more about Jesus than the vicissitudes of the Jewish nation. I was excused and did my homework instead.

I found it tucked away in my parents' 'forbidden books' section, along with *Lady Chatterley's Lover* and Harold Robbins' *The Carpet Baggers*. Harold Robbins' naughty novels were very popular with middle-class Jewish women of a certain age. Gran had kept four under her mattress. It had been a closely guarded secret until her electric blanket caught fire one night. Martin watched her running to and fro from the kitchen to the bedroom with jugs of water for some time until he decided to investigate, and promptly yanked the smouldering mattress out of the room.

'You filthy woman,' he said to her with disgust, when he saw the booty his firefighting efforts had brought to light. 'No wonder your mattress caught fire.'

I heard my mother and grandmother sniggering about it the following Saturday.

As for *Lady Chatterley's Lover*, it had generated a well-publicized trial and media furore that was impossible for any teenager to miss. That my parents had bought it in a spirit of open-mindedness to see whether it merited a ban or not, I had no doubt. And I decided that since I was expanding my education in one direction there was no harm in extending it in any other, and gathered up the Robbins and the Lady Chatterley along with the Bible.

That night, I waited to hear the gentle, even snoring from my little sister's bed, then reached for my torch. Beneath the bedclothes I had Lady Chatterley on one side of me, and the New Testament on the other. In both the language was quaint and hard to follow, but I soon realized that there was nothing in Lady Chatterley that I didn't know already. By contrast, once I got into it, John's Gospel was a revelation.

I knew virtually nothing about Jesus – except that he had been crucified and that the Jews had been implicated in some kind of way. Nicky who now attended Hebrew classes at the Reform Synagogue, such was my father's influence over my mother's weakening orthodoxy, had been better informed than I had and said Jesus was one of our great prophets, but not God. That was a Christian travesty. My father called him by a rude Yiddish name. 'Jesus, our brother', some of the Jewish community joked, laying prior claim to him, since Christians seemed oblivious of his *kosher* connections. What they actually visualized was a cold, lifeless statue with glazed eyes and a pitiful, long-suffering expression. Jesus, the Gentile God, a graven image created by the church to satisfy the imaginations of its followers, too fragile in their faith to believe in anything invisible.

Yet he had always held a fascination for me, ever since I saw the movie *Ben Hur*. Most of the time only his back, not his face, appears on camera. What we see is the powerful impression he creates on the key characters. Mum was astonished as I tried, without success, to stifle my sobs as he carried his cross to Calvary.

'Jewish girls don't cry at this bit,' she hissed.

But when, in the aftermath of the crucifixion, Ben Hur's mother and sister are healed of leprosy, I could no longer hold in the tears. Irritated beyond measure, she all but dragged me out of the cinema.

That night, as I read about him for the first time, I was confronted not with a mournful, dour, historical character depicted in paintings and statues, who had lived and died two thousand years ago and had little relevance for a twentieth-century teenager, but someone who appeared to have intimate knowledge of my hopes and aspirations, my longings and frustrations. For a start, he was relentless in his exposure of officialdom and hypocrisy – particularly of the religious kind, imposed on its victims for no greater reason than to restrict their freedoms and pleasures. But I barely had time to enjoy my smugness at such a cosmic affirmation of my various childhood resentments when the tables were turned and it seemed as if he could see every nasty piece of selfishness and spitefulness that had gone on in my little life – saw it, but didn't reject or discard me for it. No one, no matter what their failure, inconsistency or weakness, appeared to be beyond his loving compassion and unconditional acceptance.

'Get a grip,' I said to myself. 'This is a storybook.' If only he had lived now, or if I had been born in another, non-Jewish family, how different my life might have been. Here was someone who offered the kind of meaning and purpose I was after, someone who specialized in new starts, someone I might have followed.

One thing he said particularly took my breath away – the response to a question that seemed to have perplexed me for as long as I could remember. 'In my father's house are many mansions. If it were not so would I have told you that I go to prepare a place for you?' No one, not even the rabbis, ever talked confidently about life after death – despite my endless probing. 'Do your best,' they reassured us. 'Make sure to perform lots of *mitzvah*, good deeds, that will hoist you up the rungs of the ladder to eternity.' But no sooner had I lifted my foot, when bad temper, bitchiness, pilfering, lying and cheating sent me slithering down a snake. And why try so hard for what might not exist anyway? But then, if there was no life after death, what was the point of our time on earth at all?

Who was I to say Jesus was truth and generations of Jews had missed the point? What did I know about it all, anyway? Yet it seemed to me that Nicky's Hebrew teacher was neither logical nor reasonable. How could Jesus be a prophet, a great man, when he claimed to be God incarnate, the ultimate blasphemy? At worst he was a deliberate charlatan, at best deluded. The only real alternative was that he was who he said he was, the Messiah my people had been awaiting for thousands of years. The implications of that possibility were too daunting to contemplate. 'Take up your cross and follow me,' the man said. Say goodbye to family, friends and community, to the only life I knew? I shut both of the books and thrust them under the bed, switched off the torch and tried to get some sleep. This God-nonsense was getting to me.

But I couldn't shake it off however hard I tried. I had never been particularly bothered by a guilty conscience before, but now, all sorts of what had seemed fairly minor misdemeanours began to trouble me. Dodging the bus fare? That's stealing. Being catty? That hurts. Economical with the truth – especially with teachers? That's lying. I hadn't ever kidded myself that I was particularly nice, but presumed I was no worse than anyone else. Hearing that voice in my head point out my shortcomings, as they happened, I began to wonder. God seemed a ruthless judge in heaven reading out a criminal record that would condemn any miscreant to the severest of sentences.

Some six months later there was a school weekend away at the York Mystery Plays. By the first evening, the heavy rain that had poured incessantly all day had benevolently acknowledged our pleadings and petered out to a light drizzle. Waterproofed from head to toe, we trundled in a straggly crocodile into the floodlit castle grounds, climbed the scaffolding stairs and took our places on the raindrop-spattered seats. Someone handed round the toffees and we chewed contentedly, huddling close to keep out the damp and chilly air.

As darkness slowly fell, and the lights were turned up on the immense stage beneath us, I was transfixed. The crowds around me ceased to exist. The hard bench biting into my backside no longer vied for my attention. The performance had become magically, compellingly real. I hadn't realized that the Mystery Plays were a mediaeval interpretation of biblical stories from creation to the end of time, but as we moved inexorably on to the crucifixion, it struck me how much the New Testament flowed from the Old, how complete the story actually seemed. Christ is on trial, condemned, tormented, stripped and nailed to a vast cross, the hammer blows resounding throughout the grounds of York Castle, jolting and jangling every nerve end. I am there, transported back through twenty centuries, a lone spectator, as the cross is hoisted in the air with Christ splayed out upon it. I watch, entranced, and in that earth-shattering moment the kaleidoscope stops spinning, and a mass of tiny, shimmering particles in my mind's eye fall into place and form a clear picture. This may not be the kind of Messiah my people expect, but it's Messiah enough for me. And as I focus on the cross, a voice in my head whispers, 'Will you follow me now?' and I know now that I have no choice, whatever the consequences.

I sat in a daze as the performance came to an end, unwilling to move. Someone dug me in the ribs with an umbrella and reluctantly I joined the little schoolgirl snake back to the guest house where we were staying. Several times I tried to say something to Ros, but didn't know what. 'Something very odd has happened to me tonight'? It sounded thin. I had neither the vocabulary nor the comprehension to explain exactly what was going on, so crept into bed and got out John's Gospel again. 'Show us the Father and we shall be satisfied,' said Phillip, one of the disciples. 'Good on you, Phillip,' I said to him, 'My thought entirely. Where does the God of the galaxies, who created the universe and suspended the planets in space, fit into the equation?'

The Jewish God was fairly remote, and just recently, seemed fairly unmerciful. I still couldn't imagine what he was actually like.

Jesus' response was a revelation. 'Have I been with you so long and yet you don't know me, Phillip? He who has seen me has seen the Father.'

I felt a huge 'ah-ha' expand in my mind. Through the kaleidoscope several remaining particles gently realigned themselves to allow an even clearer focus. So that was it. God was neither the distant monarch of my childhood, nor the demanding tyrant and miserable killjoy of so much stereotypical Christianity. Rather, his character was reflected physically in the compassionate, compelling, fun-loving Jesus who had so completely captured my imagination. It was God himself who had been stretched out between the creation of the universe and its final redemption, bridging earth and heaven, my existence and my eternity, by wilfully and deliberately ensuring forgiveness for the bits of me I had come to thoroughly dislike. What I had come to see was that the list of my offences, however minor they might appear by some standards, would plague any ability I might have to fulfil my true potential. There was no 'good enough'; there was only the best. That's what God intended for the humanity he made with such love, and if the only way to achieve it was the sacrifice of himself, then that was what he had to do.

What I hadn't anticipated was that with the inner conviction that Jesus Christ was the Messiah would come an extraordinary sense of the reality of his presence, and a certainty that whatever following him would mean, I wouldn't be doing it alone.

'Ros,' I whispered, to the huddled shape in sensible wincyette pyjamas in the next bed.

'Ung?' she groaned, her nose appearing just above the sheets.

'I've got to a tricky bit. What's the Holy Spirit?'

'Who, you mean.'

'Okay,' I conceded, 'Who?'

She sighed heavily. 'You do ask difficult questions at funny times. I'll explain tomorrow.'

'But...'

'Tomorrow,' she said finally, turned over and pulled up the blankets.

I sat up for a long time in the dark, wide-eyed, tummy turning cartwheels, unable to sleep, knowing, inexplicably, that my life would never be the same again.

Chapter 6

Unwelcome Revelations

*S*ix of us were sprawled on our beds after a service at York Minster and a large Sunday lunch. I had gone to the Minster sporting a huge pink chiffon flying saucer on my head that I had picked up in the sales. I thought hats must be as compulsory in a cathedral as they were in the synagogue, but found myself looking like a bad attempt at a garden party diva in *Tatler* Magazine. The wide brim thankfully covered my embarrassment. I don't remember being particularly impressed by the service – apart from the goose-pimply debut from the choir singing Parry's magnificent, 'I Was Glad'. At that moment I wished we Jews could sometimes sing a psalm or two like that, but with no musical instruments allowed in worship since the destruction of the Temple in AD 70, it wasn't easy. Two thousand years is a long time to spend in mourning. But at least, in the synagogue, sitting in the women's gallery gave me a bird's eye view, while I could see nothing in the cathedral for pillars, and hear very little of the sermon because of the echo.

'The Holy Spirit is the third person in the Trinity,' Ros explained, as we lay in a post-lunch inertia. She hadn't forgotten my question, but the answer might just as well have been gobbledegook. I had no concept of a Trinity. She heaved herself up and the bed sagged several inches. 'I mean he's the third part of God, and he comes to live inside us to help us live a Christian life.'

That provoked a heated debate among the other four girls about the interpretation of the word 'Christian' and whether they actually were one. It seemed fatuous alongside my predicament, and I found myself interjecting, 'Oh, it's all right for you lot. You at least know what you are. But I don't think I'm anything any more. I'm stuck in limbo.'

'No, you're not,' said Alison, the head girl in her matter-of-fact way. 'You're a Christian.'

She might as well have hit me with her Bible. I was pole-axed. My mind reeled as they continued their discussion, totally unaware of the impact of Alison's words. How could I be a Christian? Jews did not become Christians. The very word represented everything that was most alien to me. And yet, as I sought to make sense of the experience of the previous evening, instead of seeing a mass of disconnected pieces, I had suddenly seen the completed jigsaw puzzle – a picture of eternal history and my place in it, painted with precision, forethought and care. Forgiveness had been an elusive piece. So had life after death. The crucifixion with its payment for my mess, and the resurrection with its defeat of death itself – filled the final, gaping holes. But I couldn't see why believing that would make me a Christian. Couldn't I simply believe it as a Jew?

'I tell you what,' I announced, 'my parents will never buy it.'

'Don't tell them then,' Ros said, 'Let them see a change in you for the better first.'

It was wise advice. How could I explain what I didn't understand myself? How could I say, 'Hello Mum and Dad,

I'm a Christian', and shatter their world? Besides, that wasn't a true reflection of what I felt. I wasn't any less Jewish than I ever was before. So, I would be different from now on – patient, helpful, thoughtful, loving. The startling transformation would be proof enough that Jesus was worth following. If Ros was right and I had the Holy Spirit inside me, it shouldn't be too difficult.

But it wasn't nearly as easy as I imagined. For a few weeks a new and unexpected sense of joy and tranquillity made washing the dishes, bathing the baby, and making the beds quite bearable. On even days pillowcase slots went to the right, on odd days to the left. No resentment of the rituals, I told myself. Do the most menial and meaningless tasks with patience. But gradually the ever-increasing list stirred up such a mass of frustration that I exploded with rage and marched out. I managed not to throw anything and thought it must be a sign of progress, but still felt dejected about how far I had to go if taking up my cross was ever going to be a reality.

Christmas loomed with ever-increasing dread that year. How to face the meaningless bank holiday – acknowledgment of something that now had such meaning for me?

On Christmas morning I was at my usual post by the bedroom window. The lack of heating in our home created a condensation nightmare for my mother every morning. As the ice on the inside of the windows melted, the trickle became a rivulet, the rivulet a pool, and pools could turn into floods that would cause irreparable damage to curtains and carpets. So Mum insisted that every window in the house be opened wide, and wiped down, first with wash leather and then with dry cloth.

As I mopped away at her bedroom window at the front of the house, fingers aching with the cold, heart numbed by the waste of time, I watched people making their way to church at the top of our street. I stood there for some time, consumed with self-pity, an intense and overwhelming longing to rush out and join them churning my insides. Then gradually, I became aware of a presence at my side, so close that I feared to move even a fraction of an inch lest I might inadvertently touch him and make him vanish as quickly as he had come. So real was he, such was the overwhelming sense of comfort and joy, that I was almost afraid to breathe. And somewhere deep inside me, the gentlest of voices whispered, 'I am Emmanuel, God with you. I am all the Christmas you need.'

I held onto the moment for as long as I could, dreading being left alone again, but even as the presence melted and the wonder began to fade, the deep sense of peace and reassurance did not. I knew, as I finished the drying and polishing, that whatever the future held, whatever kind of Christmas I might create once I was free to do so, Emmanuel himself was the ultimate Christmas party and present.

As the days rolled into months the double life and deceit began to feel increasingly uncomfortable. I began to realize I couldn't pretend that nothing had happened and would have to make some explanation to my parents. I rehearsed dozens of options but nothing I came up with would soften the blow or make it any less than the worst of betrayals. I could see the pointed finger and hear the gossip in the Jewish community: 'Their daughter... did you hear? Such a tragedy.' It seemed so unfair that my decision should have such repercussions for them.

So I procrastinated. I clung to the prospect of university that autumn like the victim of a shipwreck to the piece of timber that would carry them to a safe and distant shore. Durham was my first choice.

'Durham?' queried my French teacher. She had taken to spending some time with me after lessons to listen to my tales of woe or help me in my struggles to understand the Bible. 'Durham is only twenty minutes away by car. In your situation, shouldn't you be exploring further afield?'

I couldn't explain the panic I felt at leaving all my support networks behind. It vied with my longing to escape and be myself.

'Where else might you want to go?'

'Well, to do drama as my second subject, there's Manchester.'

'Put Manchester down – three hours away. It has a good French Department, and I don't know, just a certain feel about it.'

Reluctantly I agreed, never thinking for one minute that Durham would have the cheek to turn me down. I was incensed when I received their rejection slip. I flounced into school that morning in a fury. Ros emerged from behind a heavy row of coats in the cloakroom to see whose arrival had made the benches shake.

'Oh,' she said, as I rammed my outdoor shoes into a cubbyhole. She watched me with a bemused expression on her face. It was by no means the first of my rages she had witnessed. I went to the mirror and attacked my unruly curls with a comb.

'Durham,' I hissed between bared teeth, 'has turned me down.'

'That doesn't surprise me.'

I could see the gentle smile on her face behind me in the mirror.

'Look,' she said impatiently, 'didn't you say you would follow Christ anywhere? If that's to be Manchester, not Durham, who are you to argue? Doesn't he know what's best in the long run?'

She was right, of course, but I didn't discover until later that there could be no possible compromise between my need for security and the search for self-discovery. It was imperative that I go further from home, so I packed my bulging wardrobe into a vast trunk and set off for the big city.

Like any student, my first few days in Manchester were spent trailing around identical high-rise faculty buildings, combing dozens of identical corridors for obscure room numbers, sitting in endless queues, filling in piles of administrative paperwork that proved I was intelligent enough to become a fully fledged undergraduate. Entry to the main union building was forbidden, it said over the door, to anyone under the age of eighteen. I was seventeen and not used to disobeying instructions. Inside was bedlam – every wall plastered with posters, every inch crammed with makeshift stalls where student pedlars tried to sell their society. I was bombarded with handouts, deafened by the drumbeat, disoriented by the hullabaloo.

Ros warned me it would be like this. 'Make sure you find the Christian Union', she instructed me maternally. I nodded obediently. 'I don't want you falling by the way.'

I felt more like running away than falling by the way.

'Ex-cuse me,' I stammered to a young man in the statutory faded blue jeans, leaning on the reception desk, who went on tapping to the beat. He was way above my height and oblivious to my presence. 'Excuse me,' I tried even louder. 'Christian Union stall?'

'Eh? Oh, over there with all the other religious nuts,' he pointed with contempt.

I was taken aback. Anti-semitism was no surprise. Anti-Christianism was new. It appeared that antagonism was going to be my lot from now on – whichever faith marked me out.

Methodists, Anglicans, Baptists, Catholics, they were all together in one corner, along with the Muslims, Hindus and Buddhists. I noticed the Jewish Society out of the corner of my eye and suspected the young woman behind the table was fairly confident that I was heading in her direction, when I veered off towards the sign marked, 'Manchester Inter Faculty Christian Union'. The group at that table were less convinced by my approach – gazing quizzically at the red hot pants I was wearing, albeit accompanied by a pair of thick black tights, which to my mind made them perfectly decent – but managed to smile when they realized I had actually found the right place.

As I was introduced around, I felt a pair of eyes from over at the Jewish Society burning into my back. I wanted more than anything to speak to her, drawn by a sense of belonging and mutual understanding, but instead, turned around and slunk away, feeling a mixture of guilt and embarrassment. I had been seen at the Christian Union stall. How would I explain that? I couldn't face the possibility of having to justify myself, or of their disapproval. Not then. There were too many issues to be resolved.

I threw myself into university life, starting with the hall play – a naughty eighteenth-century romp – and played the first of many saucy maid parts, the inevitable typecasting for dark, little wenches with more than ample upholstery. As the curtains opened I was in full clinch with a not very attractive serving man. Learning how to do a fake theatrical snog was an urgent, if not very convincing, necessity. The Christian Union wasn't impressed. In fact, some of its members were not very sure about my activities at all. The table tennis team was fine, but student local radio? That was the era when the media, the arts, fashion and make-up were suspect to evangelicals, who, unsettled by the new morality of the sixties, clung to the safer forties, when young people knew how to dress and behave. Absolute purity required a regimented discipline that circumscribed every thought and deed, hedging behaviour in with rules and regulations. A book called *Time to Embrace* gave meticulous guidelines, in inches and seconds, on the distance and timing of first and subsequent hand touch and kiss, all the way to the wedding night.

In many ways it was inevitable. From the first week of term, many students, high on the new licence and saved by the pill, were abandoning their own beds and jumping into everyone else's like rabbits on heat. Including my new room-mate. I was shocked at the speed with which she moved in with her hitherto unknown, new man, but to my shame, immensely relieved too. Her feet were so smelly that it was heaven to have the room to myself. So much for my moral standards. But generally, at that time, we Christians, instead of constructing a whole and more positive view of sex, ran like frightened deer in the opposite direction.

Friends excused my apparent worldliness on the grounds that I didn't appear familiar with the rules regulating Christian behaviour and that was understandable, given my background. I was an oddity – the only person in the hall of residence to arrive back after a vacation, not with cakes and biscuits, but with potfulls of chopped liver and chopped herring. There were no fridges in our rooms, so I hung them on ropes from my window. I was inundated with visitors who had never seen herring in that disguise before and regarded it as one of the wonders of the world. The pots were cranked up into the room on a makeshift pulley system, and placed in the centre of the floor, with two knives and a box of cracker biscuits. Everyone dug in and those first gatherings in a new term became quite special. Despite my heritage I didn't fully understand then the power of food – not then.

To countermand the negative influences to which I was manifestly prone, I was invited to countless Bible studies, prayer meetings, planning meetings, coffee parties and house parties – innocent parties of every kind. Like a sponge I soaked up everything there was to learn. I could attend any meeting I wanted to without fear, shame or having to lie, and I wasn't going to miss any of it. But when I did occasionally allow myself to think, the deceit felt like a lump of lead in my stomach. It left a bad taste in my mouth.

My parents were so proud to have a daughter at university, in Manchester too where we had those nice cousins with the very eligible, medical student son. Realistically, what Jewish man would have me? What were the chances of my being married under the *chuppah* now, and how long could I let them sustain their false hopes and dreams? I walked back into the house through the back door at the end of my first term feeling slightly sick. In the kitchen all the old familiar objects were in their usual places – the pill bottles in neat little rows, cups upside down on saucers ready for the next drink, vegetables sitting in pans part-boiled for the evening meal, cold coffee in the old metal pot for the next morning's breakfast. How could I throw a grenade into this ordered little world?

Over supper I was bombarded with questions. How were the cousins? And what about their son, was I seeing him? I answered their questions briefly and went on eating. Mum looked slightly troubled, shrugged it off and began to clear away the dishes.

'Mum, Dad,' I said quietly, keeping my hands well beneath the table cloth so that they wouldn't see they were shaking, 'I have something I need to tell you.'

Mum put the dishes down and sank back onto her chair. My father wiped his mouth on his table napkin and laid it slowly on the table.

'I've... er... I think... er... I've become a Christian.'

No one spoke for what seemed an age. I made myself look at them, and could hardly bear the pain on their faces. I wanted to say what I had intended to say all along. 'This doesn't change anything. I'm still Jewish. I'm still your daughter. I still love you', just as I had rehearsed it over and over again, but the words refused to come.

Suddenly my mother laughed raucously. 'You, a Christian? Whoever is going to believe that? Just take a look at yourself in the mirror. Look at your nose, girl.'

'I know,' I whispered weakly. 'I'm not saying I'm not Jewish. I am Jewish – with this extra bit. I believe the Messiah has already been – and that it's Jesus.'

'You've been going to church, haven't you?' Mum demanded.

'Yes,' I whispered, as if I was admitting to taking drugs.

'That it should ever come to this, a daughter of mine going into a church.'

'Now don't get into a state, dear,' my father said calmly, 'It's just these friends of hers who've influenced her. She'll get over it. Won't you?' His face begged me for reassurance, but I only shook my head. Now it was his turn to look bewildered. 'Where did we go wrong? How have we failed you?'

Mum broke down and began to sob. 'No *chuppah*. Never to see my daughter married under the canopy in *schul*. And what's more, I'll be the laughing stock of the entire community.'

So that was it, worrying about what everyone else would think, the scourge of every small community. If that was all that mattered I could stand firm and weather the immediate crisis.

It was the first of many during that vacation. My mother spent most days wandering miserably around the house sighing and muttering to herself, 'What are we going to do?' and playing *Fiddler on the Roof* repeatedly on the record player.

'What's with all this *Fiddler on the Roof*?' Mike asked her eventually, mystified.

'It's for your sister,' she snapped, 'to remind her of her heritage.'

She'll survive, I thought.

My father worried me more. He was unnaturally thoughtful and I often caught him looking at me with great sadness in his eyes.

'You were my perfect daughter,' he said, shaking his head in total incomprehension, 'I put you on a pedestal. Now look where it got me. What I don't understand is why, when you just decided one day to believe in Jesus, you can't now decide not to believe in him.'

'Because, Dad, it isn't a matter of believing or not believing. He is as real to me as you are standing there. How can I say that he isn't when he is?'

'We can't go on like this,' he murmured, after yet another scene, when we had all begged and pleaded and wept our way through boxes of tissues. 'We're not getting anywhere, so let's be sensible about the whole thing. Honour thy father and mother is one of the ten commandments, agreed?' he asked me.

I nodded, blowing my nose.

'Well I can't help but think you'd give up this silly business if you really believed that. Still, there's a chance you may yet grow out of it. So, this is the deal. You're not twenty-one yet, so we still have some say. We can't demand it, but we want you to agree that until you are twenty-one you won't go to church or be baptized.'

'Or take that bread and wine they hand out,' my mother chipped in. 'And you'll see a rabbi who will teach you more about Judaism. I've rung him already,' she said with a wave of the hand, before I could protest, 'and he's ready to answer some of your impossible questions. And,' she added, the tears flowing copiously again, 'no going out with non-Jewish boys. And, we would like you to stop reading your Bible.'

I weighed up everything they said carefully. They had a right to see that I still loved them and wanted to honour their wishes, even if it meant tough choices. 'Okay,' I conceded, finding it hard to swallow, 'Until I'm twenty-one, no baptism, no church, no Communion, no boys and see the rabbi. But I must read my Bible.'

'As long as you read as much Old Testament as you read New.'

I nodded in agreement. They heaved a sigh of relief, and hugged me close.

'Good, so let's get on with life, shall we?' my father said.

When I arrived back in Manchester there was a letter waiting from Rabbi Gold of the Reform Synagogue who would like to see me at my parents' request. An appointment had been made for the following week. I took the letter to the small prayer group that met in my hall and said, 'Pray for me girls, because God only knows how I'm going to survive for three years with no church and no boys. All I've got now is you lot. And what the heck am I going to say to a rabbi?'

A hundred butterflies took flight in my stomach as I knocked at the synagogue door. A secretary showed me into the waiting area outside the rabbi's study door, where I sat chewing the skin around my nails, reminding myself over and over again of verses in Luke's Gospel where Jesus tells his followers not to be afraid when they're dragged before synagogue rulers and authorities, for 'the Holy Spirit will teach you in that very hour what you ought to say.' It seemed very apposite. My life was depending on it.

The rabbi emerged moments later, not as I imagined, with a long beard, but tall and gaunt, clean-shaven, with a prominent nose and small, penetrating eyes. He had his arm around a much smaller, younger man and showed him out, calling after him, 'Don't forget to let me know how you get on.'

A nod seemed to suggest I follow him, and another, that I take a chair. I perched on the edge, bracing myself for the first assault.

'So, why have your parents sent you to me?' he asked wearily, barely looking at me.

He knew, surely, so why the game of cat and mouse? 'I've become a Christian,' I said without any attempt to soften it.

'How does a Jew become a Christian?' he appealed, with an unmistakable hint of irony in his voice.

I described my experience as briefly as I could. Was it my imagination or did he seem a little shaken?

'The boy,' he said, 'the one you saw leaving just now, he has the same story.'

No wonder the rabbi seemed weary – two of us in a day. He stared unseeingly out of the window. I prayed he was reckoning I was a hopeless case and would let me go.

'Well, well, then, what do you want to ask me?' The tone was dismissive.

I tried to think of some profound theological questions. 'Isaiah, chapter 53?'

'The suffering servant, yes?'

'It says the Messiah will be wounded for our sins and bruised for our iniquities. Doesn't it describe Jesus on the cross?'

The rabbi raised his eyes heavenward, sighed and shook his head. Manifestly he had heard this one before and was not impressed.

'I think not. The suffering servant is Israel, the nation.'

I was genuinely puzzled. 'How can a nation be described as "a man of sorrows and acquainted with grief"?'

'In Scripture Israel is often referred to as a person.'

'But not as a man, surely?'

There was a long, deep silence which I didn't know how to fill.

'Have you any idea what this is doing to your parents?' the rabbi interjected, with a sudden loss of patience. 'It will be the death of your grandparents.'

Emotional blackmail – time to go. I got up and headed for the door.

'Before you go, I have a friend, a Church of England clergyman, who will help you appreciate what it means to be a Jew. Will you see him?'

I shook my head, and rushed out, walking round and round the city until I was calm enough to get on a bus. Unknowingly, I had just turned down a premature opportunity to meet my future father-in-law, who, rather than dissuade me from my course, would have embraced me with open arms. Nor could I know that within months Rabbi Gold would be caught embracing the wife of one of his congregation, and make off with her to the United States.

Not to be outdone, Ros's vicar back in Newcastle arranged for me to see a clergyman too. Once again I found myself party to a little clerical tête-a-tête in a study walled with books from floor to ceiling. This man was balding, fatherly and kind, but persuasive all the same.

'I hear you've promised your parents you won't go to church until you're twenty-one?'

'I want them to see I'll bend over backwards to honour them.'

'But you know you can't go on with that – not after a month or two?'

'I must. I've promised.' I began to feel that prickly sensation on the back of my neck that I now associated with pressure – however gentle.

'Besides, I have all the support I need from the Christian Union, without having to break my word.'

Smiling, he got up and showed me to the door. 'I'll give you a month,' he said, 'then see you in church.'

As the door closed behind me I made up my mind to be guided by one voice alone – the inner voice. If I listened to all the others I would be torn in a thousand pieces and strewn across Manchester from church to synagogue.

Most of the time obeying my parents' wishes wasn't such a sacrifice anyway. The Christian boys I wanted to date, never asked. Those who did, I didn't fancy. And I was quite relieved not to have to go to church. It was still such an alien environment that I was never fully comfortable there. But vacations were difficult.

'Yes, Sam, she is free tonight. I'm sure she'd love to go out with you.'

I am hanging over the bannisters shaking my head furiously at my mother, who smugly replaces the receiver, once the date has been arranged.

'Such a nice boy,' she sighs. 'And an accountant too. He seems so keen on you. Go out with him. It'll be good for you, take you out of yourself.'

Reluctantly, I concede. Poor Sam. If only he knew how he was being used. Then an idea dawns.

'Sam?' I said that evening as we drew up outside our house after a generous meal, 'I think I should tell you – I'm not what I seem.'

'Oh?' he wriggled uncomfortably. A shy young man, deep revelations are not his scene.

'I think Jesus is our Messiah. In other words, that makes me a Christian, so you won't want to go out with me any more.'

'Are you going into a convent?'

'No, of course not, but my life is so different now. We're miles apart.'

'You can believe what you like for all I care. It doesn't bother me.'

That was not what I wanted to hear, though it pushed Sam way up on the levels of the respect barometer.

'Well, thanks for the meal and see you around,' I shouted as I slammed the car door.

He didn't ring again for a while. Mum was puzzled. 'I've watched you from the window when you come home,' she said, 'I'm sure it's because you never gave him a goodnight kiss. Boys like a little bit of that.'

For three years the uneasy truce with my parents continued. They watched me, anxiously, desperate for the tiniest sign that I had discovered the error of my ways and that the crisis was over, giving way to utter wretchedness when they saw a Bible on my bedside table.

When I was twenty-one I moved into my own flat and began to attend a Free Church called Ivy Cottage. It was a church with a baptistry. As I watched several of my friends taking the plunge I knew it was only a matter of time before I followed them. I put it off as long as I dared, telling myself it was an unnecessary extra, that it was unreasonable to hurt my parents any further and jeopardize our uneasy truce – until I picked up my Bible one morning and it fell open at words that seemed to lift off the page in neon lights. 'Why are you waiting? Arise and be baptized.'

'You win, God,' I shouted, 'but I can't tell the parents just now, not with final exams just around the corner.'

'You know what baptism means?' The minister looked down at me with an air of gravity and compassion. 'It's a public demonstration of what you believe.'

'I know.' I hung my head and bit my lip.

He rifled in his pocket. 'Here's the vestry key. Help yourself to the telephone.'

I wandered across the church in a daze. Disappointingly, the key slid into the lock without protest. The room smelt musty, of old theological books. The phone was buried under a pile of papers. I sat down weakly beside it, waited for my heart to stop pounding, then picked up the receiver and dialled the number. It was ringing. 'Please, God, let them be out.'

'Hello? Oh, it's you, Shell, how's things?'

'Mum, I'm going to be baptized.'

The silence seemed interminable. 'I said...'

'I know what you said.' The voice was hard and cold. 'Never come home again, you're no longer our daughter.'

Click. The line went dead. I put the receiver down slowly. When the minister appeared at the door a few moments later, I was horrified to see the mascara-stained pool of tears all over his pristine white writing pad.

I was baptized on Pentecost Sunday with little elation and a great deal of pain. 'I'm doing this because you ask it, not because I want it,' I muttered to the Almighty with as much grace as I could muster. 'So don't expect me to enjoy it.'

Meanwhile, everyone else seemed thrilled, and virtually unaware of the turmoil it was causing. They hugged and embraced me, and organized a party. I went through with it all, feeling rather numb, yet reluctantly peaceful too.

Afterwards, back in my little flat and alone in the dark, I whispered, 'Oh God, why did you have to make me Jewish? If I had been a Gentile, like most other people, everything would have been so easy then.'

Chapter 7

So Who Am I, Really?

*B*y now I was having a real crisis of identity. I struggled then and sometimes struggle now with the term 'Christian', because its current meaning suggests a negation of what I really am, rather than the expanding and enriching of it. And that was something I never sought to escape.

'Of course you're still Jewish,' Christians said reassuringly. But which bit was still Jewish? Pushed, they couldn't really say. Probably because they were referring to my looks. They had little concept of what being Jewish actually meant, and although it was never said, I suspected there was an assumption that I would settle down and become the Gentile that any assimilated, Anglican-educated young woman surely could.

To be fair, if I could have afforded plastic surgery on my nose I might have considered it. In the name of peace and conformity I could have dyed my hair blond as well, if the dark roots wouldn't have shown through in days, making me look as tarty as the newspaper photos of Moors murderer, Myra Hindley. I would have quite liked to be an Anglo-Saxon goddess, instead of a swarthy cave woman with olive skin and unruly curls. I was sick of being asked if I was foreign.

'Actually, English,' never seemed to convince anyone, except one day in a crowded restaurant, when a dapper-looking gentleman in dicky bow at the next table, peering at me through the spectacles on the end of his nose, finally put down his knife and fork, leant across and said, 'My dear, allow me to say what fine Celtic colouring you have.'

The friend I was with stifled a snort with her table napkin. 'No Celt here mate,' she whispered to me.

'Semitic, actually,' I said to the gentleman, smiling sweetly, and went on eating my chocolate mousse.

That was one of the more positive encounters. In my final year at school, I went with a group of girls to the Boys' Grammar for a shared lecture. Dressed in our sack-like bottle green uniforms and unflattering pudding basin hats, we felt conspicuously unsexy, not the drop-dead gorgeous beings a girl wanted to be when confronted with the male species en masse. A gang of youths jostled past us in the entrance hall. One of them pointed straight at me and jeered, 'Look at that Yid.'

I realized then that looks are important. If people say Jew at first glance, their preconceptions will condition their attitude to me before I open my mouth. And that means that being Jewish must consist of a great deal more than looks. Before my experience in York, I never stopped to wonder what it meant. It was a fact of life, to be embraced alternately with joy and resignation.

'I may not be a good Jew, but I am a proud Jew.' It was a refrain I heard over and over again as a child, as if owning one's identity gave you such a big tick in your credit column on the day the Almighty balanced the books, that it wiped out all the debits in the law-breaking column. Gradually I understood. For a people so used to abuse that they anticipate it at every turn, it isn't easy to embrace one's heritage. More than that, debase and despise a race for long enough and they may, at some subconscious level, come to believe they deserve it. Millions walked into Hitler's death camps without a murmur or a protest, helpless and defeated. Pride is the antidote to being ostracized. Pride keeps the demons of rejection and humiliation at bay – pride and an ironic, self-mocking sense of humour that laughs at ourselves before others get round to doing it.

No one can come to terms with being Jewish without facing up to the Holocaust. How nice to see it merely as a historic event and acknowledge it for one day a year. For a Jew, the genetic bonds mean that each one of us carries within their DNA the sufferings and tragedy of the entire race. By the grace of God I was not born ten years earlier in Germany, Austria, Holland, Poland, Czechoslovakia, Italy or France. Yet I still had to face the terrible reality that had I been there, I too would have been a nameless, faceless, worthless piece of flesh, of less value than horse manure. That reality has produced the dedicated Zionist, convinced that an exclusive homeland is the only solution, the aggressive Israeli, accountable to none, discovering for the first time that the Jew can fight and win, and the materialistic entrepreneur seeking security and acceptance in wealth. But it has also contributed to the extraordinary intellectual, cultural, scientific and academic achievements of the Jewish people, fruit of a compassion nurtured by centuries of pain and brokenness.

For three years I had honoured my parents' wishes. Now, faced with a church that didn't really know what to make of me, resolving my identity issues became crucial. I could allow my Jewishness to be a negative force, read anti-semitism into the most meaningless word or gesture, take umbrage at every unintentional slight, become aggressive and antagonistic and withdraw pained and hurt. Or, I could use it positively to enrich, enlighten and liberate.

I would like to be able to say that I embraced the latter immediately, but it wouldn't be true. This was my first encounter with the institutional church, albeit in its Free Church disguise, and we didn't get on too well at first. Following Christ was one thing, being committed to one particular expression of it was another, and I felt a bit like patriarch Jacob, who having set his heart on Rachel, found he had acquired Leah into the bargain. The congregation, bless them, didn't really understand the nature of Jewish pride, or the upfront approach of Jewish women. And since religion was a serious business, nor did they appreciate the sense of humour that softened its edges. I repeatedly found myself in corners, being told that 'in love', I was, 'too emotional', 'too outspoken', 'too unconventional'.

But what was Jesus if he wasn't emotional, outspoken and unconventional? In my readings of the Gospels he was joyous, exuberant and vulnerable. He wept openly, loved eating out and having fun, and was given to sudden bursts of anger, when it was merited. I couldn't believe he was the bland, conservative Englishman they wanted to make of him. A little voice whispered in my head, that if he was really Jewish, then genetically at the very least, I had more in common with him than they did. I didn't know that Martin Buber, the Jewish philosopher, reclaiming Jesus for his people, had written, 'We Jews know Jesus in a way – in the impulses and emotions of his essential Jewishness – that remains inaccessible to Gentiles subject to him.' And even if I had, how could I have repeated it? It sounded so arrogant. I was the one with the 'L' signs on – my place was to sit and learn.

Having forfeited both family and community, more than anything I wanted love and acceptance, so for a while I tried to modify my behaviour so that I could blend into my new environment like a chameleon. But trying to hack off my past was like a botched amputation. It left me scarred and mutilated, not whole and healthy, living the kind of fullness of life Jesus had led me to expect. In the end, the pretence was too difficult to maintain. My real identity haunted me like a restless ghost, making unwelcome appearances, like Banquo in *Macbeth*, when I least expected it.

'We Gentiles...' proclaims the preacher from the pulpit.

'Speak for yourself,' I find myself shouting out, to concerted tutting.

Manifestly, interaction with the speaker is not encouraged. But I can't let go of this extraordinary irony – that in the early days of the church they would have been the outsiders, not me. And I can't help but feel, from what I've read of Jesus, that he has a soft spot for outsiders.

My culture shock was profound. The stark Victorian neo-Calvinist decor didn't help. Coloured glass windows, set in mullion stone and coated on the outside with 100 years of Manchester grime, shut out the daylight. The low timbered ceiling had been varnished an unattractive dog mess brown. In moments of boredom, in the middle of the hymn sandwich, I imagined climbing up with paint stripper and a brush and restoring it to its golden pine glory. The wooden blocks of the parquet floor clattered as we stood and sat, sat and stood, to sing. It was like being enclosed in a huge wooden coffin.

Where was the bustle and the noise, the velvets and satins, crimsons and gold of the synagogue? I never realized how much the haunting quality of the Hebraic chant, the easy alternation between prayer and chatter, the dazzling shimmer of the scrolls, carried around so that men and children could touch them with the prayer shawls they had kissed, were a part of me. In the intensity of my search for God, I had been so full of Judaism's inadequacies that I had forgotten its sheer beauty – until I was deprived of it. In church services the memory of it would flood over me in huge waves that left me disoriented and panic-stricken.

'What am I doing here? I don't belong here. Let me out.'

And then I would remember I had nowhere else to go. The festivals with their gaiety and laughter, the family traditions I had loved so much, had gone forever. At my baptism I thought I was taking on a new family, but it didn't turn out like that. Sunday after Sunday I walked home from church and ate alone in my little flat. Once, I went to the synagogue around the corner, and found myself bombarded with invitations to lunch. I felt it would have been dishonest to accept.

The more I grieved for the world I had lost, the more I sank into a morass of self-pity and anger – with the church as the primary object of my resentment. I became a hedgehog, wound into a tight little ball, covered in protective prickles on the outside.

'When the Jews crucified Christ,' says the preacher. That sets me off, but it's not as bad as, 'Now that God has finished with the Jews', or 'The church is the new Israel.'

'Finished with the Jews? Then why am I sitting here? And why are you so superior, by the way? Are you so much better than they are with these dry, dull ways of worship? If he has finished with them, why shouldn't he finish with you too?'

And woe betide anyone who tried to discuss Middle Eastern politics with me in an effort to get me to understand the Arab point of view. I knew they had one, but there was no way at that time that I wanted to see it. 'We Jews have never had a land to call our own before. We have to have one because, in the end, no one wants us.' The truth was that inside me, a voice was crying, 'And do you really want me, a Jew, in your church?'

To the vast credit of my Christian friends, they endured my rudeness, my tempers, tantrums and explosions as I wrestled to find out who I was, with far more grace than I ever deserved. They listened for hours and lovingly let me weep away the hurt and pain, not only of the recent rejections, but of the generations of it I had unwittingly accumulated in my psyche, the inheritance of every Jew. Then, gradually I began to see how Jewish Christianity was.

'Do you get the significance of that?' I asked my home group in great excitement, when we were studying, 'Where two or three are gathered together, there am I in the midst.' A sudden flashback had transported me to the times when it was necessary to say prayers at home or in the synagogue, and it couldn't be done because the statutory ten men hadn't turned up. 'In Judaism,' I explained, 'no act of public prayer can go ahead without a *minyan* – a quota of ten men. Jesus is superseding the *minyan*. He's saying, just go ahead and pray because he's always there.'

Certain New Testament passages were real for me in a way I could see they weren't for my friends. I could never hear the verse, 'Jesus has broken down the dividing wall of hostility between Jew and Gentile', from the Apostle Paul's letter to the Ephesians, without wanting to leap off my chair in a paroxysm of joy. But my smiles were only greeted with blank stares. I wanted to shake the congregation and say to them, 'Don't you see, here we are together when normally we would have nothing in common, and years of mistrust would have kept us miles apart? Take my Jewishness for granted and you take the whole reconciliation work of Christ on the cross for granted too.' Manifestly, putting the New Testament back into its Hebraic context twenty centuries after it was written was going to be a slower process than the writing of it.

Several months after my baptism I plucked up courage and rang home.

'Mum, it's me, I've got my degree.'

'Oh yes.'

'Will you come to the graduation next month?'

'We'll see. I'll discuss it with your father.'

A glimmer of hope. I clung to it – and there, among the last cars to swing into the car park was the familiar, shiny silver Volvo. My heart pounded as I went to meet them. My academic gown and hood were heavy and it was a hot day. I could feel the sweat trickling down the back of my neck. Mum checked me over from head to toe with a look and frowned at the sight of my tangled, limp curls. We walked in silence to the ceremony, then afterwards, posed together for photographs, smiling at the official photographer.

'Where's your luggage?' Mum demanded, as we made way for the next happy family.

I had packed a suitcase in a half-hearted sort of way, just in case, hardly daring to hope.

'Get the car,' she snapped at my father. 'We're going home.'

We travelled in a heavy silence for around half an hour.

'I presume you went through with it?' she asked in a controlled voice, without as much as turning her head.

'Yes,' I whispered.

I saw her reach out and pat my father on the knee.

'We could have been so proud of you today, and instead... this. You come home as a stranger, you realize, not our daughter.'

That first evening I was sitting alone, reading in the sitting room. Dad put his head around the door. He was wearing his skullcap. 'Have you a moment?' he asked.

'Of course.'

I followed him upstairs to the bedroom and saw his prayer book lying open on the bed. He picked it up uncertainly. 'I have *jahrzeit* today for your grandmother. It's ten years since she died and I've been trying to pray,' he said, the words catching his throat. 'Funny, isn't it, an agnostic trying to pray? I don't know how to.'

Not easy either, I thought to myself, given the circumstances of her death, which must have plagued him with guilt every time he remembered them.

'Will you pray with me?' he asked hesitantly. 'I don't know who else to ask.'

Together we read from the *Siddur*, the Jewish Prayer Book, in English. I slipped my arm through his and saw that there were tears in his eyes.

'You're a great comfort to me you know,' he said.

And I could do nothing but marvel at such an extraordinary turnaround.

That was the beginning of a very gradual rebuilding of the shattered relationship with my parents. But it was not as it had been before. To my astonishment it was better, less fragile, stronger, based on their acceptance of my adult decision to live my own life. No more blind dates, no more *Fiddler on the Roof* in the hope of generating some emotional return to the fold. They truly let me go, and as they did, I discovered a freedom to love them that I had never known before. I loved them for accepting me, when so many Jewish families would have turned their backs forever and even read *kaddish*, prayers for the dead, over their own child. There is an old Jewish proverb that says, 'If we do not bend, we break.' They had understood that so well, and realized that the relationship with a child is paramount. Unnatural to break such a cord, no matter what culture and community demand. One of my father's oft-repeated pithy words of wisdom was, 'Principles are all very well, but when principles come before people, fanatics are born.' My actions had called upon him to live it out, and live it, he did.

Now I was free to go home for major festivals. In an unexpected way, the Christian part of me began to make new sense of Judaism. Jesus, the Jew, had known and engaged in all the familiar rituals, and often used them as an audio-visual aid to point to his destiny. The eating bread and drinking wine of the Sabbath service was a foretaste of Holy Communion. Lighting the tiny candles on the *Hanukkah* around Christmastime, at the Feast of Lights, was a reminder that the Light of the World had indeed come. At Tabernacles, when the people cry out for the latter rain to water the crops, representing their messianic hope for eternal redemption, he had actually said, 'If anyone is thirsty, let them come to me and drink.'

Passover thrilled me the most. It was the same old service I had known and loved as a child, but now, as we read it together, I imagined Jesus eating that last meal with his disciples, his own heart heavy because he knew what was coming, using the well-known and much loved symbols to explain why he had to do what he was doing. In every Jewish home Elijah's goblet would always remain untouched. No prophet would announce the appearance of the Messiah. He had already come.

One year, two places at our Passover table were conspicuously empty, and Gran wept her way through the entire evening. My new enjoyment in the occasion was checked by the terrible pain we faced as a family. My grandfather died at a relatively early age after a stroke had left him paralysed and speechless. Gran nursed him devotedly at home, and was exhausted when another stroke finally ended his life two years later. But there was worse to come.

When their beloved son Martin was born, seventeen years after my mother, my grandfather had declared triumphantly, 'Now I have my *kaddish*.' In the synagogue, when a son recites the special prayers for the dead, he keeps his father's memory alive. Martin came home for the funeral from Peru, where he was working as a journalist for Viznews, supplying all the major TV networks with news stories. Six months later, at the age of twenty-seven, he too was dead, after he fell down a flight of stairs that led from the roof into his flat. He had no son to say *kaddish* for him. His coffin was flown home for burial in the Jewish cemetery in Sunderland. Only my father could bear to lift the lid, and look for one last time at the sleeping face, wrapped in the prayer shawl he had loved to wear. For the second time in just a few months, my grandmother and mother sat on low stools in the sitting room of my grandmother's home, as prayers of mourning were said morning and evening for seven days.

'Why?' Gran cried out to the ceiling, 'Why, why, why? There isn't a God. There can't be a God.'

The women tried to comfort her, while in the next room, my brother, Michael, only twenty-two, led the familiar prayers for the first time. They mourned a life cut short, the wasted potential, the children Martin would never have. As the sound of their lament drifted through to us, my mother took hold of my hand and said, 'I'm so glad we didn't drive you away. He was like my first child. Losing one is enough.' She looked at me inquisitively for a while, then added quietly, 'I wish I had your faith.'

'You can,' I whispered back, desperate to offer some kind of hope. But she simply shook her head and looked away.

Prayers ended and one by one the visitors filed past the bereaved to pay their respects.

'What's this I hear about you then?'

Jeremy, one of my mother's cousins, was standing in front of me.

'What?' I asked, playing the innocent.

'You've become a Jehovah's Witness or something. I know Martin defended you to the hilt. He was adamant you should be allowed to follow your conscience.'

To my surprise, Jeremy displayed genuine interest, not a hint of condemnation or paternalistic indulgence.

'I've become a Christian,' I said. There it was again, that word that implicitly implied rejection, rather than an expansion of the essence of Judaism. 'I mean, I've found something that seems to make sense of being Jewish.'

'Really? We must talk.'

It was hardly the occasion, and would have to wait. Still, it was comforting to be greeted without hostility, and sad to discover too late that Martin had been a secret ally.

If being a Christian in the Jewish community was beginning to be interesting, being a Jew in the church was even more so. I discovered there could be great advantages in having no denominational bias, no preconceived notions, no knowledge of long-standing traditions. Objectivity was very useful in discerning what was really essential, and what were merely extraneous cultural additions.

'It must be marvellous to be free from the Law,' gushed a middle-aged lady, grasping my hand to her generous bosom, after she had heard me tell my story in some church or other. Public speaking was becoming a regular occurrence. Unusual 'testimonies' as they were called, were in great demand, and I was beginning to feel a bit of a prize poodle.

'Free from the Law, lucky you.' It was repeated to me over and over again. But what did it mean? The Jewish law had never really been much of an encumbrance in our home. We observed the laws we chose to observe and ignored the rest. How could I explain that in the few seconds of a snatched conversation? 'Yes, thank you, it's lovely to be able to have a pork chop every now and then.' We had always gone out to restaurants where I could have eaten pork, had I wanted to. How could I make her see that I had noticed that some Christians seemed to have a system of laws more terrible and tyrannical than anything I had ever faced as a Jew? There was a veritable evangelical Torah:

'Thou shalt not have fun in church.'

'Thou shalt not study on the Sabbath day.'

'Thou shalt not date without intent to marry.'

'Thou shalt not tempt a man by dressing in any way that could vaguely be conceived as sexy, or let's face it, nice.'

It could all be summed up in one basic commandment, 'Thou shalt conform.'

Sometimes the church felt like a vast machine which swallowed up its members, ground them to powder, then rebuilt them into model Christians, pumping them out numbered and coded without personal identity or individuality. I fought the process with every fibre of my being. It was hard enough seeking to obey the truth, let alone a Puritan, Victorian anachronism.

One Sunday evening, while I was still at university, there was a tiny tap at the door of my room in the hall of residence. I opened it and found Ruth, who was in charge of the Christian group, standing there hesitantly.

'Can I come in?' she murmured, staring at the floor.

I suspected she had come to check on why I hadn't been in church.

'Of course you can. Why the formality all of a sudden?'

She didn't answer but shuffled sheepishly into the room in those ridiculous fluffy slippers she wore.

I was in fact unpacking my suitcase after a particularly difficult weekend at home, feeling tired and emotionally drained. Mum had bought me a brand new dress, cherry red and cut away at the shoulders. I couldn't resist wearing it for the journey back to Manchester.

'Seat?' I nodded at a space on the bed next to my suitcase, and she perched uncomfortably near the edge, examining her fingernails. I stopped unpacking and waited.

She drew breath. 'Well, er, it's just that Sylvia and I thought we ought to talk to you about... a few things.'

'And you pulled the short straw?'

She nodded unhappily. Sylvia was Vice President of the Christian Union. Sylvia was wise and spiritual – she gave up her fiancé because he only wanted to be a clergyman, not a missionary like she did, buried in the jungle, translating the Bible for some exotic, unknown tribe. Everyone was in awe of her. She spoke and we obeyed. The back of my neck suddenly felt clammy.

'What sort of things?'

'Well your hemline for a start. It's barely decent. Men

have a hard time keeping their urges in check. You're just making it harder for them.'

I looked down at my legs. They were short and not exactly sexy. I wondered whether to feel flattered.

'And just look at that dress.' Ruth was beginning to warm to her subject. 'Just look at the stitching. Talk about suggestive.'

For the first time I noticed the two rows of white topstitching encircling the two mounds on my front.

'Oh, yes, I see what you mean. Do you think it will upset someone?'

'Sylvia and I think that you should probably succeed me as leader of the Christian group, but it really does depend on your... on, well, your behaving like a Christian.'

'But I'm Jewish too. Mum still buys me clothes fit for a *Bar Mitzvah*. You wear a hat on Sundays because your mum belongs to the Brethren and expects it.'

She looked uncomfortable and it didn't seem fair to push her any further.

'Okay,' I said wearily, 'I'll try.'

'Oh, and by the way,' she delivered her final shot from the safety of the doorway, 'Even your nightie's bright red and frilly.'

Drat, I thought, she's even been peeping under my pillow.

I flopped onto the bed and lay there thinking for some time. It was a bit daring to reveal so much leg – especially when mine weren't very long to start with. More than anything, it was an act of rebellion, a determined attempt to retain some colour and not become dowdy or old-fashioned. Surely faith should be attractive to outsiders, not a turn-off. But then, the demure girls got the men and I rarely did. I suspected I seemed too fast, too foreign for the timid, mild-mannered blokes I was meeting. Years later I checked it out with one of the more together examples of the species I knew in those days, and he said, 'Yes, you had a big pair of knockers and knew how to use them.' I had no idea I was 'using' them. Jewish women tend to be rather well endowed, and it's hard to hide them without hunching the shoulders. But perhaps, for the sake of happy relationships, I might just have to reform a little, and not be quite so much in their faces. Being a follower of Christ and remaining true to the Jewish woman he had made me was more of a fine art than I had anticipated, but once I began to acquire it, the comfort eating that accompanied my quest for loving acceptance vanished. I lost a great deal of unwanted puppy fat, and felt more comfortable in my skin. The only problem was that I had a French degree, and no idea what to do with it.

All that was certain was that I now wanted to use my Jewishness to enrich the church, if that were at all possible. If there are hundreds of years of rejection locked in the heart of any Jew, there are also hundreds of years of riches waiting to be unlocked and shared. I hadn't discovered a new religion, or even a new God. It was the same God who had been with my ancestors down through the centuries and was there in the rituals of my childhood, only I had not recognized or known him. If I was Jewish through and through, then so was the church, from its founder and foundations, to the book that inspired it. One day it would wake up and begin to rediscover the Hebraic cultural roots that had been buried for so long beneath the soil of misconception, incomprehension and anti-semitism. My mistake was that I thought it could happen overnight. But happen it must, of that I was sure, and I was going to do everything I could to encourage that process – introduce celebration, feasts, festivals, all the colourful treasures of my heritage, which was not mine alone. Besides, the wind of change was in the air. The Charismatic Movement had already started to blow the topsoil away. Old preconceptions were being shaken, conventional attitudes overturned, creating a lighter, fresher, more open attitude, and a demand for Hebraic music and dance. The time was ripe for innovation.

Chapter 8

On the Streets

*I*never meant to fall in love. It was an added emotional complication I could have well done without. The object of my infatuation was a six-foot-four gentle giant with soft brown velvet cow's eyes, and a grace and dignity unusual in the men who tended to cross my path. Jewish men aspired to cars with attitude. Christian men did not aspire to women with attitude. Or if they did, they certainly didn't let it show. Neither types of the species had much appeal for me. But here was a man who appeared to enjoy my quirkiness. I was suddenly overtaken by daydreams of romance on desert islands, white wedding veils and nappies on the washing line blowing in the breeze.

I first became conscious of his existence in my 'no-non-Christian-men-allowed' era, during a year in Paris as part of my degree. A young French woman who had become a close friend had fallen in love with an English boy. She thought I might know one of his school friends because he was at Manchester University. 'His name,' she said, 'is Peter Guinness.' She had met him, briefly, when he and her beloved were touring Europe together. I had the vaguest memory of a smile across a crowded room, nothing more, but when I got back to Manchester, I went to seek him out.

I liked the way he pulled up a chair, turned its back to me, effortlessly stretched his long legs over it and sat down, so that he was now at my level and could look me in the face. I told him we had mutual acquaintances in France. He told me he had been waiting for me to come back to tell me about his family's long involvement in Christian–Jewish relations. There was an immediate spark between us, I knew, I could tell, which for me grew quickly into something far deeper, but for him, never progressed beyond special friendship. Perhaps, in this time of 'purdah', divine intervention was forcing me to stay true to my promise to my parents. If so, I wasn't pleased. 'I've given you home, family, community, what more do you want? How can you refuse me the man of my dreams as well? You can make him fall in love with me, if you want to. It shouldn't be too difficult for you.'

I had reconstructed the Almighty into some kind of celestial Eros who could either fire a dart in the direction I specified, or remove it from my heart if it had found its way to an unintended target. When the foot stamping and tantrums failed, I tried reasoning. 'You'll never find me anyone as suitable. There's our joint interest in France and the Jews.' But God would not submit to either bullying or blackmail. I would simply have to trust he had the best in store, even when Peter moved into a flat around the corner and started to attend the same church, and it felt as if I were being taunted. In my imagination I made a little altar in my room, and like Abraham with his beloved son, Isaac, pretended to put him on it every day – usually through gritted teeth. Even if I had to watch him walk down the aisle with someone else, I told myself, I would find the grace to be happy for him. Real love was like that. This was its test.

My Great-Grandfather Fishkin, who got his name from a man filleting fish on the Tyne Quay.

The wedding of Abe Davis and Elsie Fishkin, my maternal grandparents. 'I'll bring him down a peg or two'. And she did.

My Great-Grandmother Fishkin in her favourite fur coat on the right – with from left to right, my tragic Uncle Martin, Michael, my Grandmother Elsie, and me.

All feathers and furs – my Great-Grandmother Fishkin on her way to a ball, with my Grandmother Elsie, in veils, fashionable in the 1940s.

My paternal Grandparents Gilbert, with my father and 'purple' Aunt Ida. My grandmother, Rose, was never a happy woman.

Ida embarks on a long, embittered marriage. My grandfather had to go back to tailoring to pay off the extra dowry his son-in-law demanded, and died an early death. My father on the right makes a very dapper page boy.

My parents' wedding in 1947 – so many cousins meant there were plenty of bridesmaids. My mother was only nineteen.

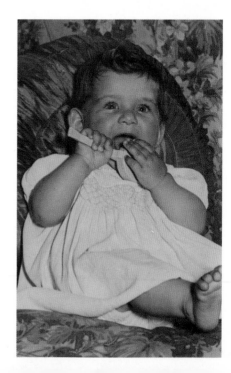

A few months old in my great-grandparents' home – the first great-grandchild.

Four years old, in my father's arms, and bridesmaid for my mother's cousin, Eddie Arnold, a well-known comedian and impressionist who played regularly at the London Palladium.

Eddie Arnold married Mary, one of the 10,000 Jewish children given asylum in Britain from the Nazis, known as the 'Kinder Transport'. Adopted by a non-Jewish family at the age of three, she was used as a servant and didn't discover she was Jewish until after the war. After her marriage she went on to run a very successful theatrical agency that included Tom Jones and the Walker Brothers.

A new baby sister – I am nine years old.

The dress for my brother's Bar Mitzvah. I wanted to look like Walt Disney's Snow White.

One of the most significant weekends of my life: The York Mystery Plays 1966.

York Minster – sporting the pink chiffon hat!

Graduation at Manchester University – the smiles belying some of the strain of the occasion.

After four long years of waiting – 'I've got him at last'.

My beloved Aunt Ida (left) with Norah, her Irish live-in companion/maid. She decided not to wear purple to my wedding, which was a surprise.

The family in Normanton – with Joel (aka Spiderman), and Abby.

When Ernest Saunders, CEO and Chairman of Guinness, was arrested for fraud, just as I was writing a biography of the family, the press virtually camped outside our front door in Normanton. Local folk got used to directing journalists to the curate's house. *The Daily Express* made Peter pose in a clerical shirt for this photo of us. I had no idea my thumb was strategically placed!

The Rabbi is obviously bending my ear! Just checking my earpiece whilst presenting a series for Central TV called, *Right or Wrong*.

It's *Children in Need* night at the BBC. Fundraisers who came to BBC CWR (Coventry and Warwickshire) with their takings offered an extra £5 in exchange for a kiss from the presenter! On the right is Jim Lee, my director, now continuity announcer on Radio 4.

With Helen Shapiro at one of her gospel concerts in Morecambe. It was the first time we met.

Filming in the Galilee with Matthew Kelly for a programme called, *Paradise Found* which gave celebrities a chance to go on retreat to a place with spiritual significance. I resisted the urge to say, 'Tonight, Matthew, I'm going to be …'.

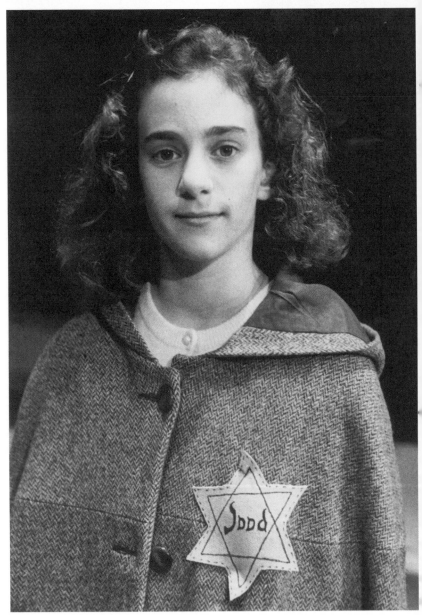

At fourteen, Abby played Anne Frank at the Grand Theatre in Lancaster. It was a very moving experience for the whole family. The local papers were all taken with the striking resemblance.

Joel marries Sarah, who was raised in the Lebanon, where her father, Colin Chapman, was a CMS missionary, and well-known in his support for the Palestinian people. The joining of our two families could be seen as one of God's little jokes – or symbolic of the reconciliation so badly needed in the Middle East.

And now I am a grandmother. Livvy at six months.

Great-Grandmother's Baked Cheesecake – a melt-in-the-mouth treat, either for Sunday tea or as a dessert.

Stuffed Cabbage Leaves – a traditional and economical way to celebrate the feast of Hannukah, or any occasion.

And meanwhile, at least, I had his friendship, his presence at social events, and the chance of a surreptitious glance or two from behind my hymn book every Sunday morning. But for a long time, that was all I had.

'Don't get tied down too soon. Have your fling, dear,' my father said with a knowing wink, when no man appeared on the horizon to take his daughter off his hands.

'Fling, fling?' my mother snapped, 'That's all right for a man, but at her age I had two children.'

She had taken to making comments about glamorous young grannies. But the 'children' I acquired were not quite what she had in mind.

In the 1970s some women were beginning to think in terms of a career. I wasn't one of them. Child of my upbringing, my ultimate goal was full-time wifedom and motherhood – with a man wealthy enough to support them. But the present reality was that I was alone, with the rent to pay and food to find. My only other plan had been teaching, and experience in a junior school in France had shown me that I had about as much control over a class full of children as a field full of sheep.

For two years I staved off having to make any long-term decision about my future by studying for a Master's degree in Wagner's influence on French literature, but my tutor disappeared back to France and I never completed it. Such earth-shaking research – its results lost to the world forever!

'The eternal student,' my father said wearily, with one eye on his bank balance. But I soon tired of spending all day in silent libraries with nothing but musty old books for company. Little did I know then that this was the perfect preparation and discipline for a lifetime of writing and journalism.

It occurred to me that since I enjoyed young people, but not teaching them, youth work might be a reasonable alternative, so called into Manchester Youth Services to see what voluntary and training opportunities were available.

'Experience?'

'Summer camps.'

'None, I see.'

This particular manager had manifestly never been on a summer camp.

'I stopped a young woman carving open her veins with a pen-knife.'

'Fascinating. How about doing the real thing then, say, one or two evenings a week at a club?'

He was manifestly unaware of self-harm, but then, many were in those days.

'What do you have in mind?'

I felt my face coming under close scrutiny, and sensed what was coming next.

'How about a Jewish Youth Club, the one just around the corner from where you live?'

'I'd quite like to work with drug addicts.'

'With your experience? Stanley Bates, the youth worker at the Jewish club, is one of the best. He'll train you well, and you may find that youth work is what you really want to do.'

That evening I walked down the road to the local synagogue. I had often watched the congregation coming and going from my flat window and wondered about joining them. Now here I was, standing outside the wrought iron gates. They opened at my touch and I followed a beam of light and the blast of pop music into a large hall full of teenagers, who stopped their chatter to dissect the total stranger who had just walked in. Eight years instantly melted away and I was transported back to Newcastle, to *Maccabi* and my own adolescent fear and anxiety.

'Michele? Come into my office, darlin'.'

The strident cockney accent jolted me back into the present.

'Yer don't smoke, do yer?'

'No.'

'Good, ruins the natural body odours.'

Stanley Bates was a small, middle-aged man with a round head and penetrating, dark eyes. Everything about him from his thinning hair and old-fashioned tweed jacket to his badly cut trousers and heavy-duty shoes shouted determined conventionality. A more obvious Gentile in a room full of Jews would have been hard to find.

'I'm a Goy, yer know.'

'Yes, I guessed,' I said wryly, and saw for the first time the flicker of a twinkle in his eyes.

'But I don't stand for any nonsense. If any non-Jewish youngsters come in here they keep their hands off the opposite sex. No marrying out. It's more than my job's worth.'

'In that case, there's something I'd better tell you.'

'Oh yes?'

'I'm a Jew... but I'm a Christian too, by conviction.'

'Oh gawd, not one of them. You're not going to convert us all, are you?' he laughed raucously.

'If I'm asked about it, I can't lie.'

'All right, darlin', only don't cause me any trouble.'

Stanley Bates lived up to his reputation. Over the next months I was immensely grateful for his astute and honest assessment of my work, which I enjoyed enormously. With all expenses paid by the Association of Jewish Youth I joined a training programme he had organized for volunteers across the Manchester area.

'Where did you say you were based, a Jewish Youth Club?' the other volunteers asked disparagingly. 'You can't call that the real thing. Those kids are hardly socially deprived.

They're middle class. They've money – too much of it – that's their problem. They need a good spanking – not your help.'

Youth workers in the early seventies were edgy, radical, left wing – and bigoted.

'Let me tell you about them,' I flashed. 'There's Simon, struggling with eighty per cent deafness, there's Jackie with special physical needs, one of the most intelligent kids there, but totally rejected by her parents, there's Becky, adopted by an orthodox family, who doesn't even look Jewish and is totally confused about who she really is. On top of that, all the kids are trying to come to terms with belonging to a minority group, with anti-semitism at school, and with the enormous pressures they face to achieve, marry well and conform to the standards of their community. Since when does money spare any youngster the trauma of adolescence? And if you, of all people, can't deal with your prejudices, what hope is there for the rest of society?'

I was never baited again. But prejudice – from a very different source – finally put paid to my efforts nonetheless, and the crisis, when it came, was immensely painful.

A journalist from one of the local Jewish newspapers decided to write a feature on the club, and popped in one evening to see what went on.

'And what do you do?' he asked me.

'I sit in the Ladies' most of the time and chat to the girls while they put their lipstick on.'

'Youth Worker Spends Time in Ladies' Loo', the headline read. The kids were highly amused and pinned the cutting to the wall behind the bar.

The editor of a rival Jewish newspaper was even more entertained. He had heard me speak on BBC Radio Manchester about my faith, had jotted down the name for future reference, and could hardly believe his luck. This time the headline read, 'Christian Proselytizes our Youth'.

'Stanley, I'm so sorry,' I whispered down the phone. 'He tricked me into an interview, said it was about youth work.'

'I don't suppose you've seen the editorial – "How long must we go on employing a Gentile youth worker?" It's me they want out. Ah well, I've weathered worse storms than this.'

'Can I come and explain, say goodbye?'

'You're joking, though, aren't you? Do me a favour, don't show your face round here again.'

When I next heard about Stanley Bates he was teaching youth work at a polytechnic.

Becky contacted me a few days later, asking if I would meet her in town for coffee. As we sat in the Kardomah Café, she giggled into her cona-machine coffee.

'My dad would kill me if he knew I was here with you. It would be worse than being seen with a non-Jewish boy.'

I could imagine. Dad was a bigwig in the synagogue, chair of the youth club committee. I was unlikely to be on his list of favourites. With her blond curls, vivid blue eyes and freckles, Becky was already creating havoc among the boys, but behind the girl-who-has-everything facade, the bounce and sparkle, was someone who felt very unloved for who she was, who would have to decide whether she ever pursued her real parentage against immense opposition at home.

'That article in the paper...'

She struggled to put her feelings into words, and only then did I see the hurt and anger in her eyes.

'Was it true? Did you only want to convert us?'

'What do you think, Becky?'

'I don't know, I'm so confused. Everyone says you did and they feel betrayed. They're furious, but that night when I was so upset and you sat with me for ages, you never said anything, even though you had the chance. I thought, here's someone who really cares about me at last. Now I don't know any more.'

'Becky, I do care. You have to believe that. I wouldn't do anything to hurt you if I could help it.'

'Then why did you do it? Why did you convert?'

'I suppose the article was right about one thing when it said that I was looking for something I didn't find in Judaism. I was fed up with religious hypocrisy, and like you, dissatisfied with the social routine. I read the New Testament, and though it's hard to explain, when I read about Jesus Christ, I knew he was the missing link. Suddenly Judaism made sense at last. But I'm not any less Jewish because of it.'

'You amaze me. You're not bad looking. You could easily find a nice Jewish boy, settle down and have a pleasant life. But instead you choose this.'

'Life's a funny thing, isn't it? It amazes me too, but I wouldn't have it any other way. When you find something that answers the questions about why you exist at all, it's worth any price you might have to pay. And had any of you asked me, I wouldn't have hidden it. But as for converting anyone, you're all intelligent enough to make up your own minds.'

'I think I understand a bit better,' Becky smiled at me. 'Can we meet up again?'

She was the first of several young people from the club to contact me. The newspaper editor achieved more than he could have ever imagined. But by now the Wagner research grant had run out, I was unemployed, and there were no youth work jobs advertised in the local newspapers. I suspected something might just turn up, as things had a habit of doing, and one day the phone rang, and a soft voice with a familiar Geordie lilt said, 'Hello, I'm Frank White.

I've just arrived in Manchester to work for the Catacombs Trust, a Christian detached youth work project. It's grant aided by Manchester City Council, which is represented on our committee by Stanley Bates. I need a colleague and he tells me you're the girl I'm looking for.'

It sounded like a proposal.

I liked Frank enormously from the moment I first met him. Raised in a large, loving Catholic family, his own faith had only recently been awakened, and he was struggling to shrug off the excesses of his old life, cut down the beer and cut out the fags. He was warm and cuddly to the point of chubbiness, owing an extraneous couple of inches around his midriff to a diet of fish fingers – the only meal he knew how to cook. He sucked endless peppermints, but could still be tetchy when cigarette smoke wafted beneath his nostrils. Trailing the streets in his ill-fitting jeans and battered, khaki hat, he reminded me of a stray mongrel. It was that touch of the vagabond, and his self-deprecating smile, that was his special charm. Such is the very human stuff of which future bishops of the Church of England are made. And it is probably a very good thing.

'What do we do then?' I asked him.

'We walk the town.'

'Why?'

'To find out what goes on.'

He must know. He had the university degree in Social Work. So inch by inch, hour after hour, we scoured the alleyways, until the soles of our shoes were so worn I reckoned Manchester City Council deserved what we were paying them in rates for pavement repairs.

One autumn evening, just as our breath was beginning to condense in the cold night air, I stepped over a large human bundle and walked on.

'Hang on,' Frank called out to me.

I turned around and saw that he had stopped to examine the mound at his feet.

'It's only a drunk for goodness sake,' I said irritably. I hated this walking around in endless circles. And besides, the damp made my curly hair frizz.

'We can't do that. The next bobby who comes along will book him and that's a night in the cells.'

The stench of alcohol and vomit was beginning to waft in my direction. 'Good. He has it coming to him.'

Frank looked up at me in surprise. 'Jesus wouldn't have just left him lying here.'

I felt ashamed. And yet, this wasn't what youth work was all about – picking up middle-aged men who couldn't hold their booze. It was glamorous and exciting, Sir Galahads rescuing the perishing. Blow Frank and blow his good Samaritan charity.

'I'll take his arms and you take his legs,' he called to me. 'Where do you want to be, pal?'

'Hotel Piccadilly,' murmured the semi-conscious form in a strong Irish accent.

'Phew, we've got a posh one here,' whistled Frank.

Somehow we managed to manoeuvre the retching dead weight through the streets to the doors of his hotel, then propping him between us, dragged him nonchalantly past the page boys and porters into the lift, and along the corridor to his room, where we dumped him on his bed and left him to snore in peace.

It was a relief to suck in the sharp, clean night air again.

'Frank?'

'Yes?'

'You don't half smell.'

'Thanks,' he said, examining his front. 'I don't think this shirt will ever be the same again.'

'You won't find any more like that, will you?'

'No promises.'

It was just as well. Over the next months I lost count of the number of drugged and drunken youngsters we rescued from clubs, pubs, and bars, bundled into our car and deposited on their own doorstep. But from that night, it never bothered me again. I had learned an invaluable lesson, that in every situation the inner resources are always available for whatever we have to do.

My heart went out to the young people who frequented the city centre, and so often made themselves a total nuisance, pick-pocketing, shoplifting, mugging to survive. In a society that dazzled them with mouth-watering images of the material good life, dangled like brightly bejewelled carrots under their noses, theft was an addictive way of life. There was the adrenalin buzz of the risk of being caught, and then – if they were clever enough to get away with it – of having money in their pockets to spend. It was anonymous. It didn't really hurt anyone, as far as they could see. And, in a world that offered them no opportunity, no achievement, no hope, it fed their need for self-worth and status. Booze, drugs, and especially free sex since it was the cheapest, were a welcome, accessible escape from the unacceptable reality that they might have no real value, that life would never be any better than it was now.

Sitting in court one day with a young woman accused of engineering the burglary of her parents' home, we heard the magistrate threaten her with detention in the dreaded Risley Remand Centre unless bail could be found. No kid deserved to be in Risley, no matter what they had done. They all emerged distraught and demoralized to a life of far greater crime and desperation.

'We'll stand bail,' I heard myself saying.

It was Frank's turn to look shocked. 'What will we do with her?' he whispered urgently. 'Where will she stay?'

'Someone in church will have her,' I said with a great deal more confidence than I actually felt.

'She's burgled her parents' home. Who'll take the risk?'

To their eternal credit, one couple did, and it was a costly venture. Naively, I thought she would be grateful, but she took advantage of their generosity. She knew no other way, and despite the quality of care and freedom they gave her, ended up spending a long spell in prison for stealing handbags in a nightclub.

I have no doubt that in the fullness of time such self-sacrifice wouldn't be wasted, but the problem was that there was only a limited amount individuals could do. We could hold out meaning, acceptance and love. They could touch it, take it and try it, but the moment they returned to their old haunts, the youngsters didn't stand a chance. They were as embedded in their culture as the Jewish young people. It offered the same reassuring yet demanding mix of familiarity and safety, of belonging and conformity. Breaking away from that emotional support network was just too threatening for such vulnerable human beings. And that was something I understood. Only a radical Christian community that would be there for them, day in, day out, for as many years as it took, could offer any real long-term alternative. And in those days, communities like that were almost impossible to find.

Chapter 9

Of Romance and Its Consequences

*F*our years had passed since my affections had first been hijacked and the inadvertent perpetrator was no nearer making any response now than he was at the beginning. If anything, he was more remote. I engineered countless opportunities for romance – including a trip à deux to magical Versailles, the day after his school friend married my French friend in Paris. But he was susceptible neither to its charms nor mine. In fact, once my intentions had become clear, he felt it would be less painful for me if we discontinued our close friendship. This was not, in my dreams, how the day was meant to turn out. Never has a couple walked around Versailles so oblivious of their magnificent surroundings. I registered very little except the huge lump of pain that seemed to be expanding like builder's foam in the middle of my chest.

From that day on we saw little of each other. Peter made very sure our eyes never met across a crowded room – or church, and that we were not alone together for any length of time. Meanwhile, there were several men in my life – and even one or two proposals. But faced with the ultimate decision, knowing I could never love anyone as I loved Peter, it was only fair to turn them down.

On one occasion, I really was severely tempted to take the fruitcake available and not wait for the chocolate cake that wasn't on offer – especially as the fruitcake was of a very high standard.

'Gorgeous, isn't he?' a close friend said to me, of one particular interest, 'Handsome, like a Greek god?'

I couldn't have put it better myself, and basked in her approval of my man.

'A pity he's so boring,' she added.

The warm glow turned to a sudden chill.

'Wait,' she urged me, 'be patient and wait – for Peter.'

Looking back, I realize how blessed I was in my friends and their ruthless honesty. But love-sickness was blighting my life. Time to take remedial measures, leave Manchester, start anew. In the summer of 1974 I handed God my ultimatum. If there was no sign of a thaw in the romance climate by Christmas that was exactly what I would do.

The phone call, when it finally came, without any prior warning and a fortnight from the deadline, was nothing short of a miracle. Anita, one of my flatmates, was on hands and knees in front of the fire, sorting out a tangled heap of Christmas paper chains that she intended pinning across the wall.

'I'll go,' she said, jumping up. 'You never know – my prince may have found me at last.'

When she came back into the room, I could tell from the way she looked at me, with an expression of disbelief on her face, that this was no ordinary call.

'It's for you,' she said, a huge grin breaking through the consternation. 'Guess who?'

My legs felt weak as I walked out into the hallway. Anita followed me, her eyes fixed on mine as I picked up the receiver.

'Hello. The 23rd? Yes, I'm free that evening.'

Pam, the other flatmate, appeared at the top of the stairs, drawn irresistibly by something in the air, her mouth wide open. I put the receiver down and we stared at one another in silence for some time.

'He's asked me out for dinner,' I whispered, as if the Prince of Wales himself had asked me for a date. 'After all that's gone on between us, he wouldn't do that unless it was serious, would he?' I asked them nervously, looking from one to the other. Simultaneously we all broke into shrieks of laughter and cavorted around the hallway, until the landlady's stick banging on the wall restored our decorum.

On December 23rd Peter proposed to me outside Woolworth's on Bolton High Street. In his memory the actual offer was made during the fairy book, candle-lit dinner at the Last Drop Hotel, some time between the chestnut soup and the mincemeat meringue, accompanied by carol singers in Dickensian dress. I recollect that it was later, when, not wanting the evening to end, we drove around the town and eventually found somewhere to park. Wherever it was, once his mind was made up, he moved with the same determination that had earned his beer-brewing ancestors their millions.

For the first weeks of our relationship I felt permanently giddy, as if I'd had a glass or two of wine too many. Having waited so long for the daydream to become reality, I could barely cope when it did.

'I knew I must be in love,' he admitted, 'when I spent so much on a meal. I've never done that in my life.'

'But how could it have happened, after all these years, and especially the last months when I've barely seen you?'

'When I discovered you had designs on me, I felt sorry for you, and thought you were wasting your time. You were always a special friend, but I wasn't ready for marriage and it didn't seem fair to encourage you. Then one day, as I was spending some time in quiet reflection, an inner voice seemed to say to me, 'Peter, why don't you get married?' It was an extraordinary conversation. I said, 'Who then, Lord?' And yours was the name that popped into my head. I said, 'But I'm not in love with her, so you'll have to do something about that.' And from then on I couldn't stop thinking about you. By the end of the week I was totally distracted. That's when I called you to make the date. And then it occurred to me you might no longer feel the same about me, that you might have found someone else. It was an agonizing wait.'

'It was a close call,' I admitted. 'I was about to start job hunting elsewhere.'

But not feel the same? I couldn't eat, sleep, work, or even think straight. I travelled several inches above ground level, carried along on waves of bliss. Only an occasional gust ruffled the calm sea of joy. What would the parents say? Had I already committed the ultimate crime, or was marrying out still far worse?

I felt sad for them, as my train jerkily shunted the last few yards into Newcastle Central Station. Things never seemed to go their way, as far as I was concerned. But as we crossed the Tyne and I saw the familiar five bridges, everything looked so different, so welcoming. This time there was no heart sink. There was someone back in Manchester thinking about me, rooting for me, waiting for me. I wasn't alone any more.

'Still picking yobbos out of the gutter and dropping them back in, dear?' my father asked over supper.

'Yes, Dad.'

My work wasn't going to be the start of an argument – not this time.

Half amused, half wistful, Dad shook his head. 'If only you'd been a doctor. You'd have made such a good doctor.'

'You always said women doctors were horses, Dad,' I reminded him.

'Most of them are, but you wouldn't have been.'

'What's more to the point,' my mother intervened, 'Any boys on the horizon? Any nice boys?'

There seemed no better moment to break the bad news, so I said, 'Yes, actually. A very special boy as it happens. I'm going to marry him.'

There was a heavy, difficult silence, for what seemed a very long time.

'I suppose there's no need to ask if he's Jewish?' my mother said finally. She was pale, tight-lipped, but much calmer than I had anticipated.

'Well, I can't say I didn't expect it. Marry him. You don't need our permission, but don't ask for our blessing, either. When I think of all the dreams I've had for you.'

Dad waited for her to get up from the table, then leant over to me and whispered, 'Give her time. She's ready for it. She'll accept it.'

I nodded, amazed at how resigned she seemed to be.

'It's strange how things go,' Dad continued, 'I had made up my mind to speak to you this weekend. I was going to say to you, you're twenty-five, don't stay single just for us. If there's a non-Jewish boy you want to marry, marry him. You'll have a life to live long after we are dead and buried.'

I took his hand, and knowing what pleasure it would give the son of working-class Jewish immigrants to find himself in the official pedigree of one of the wealthiest families in the United Kingdom, delivered the coup I had until then kept in reserve, 'And after all, Dad, he may not be Jewish, but Peter is the great, great-grandson of Arthur Guinness, the brewer, and you will have your name under mine in the Guinness family tree, where it says, daughter of...'

An appreciative grin spread from ear to ear, then vanished as he said, 'I have just one quibble. Did you have to pick one of the poor relations?'

When my mother came back into the room, I hugged them both.

'We can't come to a church wedding,' Mum said quickly, before there was any chance that I might take acceptance as approval, 'but we will come to the reception.'

That was already more than I ever dared to hope.

'So now I have to work out what to say to all the relatives,' she sighed.

'When can I bring him home to meet everyone?'

'You can't.'

She saw my crestfallen expression and relented a little.

'I have your brother and sister to think about. I don't want them to think they can marry out if they please and it won't make a scrap of difference to us. I must set an example. Once he's your husband and nothing can be changed, then you can bring him home. Meanwhile, we'll have to find a convenient place somewhere half way between Newcastle and Manchester where you can introduce him to your father and me.'

One Sunday in February Peter and I slipped out of church before the end of the service and drove to Harrogate. We had arranged to meet my parents at the Majestic Hotel for lunch. They were already there when we arrived and walked down the hallway to meet us, greeting Peter, to my relief, with genuine warmth. They both bent their heads back several inches to look up at him, like tourists in front of the Eiffel Tower.

'Good grief, what a height,' my mother gasped.

Peter bent almost double to speak to her.

'They called me Everest at school. My family are all tall. But never mind, marriage with yours should bring us down a peg or two.'

My father, at least, was amused.

We went into lunch and I noticed there was gammon and pineapple on the menu, Peter's favourite. I watched his face with interest.

'Lamb, please,' he said, with admirable restraint.

'And the gammon for me,' my father said to the waitress.

I saw Peter's mouth fall open, and threw him an apologetic look.

'Let me see the ring then,' my mother said, grabbing my left hand during the starter. 'Hmmm,' she sighed, comparing my pretty little stone with the sparkling knuckle duster on her third finger, 'You call that a diamond?'

Over coffee my parents got down to the real financial business. They had a certain amount of money they intended to give away with their daughter, not exactly a dowry, but 'a little help' all the same. What had Peter to offer? What did he earn, how much had he saved, what were his prospects? It was acutely embarrassing. I almost expected him to say, 'six camels and two donkeys', but if the question made him uncomfortable, he managed not to show it.

'I've saved around £500,' he said proudly.

'Nothing at all then,' my mother said dismissively. 'And what prospects has a schoolteacher? You're not exactly what we wanted for our daughter, but I suppose you'll do.'

We were married five months later in the Free Church we attended in what was a fairly restrained kind of service compared to a Jewish wedding. There was no *chuppah*, no stamping on the glass, no dancing and none of the ceremony that had been the fabric of my childhood. But since Dad couldn't give me away, and since I hadn't yet worked out how to weave my two worlds together – and we were paying the bill – it seemed best to keep things fairly simple. I did raise the idea of having a *chuppah* with the friend in charge of the flowers.

'You want a what?' she asked, looking at me as if I wanted to be wed on a traffic island.

'A canopy of flowers, symbolic of marriages in ancient times, when the bride was brought to her bridegroom's tent. It's a reminder of the forty years in the wilderness.'

Since I had just survived my own four-year wilderness without my man, it seemed relevant somehow.

'Don't be daft,' she said. 'Think what that would cost.'

I didn't argue.

Not all went according to plan. The minister of the church, invited to give the final blessing since Peter's father performed the actual ceremony, prayed for 'Frank and Michele'. Since we had worked together for two years, the names, naturally, were associated in his mind, but Frank, our best man, shook his head violently and said, in a stage whisper, 'She's nothing to do with me now, mate.'

And then, at the reception, a previous minister sidled up to us, and explained that since Peter's father had conducted an Anglican service in a Free Church which has no reading of banns, the vital, legal, 'I know not of any cause or impediment...' clause, which both parties of the couple should be called on to say in public, had been omitted, and therefore we were not legally married.

'Don't worry,' Peter whispered, reassuringly. 'The registrar signed the papers.'

'We'll just have to live in sin,' I whispered back, 'and enjoy it.'

The caterers stole our wine and champagne, and fobbed the guests off with the non-alcoholic refreshment we had bought for teetotal friends. My father stuck his nose in the fruit punch, sniffed, and shook his head. Manifestly he thought it a very poor do. The caterers were sacked by Manchester City Council the following week – too late to rescue our reception.

But given the potential tensions of the situation, the heady mix of church friends and Jewish relations, the event went off as smoothly as we dared hope. As we drove away in the antique Rover I had called Barnabus, or a 'son of consolation', with its real leather upholstery, which Peter had just bought from Frank for a song – nicking his colleague and his car in a single blow – the sun broke through the clouds, and we heaved a sigh of relief.

'You're going to travel a lot,' I said to Peter.

'Me? No. What makes you think that?'

Alec Buchanan, who had preached for us, and was known in the wider church for his prophetic insights, had finished his wonderful sermon with, 'Partings there will be, when the way of the cross demands it.'

'Oh,' I said, and shelved it at the back of my mind.

Few couples spend their honeymoon with their in-laws, but mine just happened to live in Ibiza. In the late 1960s house prices in the UK had begun to rise at an alarming rate. Unable to afford their own property after many years of Church of England ministry, Peter's parents had bought in retirement a lovely, whitewashed home, built into a steep hillside high up over San Antonio Bay. It commanded some of the most magnificent views of the island, a golden paradise before the locals had ever caught sight of an English beer belly. 'My island in the sun,' my father-in-law sang out loudly from outside his rooftop study, scanning the miles of coastland, which curved and dipped into countless rocky inlets and bays, way beyond the pine forests which swept down to the sea.

'A shame he's not quite Harry Belafonte,' my mother-in-law would say with a bemused shake of the head.

How they loved their tranquil haven. To me, it almost seemed a favour from above for faithful service rendered below. Theirs had not been an easy ministry. For four years my father-in-law, an army chaplain, had been a prisoner of war, beaten, abused and starved, giving away his meagre food rations to those whose need seemed greater. It left him with a slow wasting of the nervous system caused by vitamin starvation, which meant that his large hands and feet now refused to move at the brain's command. He needed the heat to stir his benumbed, aching limbs into any kind of action.

'Close the windows,' he would call out in the evening, as we sat in sweltering temperatures, the perspiration pouring from pores we never knew we had. 'There's a terrible draught'. And we would go out onto the terrace to finish our game of scrabble, to enjoy as much of the 'the draught' as we could.

Years of overwork in a parish back in the UK, a time of disappointment, false accusations and delayed, post-traumatic stress syndrome, of scrimping and scrounging on a stipend that was never enough to heat their vast and draughty vicarage in depressing Ashton-under-Lyme, eventually led to a breakdown. The necessity of an early retirement abroad seemed out of reach. But it turned out to be much cheaper to build in Spain, and for some reason their particular site had been overlooked and underpriced. A small Swiss pension in acknowledgment of several working years there finally made the idyll a reality.

It was here my father-in-law managed to fulfil a cherished ambition to write a book on his involvement in Christian–Jewish dialogue. It was the culmination of a lifetime's work and study, dedicated to encouraging Christians and Jews to understand their joint hope and destiny. Jews were awaiting the coming of the Messiah. Christians were waiting for him to come back. Both had been entrusted with the responsibility of communicating and demonstrating to a hostile world the benefits for a people of living in relationship with God. Israel, refusing to proselytize since the fourth century, had, like Jonah, run away from its calling. Christianity had appropriated sole rights. Now both must come to see how much they needed the other so that God's promise to bless all nations through Abraham, including the Muslims, could be fulfilled.

Born when his father Henry Grattan Guinness, the famous preacher and visionary, was seventy-two, and only two when his father died, my father-in-law felt he was born to continue his father's work. Grattan Guinness, who died in 1910, had written in several of his books that from his studies of the prophets, Daniel and Ezekiel, 1917 and 1948 were key years for the restoration of the Jewish people to a homeland. In 1917, Balfour, the Prime Minister, who was very familiar with Grattan Guinness' books, granted the Jews full access to Palestine. In 1948 the new State of Israel declared its independence. These events, said Grattan Guinness, were signs that history was slowly and inexorably moving to its great and final climax – though he never made any attempt to suggest when that might be.

But as the centuries rolled on, Grattan Guinness' voice was forgotten. Israel became a political, rather than a religiously motivated, state and my father-in-law dreamed of reawakening the Jews to their spiritual duty, and Christians to their joint task in heralding the dawn of a new age. With one foot in each culture, fighting for a way to integrate the two, I suspect that I must have seemed the visible symbol of his hopes and aspirations.

Conversation over the dinner table in Ibiza was always lively and intense.

'It was Jews for breakfast, tea and supper in our home when I was a boy,' Peter had warned me before I met his parents. 'It was my father's favourite topic of conversation.'

It wasn't just my father-in-law's favourite topic of conversation. It was his only topic of conversation.

'Dad,' I said to him, over dinner one day, in utter exasperation, 'If you don't turn the record over, you'll turn me into an anti-semite.'

'You can't hold back Niagara,' interjected my mother-in-law, who never stopped trying.

One day I wandered up to my father-in-law's rooftop study during siesta hour when everyone else was dozing, and idly began to explore his bookshelves. An old, musty-scented biography, well over seventy years old, caught my attention. I took it down and began to read – and was still sitting on the floor several hours later when Peter came to find out what where I was. 'I had no idea about your missionary relatives and their extraordinary adventures,' I said to him. 'Why does no one read these books today?'

As I enthused over dinner, my father-in-law mentioned in passing a trunk in his study cupboard, 'full of bits and pieces', he said with a dismissive wave of the hand, poems, letters, the memorabilia his mother had collected over the years. He wasn't sure what was in it. She had been a great hoarder.

I rushed to the top of the house as soon as the meal was over, heaved a large, antique trunk out of the study cupboard, prized it open and could hardly believe my eyes. It was stuffed to the brim with papers, withered with age and the drying effects of the heat. There were letters dating back to the eighteenth century, some in packs tied up with ribbons, newspaper cuttings from as early as 1815, volumes of poetry, postcards, diaries and notebooks. Peter's grandmother Gracie had married the legendary preacher, Henry Grattan Guinness, in 1903, when she was twenty-six, and he was sixty-seven. They had had two sons, of whom my father-in-law was the youngest, and a mere seven years together before his death. Everything in her possession relating to her marriage and her husband's family history had been carefully preserved – as if she knew that one day someone would recognize their importance. I knew then, in 1975, that one day, I would write their story. It would be a long time in the making.

To the horror of both our mothers, Peter and I bought a little wreck of a house, run into the ground by two hippies whose alternative taste in decor involved papering some of the walls with newspaper, and painting the rest black. We reduced it, in the days just before the wedding, to bricks and rubble and a single standpipe in the kitchen, and had the misfortune to come back from our honeymoon with salmonella after a romantic meal in a restaurant. There's no earthier way to test the durability of romance. Happily, Frank had started decorating our bedroom in our absence, so we had at least one clean space. And since Peter was not allowed to return to teaching at the beginning of term, he managed, between bouts of the gripes, to start work on our bathroom and loo. In fact, there was no handier place to be. It took us a few years to finish the work and prove to everyone that we could turn such unpromising material into a cosy, comfortable home.

Youth work's unsociable hours didn't coordinate with a teacher's, so I decided, with Peter's encouragement, to give it up and become a kept woman.

'Did we educate her for this?' my father said to my mother, as he watched me, with immense disappointment, sanding down a skirting board.

It was my mother's turn to put a restraining hand on his arm.

'Wait,' was apparently what she said. 'Just wait.'

Those two years at home without any real ties and few responsibilities were an immense, never-to-be-repeated luxury, a chance to take up new skills and experiment with creative home-making. One evening Peter lugged in a heavy object in a large, zipped-up plastic bag.

'Present,' he said proudly.

I unzipped the bag and in it was a second-hand sewing machine.

'What am I meant to do with this? My mother couldn't sew on a button, remember?'

'And your paternal grandfather was a tailor,' he retorted. 'I don't think I'll be a teacher forever. In fact, I've no idea what I'll do, but I know I'll never be rich. So if you want nice clothes, make them.'

I did – and took my revenge. I went to tailoring classes, learned the complex and tender art of putting flies in men's trousers, and made a pair for Peter, which, with a loud rip, tore from the aforementioned to the rear waistband as he stood at the blackboard in the middle of Year Six algebra. Walking backwards he managed to extricate himself from the classroom with his decorum still intact, even if his trousers weren't, and held them together with a safety pin until he could pop into town for a pair on the way home.

Most important of all, I taught myself to cook. It was strange. Even though I had spent hours of my life learning how to keep a *kosher* kitchen, soaking the meat in salt water to ensure that no blood was left in it, making Yorkshire Pudding with water not milk and creating delicacies for special occasions like Passover, I had never really learnt how to put a meal together.

My mother belonged to a generation that peeled their vegetables in the morning, and left them ready-boiled, to be warmed up again for the meal so that they became the mushy, unappetizing offerings that were a school-dinner way of life. Not only that, but my father was a 'meat and two veg' man. He didn't like 'gravy', which ruled out casseroles. Salads, as in most other homes in the fifties and sixties, consisted of a dreary piece of lettuce, two slices of tasteless tomato, a piece of cucumber or two, a hard boiled egg and a dollop of bright yellow salad dressing. TV's first ever cooking guru, Fanny Craddock, was doing her best to encourage the Brits to make their food more interesting, by adding a spoonful of seasoning or a splash of colour, but she was severely hampered by what was available in the shops. The only concession to originality in the food department in our home was chopped liver, chopped herring, chopped fried fish and smoked salmon – usually chopped too, since only the offcuts were affordable in vast quantities.

The seventies, however, heralded a national revolution in food. Yogurt, which I had only ever eaten in France when staying with a penpal, made its debut on the other side of the Channel. There were new vegetables to be had – courgettes and broccoli, instead of standard tinned peas and carrots, or boiled cabbage and mashed swede. The Italians introduced the country to real pasta and tomato sauces that tasted nothing like tinned spaghetti hoops. They used a substance that was initially treated with great suspicion and derision – garlic. That's what made the foreigner's breath smell, said the English, blissfully ignorant of the effects of fish paste. Throughout the decade Englishmen resisted being fobbed off with 'foreign muck' – until they discovered the Saturday night vindaloo.

Historically the Jews have always had a very eclectic palate, not to mention a total obsession with food. 'Oh the leeks, onions and garlic back in Egypt,' lamented my ancestors during their forty-year wilderness wanderings, as if they had nothing better to worry about. Fancy wanting to exchange your freedom for a bowl of vichyssoise. But I suppose, after a while, manna stew, manna burgers and manna pudding seemed rather bland and limited in their appeal. Even manna fries and manna lasagne soon lost their charm for a nation sated with the luxury of variety in flavour and taste. It is so easy to forget that most people survive in developing countries with one basic commodity as their staple diet.

'You want meat?' the long-suffering Almighty finally capitulated, 'I'll give you meat!'

And it rained poultry from heaven – presumably the start of the Jewish love affair with the chicken.

My mother did teach me to get the best out of a chicken. No non-Jew, she declared, really knew how to roast it properly.

'First, they don't kill it right. Then they don't clean it right. Then they don't stuff it right.' Packet stuffing mix was one of the greatest evils of the age – minced-up cardboard. 'Ultimately,' says my mother, in a conspiratorial whisper, with great smacking of lips, 'they don't cook it right. What the *Goyim* don't realize is that the skin is the best bit – and it must be dry, crispy and tasty, not greasy and slimy, as if the poor animal spent its last days swimming in the sea, rather than trotting around a farmyard.'

Roasting a chicken and chopping its liver was the extent of my practical know-how in the kitchen. Familiarity with the dietary rules wasn't very helpful to anyone married to a Gentile. According to my father there was firm, medical foundation for the Jewish food regulations, revealing an insight into hygiene unusual for its time. The pig is renowned for internal abscesses, worms and other nutritional delights. Seafood, another taboo, for the humble prawn and lobster have no gills, is a major food poisoning risk. Mixing milk and meat may apparently cause digestive problems. God, it would appear, was as concerned about salmonella then, as any government health and safety official today. And though now, in these hygienically enlightened days, I contravene most of the dietary laws, I cannot bring myself to eat animal blood for its own sake. Why would any sensible human eat black sausage?

But then, hygiene wasn't the only motive behind the dietary laws. They were designed to make us reflect on what we're eating, so that we partake thoughtfully and appreciatively, not simply to satisfy a basic appetite as the animals do. Food was given a moral dimension. Blood is a symbol of life rather than a nutritional hazard. And life, for the Jew, since that is all that you have, is infinitely precious.

I remember so well the first time I realized food could be an important symbol, accessing all kinds of subconscious associations and memories. I was in a restaurant, and to my surprise, discovered I had picked up the piece of parsley which so daintily decorated my plate, and was swinging it to and fro between my thumb and index finger. As I popped it into my mouth and experienced that strange, almost bitter taste, the memory of so many Passovers came flooding back. The sprig of parsley represented the hyssop, used to daub the lambs' blood on the doorposts of the children of Israel so that the Angel of Death would pass over them. I was transported in a moment back through my own history and beyond, into the history of my ancestors and their experience of redemption.

The famous twentieth-century French novelist, Marcel Proust, who wrote a series of novels entitled, *In Search of Lost Time*, based his entire philosophy of life on a similar experience. As a young man, his inability to prevent every lovely moment from slipping through his fingers like sand, left him with feelings akin to despair. Then one day, as he was drinking his tea, he took a 'madeleine', a sponge finger, and dunked it in his mug. As the soggy biscuit touched his palate, his life was transformed. The smell, the taste, the feel of that sponge cake on his tongue, evoked one particularly precious event and enabled him to relive it as fully as he had the first time around. If eating was all it took to recapture our lost youth, our weight would probably drive the needle off the scales altogether. Nonetheless, I can identify with Proust's sense of wonder at inadvertently rediscovering, with the help of his taste buds, the door to a long-since vanished past.

Legend has it that the art of Jewish cuisine began on the day that our great-grandmama, Rebecca, with a clever use of herbs and spices, managed to convince her husband that the insipid flesh of a young goat was really wild venison. If you can hoodwink a man that easily, said her descendants, you can get away with anything. Rebecca must have been quite a cook if one of her sons was prepared to sell his inheritance for a bowl of her lentil soup. It's hardly surprising that no Jewish woman has ever quite overcome the notion that a man with a happy stomach is putty in her hands.

Many of the more familiar dishes, like *gefilte* or chopped fried fish, migrated from Eastern Europe with the masses like my great-grandparents, who fled poverty and persecution at the end of the last century. Fish was plentiful and cheap on the Baltic coast. Mixing it with onions and breadcrumbs made it go even further. Presumably chicken was the only affordable meat, and such a luxury that it became a tradition to squeeze as much out of the poor bird as its carcass would allow.

Traditional culinary secrets which are centuries old and have travelled the world, are passed from one generation to the next, learned and taught wherever the Jewish people have settled. At Passover they still make a sweetmeat of chopped dried apricots based on a recipe acquired when they were slaves in Egypt.

Whereas most of us eat to live, occasionally stopping to savour what we're shoving down our long-suffering gullets, Jews live to eat. Food is a thrice daily cause for celebration. And there is no celebration without food. I often wonder, in the age of the freezer, and mass, globalized production and storage, when in the West all food is becoming plentiful all year round and no food reserved for any one season or occasion, whether our children aren't robbed of some important, magical sensations – the first raspberries of summer, autumn red cabbage cooked in brown sugar and wine vinegar, spicy winter sweet mince, spring new potatoes dripping in butter. Shouldn't food have seasonal associations – recalling previous autumns, winters, summers and springs, giving a sense of rhythm, anticipation, and the continuing faithfulness of God? When we eat everything all year round there are no more special treats reserved for certain festivals, reminding us of the stories and legends of our people, enhancing the occasion with their particular taste and smell – apples and honey puddings at New Year, the sweet, plaited loaf on Friday evenings and cheesecake at Pentecost, a symbol of the purity of the Law. Few non-Jews appreciate the history and significance of the food they eat, let alone its value as a spiritual aid. In Jewish thought there is no distinction between the physical and the spiritual, so food feeds the spiritual life as well as the body.

Gradually, however, my time was consumed with speaking invitations to women's luncheon clubs – including one in Dublin. I was walking down O'Connell Street, enjoying an hour's sightseeing, when the strap on my sandal snapped. They were the only shoes I had with me, and my meagre resources in those early-married days couldn't possibly rise to a new pair. My hostess, an American missionary, shared my impecunious state, and we rushed into the first shoe repair shop we could find.

'Could you do something with it now?' I asked, urgently, 'I've no other shoes with me.'

The assistant shook her head slowly, unmoved by my predicament, or, so it seemed, by any other emergency that might cross her path that day. Time has no meaning in Ireland.

'There's a long waiting list. Sure, it'll take two days.'

'Two days!' I groaned. 'It only needs a stitch.'

There was still no response and I would have marched out of the shop with my head in the air, were it not for the fact that no one can go far – let alone with dignity – wearing only one shoe. That fact appeared to dawn upon the young woman, as she observed with some surprise that I was still standing, or rather perching like a pelican, on the other side of the counter.

'Name?' she asked suddenly.

'Guinness,' I said.

There was a moment's silence, and, when she lifted her head, a perceptible change of expression on her face.

'Your shoe will be ready in five minutes, Mrs Guinness,' she whispered deferentially.

And to be sure, it was.

My companion was awe-struck. 'Oh gee,' she gasped, as we walked back out into the street, 'it's just like being with one of the Kennedys in New York.' I felt slightly punch-drunk too. I had never had that effect on anyone before, and never have since, it must be said. One of the cuttings I had found in my ongoing research on the family, from the *Daily Express* in 1969, claimed that 'all the members of the world-famous Guinness family are reputed to be worth a fortune.' We had certainly never seen any of it. However, in the next few years, there were so many bizarre Guinness deaths reported in the media, that my mother began to wonder if her son-in-law had been watching the film *Kind Hearts and Coronets*, and was making a bid for a peerage by removing the obstacles one by one.

Motherhood curtailed the cookery, the speaking engagements and the research. It was definitely not all it was cracked up to be. For the nine months of pregnancy I couldn't stop being sick, and the self-appointed star of the culinary arts sat in a corner, a shivering, quivering heap, unable to look at food, let alone cook it. And then, all the soft focus images of serene-looking women with placid babies nuzzling contentedly at the breast let me down badly. Joel wouldn't breastfeed at all. It was far too slow a process. From the moment he arrived he wanted to get on with life, and screamed with frustration whenever any developmental limitation held him back. A deacon in the church, Peter went out to more and more meetings and my role was simply to send him out with a full belly and a warm heart. I once tried to make dinner for six, filling profiteroles with cream with one hand, mixing a feed with the other, while frantically rocking a bouncing cradle with my right foot in a vain attempt to pacify a screaming baby, blue with hunger, boredom and rage. Then in comes himself from work, the meal is far from ready, and that look says it all.

'My dear, you're at home. What have you been doing all day?'

She who once catered for a dozen without batting an eyelid, whose home was museum-immaculate, who met him at the door in full war paint has been deprofessionalized, de-skilled, by life alone with a mini-tyrant inside four brick walls. It was not what a Jewish woman expected.

There wasn't even time to pray. I had been inculcated with the notion that in order for the day to go well I should set aside at least twenty minutes every morning for a 'quiet time' of meditation and devotion, as if God sat in heaven waiting to see who had and had not clocked in for work that morning. And in my case, there would certainly be no bonuses for overtime. Once Joel was a toddler I couldn't even go the toilet without him banging on the door. I felt guilty and depressed about my failure.

Then I was struck by a series on television on women and religion. In the programme on prayer, a Hindu woman sat quietly before the shrine in her home. The Muslim woman took out her prayer mat. The Christian woman sat on a settee in silence with her Bible. The Jewish woman was getting her little boy ready for nursery school as they said morning prayer together. There were constant interruptions from a glove puppet which the little boy had on his hand, who was supposed to be Mrs Mandelstam, his teacher.

'Why do we need to thank *Ha' Shem* every morning, Davey? For a new day? For lots of new things to do? Yes. Oh, hello, Mrs Mandelstam, what's the class going to do this morning? Painting? That's nice. *Shema, yisroel, adonai, elohenu, adenai echod*. My, Mrs Mandelstam, what a big mouth you have. You must let me fasten Davey's buttons though. Hear O Israel, the Lord our God, the Lord is One.'

What was abundantly clear to me was that the Christian prayed more like the Hindu and the Muslim than the Jew – despite the fact that Jesus, the Jew, when asked how to pray, didn't fold his hands, close his eyes, demand absolute silence, or even construct a long and complex extemporary piece of verbiage. He simply reminded his followers of one of the most earthed and gutsy prayers in existence, rooting it firmly in everyday experience.

For the Jewish woman prayer was integrated into the daily routine. There was no difference between talking to God and talking to her child, between prayer and play. Far be it from me to suggest that we never need silence or stillness, but sometimes it isn't practicable. I decided then that most of the prayer gurus must be men. It was all very well for them to recommend silence and stillness, I said to myself, as I fed and changed the baby, threw him in the buggy, took him out and changed him again because he had filled his nappy or been sick down his front, then raced the mile to playgroup, already fifteen minutes late.

But what if prayer wasn't a separate entity in its own little box, something to be done apart from the rest of the day? What if life is perpetual prayer, like breathing, spontaneous, natural, almost subconscious? That was when I understood the point of all those blessings or thanksgivings I learned at Hebrew classes. Getting out of bed, brushing your teeth, driving, eating, seeing the sun, or the rain, even going to the toilet, could all provide the stimulus for ongoing communion with the Almighty.

A Jewish man at prayer won't kneel or close his eyes. He will go on rocking and praying when the kids or the wife burst in on him to complain about each other, ask for the bus fare, or enquire what time he intends coming home that evening. After all, almost every conversation, even one with God, must have its diversions and distractions.

Prayer in the synagogue continues even when there is such a racket all around him that a rabbi can hardly hear himself think, let alone pray. But he knows that his congregation will dip in and out of the service, one minute joining in the unsynchronized, communal muttering and chanting which is prayer, the next discussing the unpredictability of business, the weather, or the performance of the football team – which is another kind of prayer. The synagogue is the community's meeting place, not a place for private devotion. If you want silence, why come to *schul*? Go find it at home. Jesus himself, when he wanted quiet, headed for the mountains. He knew better than to expect it from Temple or synagogue.

But say 'prayer' to someone who isn't Jewish and it's like 'walkies' to a dog. There's an almost automatic response – head down, eyes closed, vague attempt at suitably pious expression. Look no further than church council meetings. A dozen or so worthy committee members gather in a front room to discuss the independent lifestyle of the church boiler, the pigeon droppings on the porch, the inadequacies of the hall plumbing, or some other vital issue which makes up the average spiritual and intellectual stimulation of the people of God. They laugh and chatter and unwind as the steaming mug in their hands defrosts the senses numbed by the daily drudgery at the office, school or factory, and loosens the emotions and the tongue with its tingling warmth. Then a voice says, 'Let us pray', and this is a signal for the gathered throng to go into holy mode. Some stare at the ceiling, some study the pattern on the carpet, others screw up their eyes as if blinded by a sudden light. And an angel in heaven must obviously whistle at the Almighty and say, 'Jump to it, Sir', in case he hasn't noticed that his presence is required.

There is a very fine dividing line between superstition and prayer, between placating a deity and acknowledging the omnipresence of a loving Father. And the change which comes over us when we 'say a prayer' seems to suggest the belief that one minute God isn't there, and the next minute he is – if we ask him nicely, like shop floor workers requesting a visit from the managing director.

As I began to experiment with new ways of praying, I was horrified when Joel, at three, started to put his hands together, close his eyes, bow his head and say Grace in a parsonical voice. That was how they did it in school assembly. And then, instead of thanking God for the warmth of the sun, the wind in his hair, the giggles of the little girl next door, he began to say, 'God bless Mummy' and 'God bless Daddy', prayers I knew would cease as soon as he realized that grown-ups didn't say them. Not unless they thought that God was an automaton, swallowing the information, spewing out responses.

Presumably making children close their eyes and fold

their hands together was a way of teaching them to switch off from outside distractions. But I had a sneaking suspicion that it actually taught them that God exists only in their own heads, and that talking to him is a rather weird activity, which they can drop, along with any belief, when they're old enough. He did find it hysterically funny when a teacher once told him off for not closing his eyes.

'How did she know,' he asked, 'unless she didn't close them herself?'

I realized that if traditional prayer hadn't worked very well for me, it might not for him and began experimenting with a more Jewish approach, like the Jewish woman in the TV programme, to enable him to discover a sense of God's presence everywhere, all the time. We never taught him to 'say his prayers' at bedtime. We prayed with him every morning in our bed, trying to weave it into conversation about the events of the day, without changing our tone of voice, or the kind of words we used. Let's be honest, I was often the sleeping partner in this activity, dozing through it all, vaguely aware of the gentle murmurings of Peter reading a Bible story. I was imbibing the atmosphere, I told them, through my skin cells.

My parents came to stay from time to time, more often once the first grandson was born.

'You know,' Mum confided in me one evening, 'I never intended liking Peter, let alone loving him, but somehow he's just crept up on me.'

Little did I guess to what extent that newly acquired affection would be tested in the coming months.

We had barely finished painting our final skirting board when Peter rocked my contented, even little existence.

'I think I may be called to the Church of England ministry.'

It was a hot summer afternoon and he had just come in from school and was stretched out on the bed, hands under his head, staring blankly at the ceiling. I was sitting beside him, trying to find some fresh entertainment for our lively toddler, who was never entertained by anything for longer than three seconds.

'Great love,' I said distractedly, 'A deacon in the Free Church – the Church of England will welcome you with open arms.'

'I mean it, I'm serious. I've been thinking about it for ages. When we got married I told you I thought we'd be in some kind of Christian ministry one day.'

'But you never mentioned the Church of England.' There was no response and I began to feel really disturbed.

'How can we leave our friends and community, the people we love so much? How am I going to cope with the Anglican liturgy and a whole set of traditions that mean nothing to me at all? I can't even say "The Lord's Prayer" without reading it from the prayer book. Some vicar's wife I'll make. And what do we say to our church? "Thanks for the last eight years, but we've just had this revelation that we're meant to be Anglicans."'

'But darling,' Peter said in that supplicatory tone of voice I had come to recognize as, 'I have made up my mind, so do try and accept it' – it made my toenails curl – 'I've explored the Free Church ministry, you know that, but no door ever seems to open. I'm thirty. I can't sit around waiting any longer, not when the Church of England has issued such an open invitation.'

'When? I hadn't noticed.'

'You remember that Sunday the Archbishop of

Canterbury's letter appealing for men to come forward for the ministry was read out in every Anglican church in the country, and we were staying in Rugby that weekend and just happened to be sitting in an Anglican church?'

'I didn't realize it had such an impact on you,' I muttered, as an awful awareness seeped like icy water into my consciousness. What if my husband was better acquainted with what God wanted than I was?

'I don't want to be a vicar's wife, condemned to a life in purple crimplene.'

I had visions of brogues, awful hats, or running women's meetings and organizing jumble sales.

'At the moment, all I want to do is explore whether this is the way forward. We'll have to start attending an Anglican church, of course, but we've friends there. It shouldn't be too hard.'

It was harder than I anticipated. In 1979 many parish churches were still very formal and traditional, and certainly not child-friendly. I spent most services in the rain and cold, out in the graveyard, where a hyperactive toddler could clamber merrily over gravestones and 'yahoo' loudly without causing disruption or offence. Where a child isn't welcome, neither is the parent. But since I had little inclination to face up to my cultural alienation from this quintessentially English, fundamentally un-Jewish environment, being banished suited me well.

But there was no escaping Peter's growing sense of call, and its implications. I wandered around our little house, feeling utterly miserable. I loved every bit of it – the Victorian pine dresser built into the kitchen wall that we had stripped with such meticulous care, the Georgian window Peter had built into the dining room, making every joint by hand, the little brick hearth in the front room that we had designed ourselves, balancing the bricks around an arched coat hanger overnight, then rushing down the next morning to see if it had survived the night. And now I had to leave my own home behind, to live, probably in bigger houses, but properties that didn't belong to us, that were hard to heat, with other people's designs and decorations. It was easy enough to say I would follow Christ wherever he asked when there was not a lot to lose, but now, when materialism had crept up on me and obedience meant being yanked out of a comfortable rut, promises were much harder to keep. Yet if I didn't, we could end up stuck, middle-aged and set in our ways before our time. What was this house but bricks and mortar? There would be other, just as precious, piles of stones somewhere else. Giving up our home and a reasonable salary might seem like madness, but at least it wasn't boring.

'Okay, we go for it,' I said to Peter, one day when he came in from work. 'And you'd better contact the bishop quick – before I change my mind.'

I still had one major worry. 'I'll try to be an Anglican – but I don't much look like one. What if I don't really settle? What if I hate it?'

He took me in his arms. 'You'll be fine', he said, smiling down at me. 'After all, this isn't the first time you've had to make some major adjustments.'

'Well, I'd better go and buy a tweed jacket then.'

'Don't you dare. I love you just as you are. That's why I married you.'

He was halfway out of the door when my parting shot wiped the grin off his face.

'So you can tell the parents then.'

He stopped, turned to face me, took a deep breath, and nodded.

And there we were, weeks later, in my parents' sitting room, ready to deliver yet more bad news. But at least this time I wasn't going to be the one to break it.

'Mum, Dad, I have something to tell you,' Peter said gently.

I could tell from their stricken faces that they were still not totally immune to the pain I was in the habit of inflicting.

'Don't get hysterical, dear,' my father commanded, more for his own benefit than for my mother's. She already had that fixed look of disapproval on her face that I knew so well.

'I knew it, I knew you'd do something like this to me,' she raged, when Peter outlined his sense of vocation.

'Oh, I don't know,' my father said reassuringly, 'a clergyman is a professional man after all. That's better than being a mere teacher.'

'Hardly one of the professions Jewish parents wish upon their children,' my mother snapped. Then suddenly, listening to herself, her face expanded into a grin. 'Hmmmm, my son-in-law, the vicar. It has a certain ring about it. What would the rabbi say to that?'

We all managed to laugh. I marvelled at the quality of a love that could stretch to encompass so many knocks and shocks.

'And who knows,' she continued, warming to her subject, 'I may yet be mother-in-law to the Archbishop of Canterbury.'

A few months later, when Peter had been accepted as an ordinand and we had begun to plan our two years at theological college, my parents treated us to a few days' holiday in Blackpool – inevitably, at the Norbreck Castle Hotel. The car was packed up and we were ready to go when I had an afterthought.

'Love, go and get my grandma's ring out of its hiding place. I might as well wear it while we're away.'

'Peter,' my mother parroted, 'You heard the vicar's wife, she wants her diamonds.'

My mother used irony like a sabre when she wanted to thrust home her point – that whatever title I was given, whatever stereotype the world thrust upon me, I would never be any other than the Jewish woman I had been born. Even so, there would always be an element of something she could never quite identify or understand. That incomprehensible, intangible Christian bit.

As she followed me out to the car, she said, 'By the way, when I die and you inherit all my wonderful furs, you'll wear them to the parish fêtes, will you?'

'Mother,' I laughed, 'what on earth would I want with your furs?'

'Exactly,' she said knowingly. 'That was my point. Well, don't sell them at the jumble sales, that's all, or I may come back and haunt you.'

Chapter 10

In the Vicar Factory

*M*y first year in Nottingham, where Peter was studying theology, was blighted by problems in the reproductive department.

Joel had timed his conception perfectly to fit with summer holidays abroad. That he almost arrived at Christmas, the bane of my life ever since, was a fact we somehow overlooked. Strange how we mortals now feel ourselves in control of birth, even if death still defies us. At every *Rosh Hashanah*, the Jewish New Year, the story of Hannah is told – she who suffered such agonies over her childlessness that she rolled around the Temple in a wordless prayer of sheer desperation. With real religious sensitivity Elijah the Priest dismissed her as a drunk – until she told him her tale of woe. The outcome was a very special son – Samuel, the prophet. The moral of the tale, the Jews tell us, is the power of prayer in determining destiny, hence its importance at the start of a new year, a clean slate, its possibilities as yet unwritten.

It sometimes seems today as if we rewrite the lesson of Hannah, and rather than playing a part in destiny, take it firmly into our own hands. Naturally I assumed that since our fertility had gone to plan the first time round, the second time would be just as straightforward. It wasn't.

Before we left Manchester, after several barren, increasingly unnerving months I took myself to the doctor's for the examination which every woman dreads.

'There's no way you'll conceive through that lot,' he concluded, which wasn't very enlightening, since I wasn't privy to the same view of the situation.

'Through what?' I asked, unsure of how detailed an answer I wanted. He explained, in the verging-on-the-incomprehensible way that doctors sometimes do, that damage had been done when Joel was born, that I would need a little minor surgery, and that he would refer me to a gynaecologist.

The 'little minor surgery' grew by the month. It began with an attempt to burn away the problem. When fire failed they tried the deep freeze treatment. No one had warned me not to turn up for my appointment on a bicycle. I defrosted on the way home. When that failed too, I was sent for surgery under general anaesthetic. It turned out to be one of the most negative experiences of my medical life, for I was wretchedly bullied and browbeaten, as were all the other patients on the ward, by a harridan of a nursing sister who couldn't have been more at home in a concentration camp.

'Where do you think you're going? Stay on your bed. Put your shoes in your locker. Lay your dressing gown straight. Go to the toilet when I say so.'

Only now, many confidence-building and assertiveness-training years later, do I realize that no one has the right to abuse their authority in that disgraceful way. Nor is it necessary to submit to that kind of humiliation. Christ himself, though subjugated physically at the end, was never subjugated mentally and remained, in an extraordinary way, in complete control of every situation. How I wish I had found the strength then to do what I hope I would do now, and stand up for every patient on that ward, and those yet to come.

I went home a wreck. And though the world swam before my eyes as the anaesthetic still swirled its way round my system, Peter was unable to take time off from his teaching job, and I was left with a hyperactive toddler rampaging round the house. What does a poor Jewish girl do caught in such extremity? She calls for Mama, what else! And Mama cooked and cleaned, made chopped liver and minded the baby, while Pop, as doctors do, lambasted 'that horse of an anaesthetist' (it was a lady doctor of course), who in removing the tube from my throat had also removed most of the skin from my bottom lip.

When we moved to Nottingham some weeks later, convinced that all was still not as it should be, I went to see my new doctor, and was told that my ordeal, far from curing the problem, had made it even worse. There would be no baby for the foreseeable future. A course of antibiotics and stinging iodine pessaries were prescribed. I was to return in two weeks for referral, yet again, to a gynaecologist.

In a state of utter dejection I trudged around the square where we had rented a house, to see another couple from the college, the only people we knew at that stage. John and Ros Harding, with their three boisterous children, struck me as an approachable, caring family. Instinct proved right. They listened to my woes with sensitivity and concern, and that was all I needed. I was resistant to any prayer in this department, having convinced a close friend in Manchester with secondary infertility that she would have a second child. She never did, and I suspected that the false hope had hurt more than the childlessness. The Hardings prayed anyway, and two weeks later I went back to my doctor, sample in hand, and asked for a pregnancy test. That was the beginning of the little miracle that was Abby, 'Father's delight'.

Apart from severe nausea for the entire duration of the pregnancy, Joel's entry into the arena of life was uneventful. I told Peter when we married that I was rarely ill and never sick, and spent eight horrendous months disproving it, carrying a bowl around with me for good measure. I took the now-banned drug Debendox throughout, and it helped me survive, contributing to very real concerns I have about our increasingly litigious society, apportioning blame and hunting compensation for every possible mishap in life. My father prescribed the drug for thirty years, and never once had the slightest cause for fearing it might have impaired a foetus. It was the last available drug to control vomiting in pregnancy. Now women have to survive alone, without any help. The writer Charlotte Brontë died of pregnancy sickness. That fact was a comfort to me. I always knew, in whatever loo, behind whatever tree I was, that it must be possible to die of how I felt.

Along with a repeat of the 'mal-de-mer', Abby's development was one worry after another. I had been taking antibiotics at her conception. The uterus was too high, the doctor said. She seemed to sit halfway up with the crown of her head pushing into my lungs and rib cage. I could hardly breathe. All the signs of the trauma to come were there, but fortunately I wasn't medically minded enough to know it.

Eventually, weakened by nausea and the stress of acclimatizing to a new life, scarlet fever struck and I was ill for weeks.

'I thought coming to a theological college would be exciting, stimulating, and stretching,' I wailed at my poor husband, who took himself off into another bedroom at night, while I paced the floor, itching, and daubing my weeping skin with phenol oil, 'The only thing to stretch is my stomach. And that means there's more of me to itch.'

I visited the doctor daily so that she could monitor the baby's heartbeat, which thankfully remained loud and strong, but even that did little to eradicate my neurotic fantasies of a poor, puzzled little creature, floating *in utero* with flaking, itchy skin.

The Hardings were there to support me yet again. The baby's name, John believed, was 'Faithful', for its hand would never let go of the hand of the Almighty, nor would his hand cease to protect it, all the days of its life. How I clung to those words the long, frightening night of her birth.

I was admitted after what had started as a routine ante-natal visit. An X-ray, taken the previous week, had revealed what was known already, that the foetus was sitting head up, not down, but also that being barely five foot, I was unable to deliver a breech baby.

'Why doesn't this X-ray show me where the placenta is?' demanded the consultant, the formidable, wonderful Miss Baker. I felt safe in her hands.

Her registrar shrugged.

'I'll turn the baby,' he said. 'She delivered normally the last time. There's no reason why she shouldn't this time.'

I managed a grateful smile. Joel's delivery had been a disappointingly mechanical affair. I had been wired up like a battery hen, pumped full of drugs, and then he had been bottle-fed before I had a chance to feed him myself. It had left me feeling cheated and inadequate. This time I intended being in control of the birth.

'And do you know what you're doing?' Miss Baker barked.

My gratitude evaporated.

'Yes,' said the registrar uncertainly, and proceeded.

He pushed until my entire insides seemed to give way and revolve. Almost at once a young nurse, struggling to curb the alarm in her voice, said, 'The heartbeat's gone!'

We watched the machine in silence, and slowly it revived, 'Beep, beep, beep... beep... beep', an irregular, half-hearted affair. I breathed again.

They left me attached to the monitor for some hours, popping in and out to listen to the feeble little beep, shaking their heads and tutting as it faded and revived. One of the midwives, married to a student at the college, said, 'I wish they'd just get on with a caesarian', and unknown to me, went back to the Thursday night Communion service and told them to pray hard if the Guinness baby was to live.

In the early evening they decided to induce the baby by breaking the waters, my last chance of a normal delivery. As the registrar stood over me with open scissors, ready to lunge, I remember hoping that it wasn't too disturbing for Peter, at his end of the spectrum. The waters broke in a gush, and with them, down came the umbilical cord. I felt it against my skin, warm, damp and slimy, as the doctor barked tersely into an intercom, 'Emergency section'. I was turned onto my knees and ordered to keep my head down, as low as possible so that the baby would slip back into the uterus. No one spelt it out to me but I was vaguely aware that the cord ceased to function after a certain length of time, starving the baby of oxygen. How long, I couldn't remember.

Within seconds we were hurtling along the corridors, TV soap-style, I on my knees, face pressed against the trolley, and the Sister, who wheeled us along with one hand and held the cord up inside me with the other. A young nurse stopped us and asked if she could have, 'a quick word, Sister.'

'Can't you see I'm busy?' the Sister hissed, nodding in the direction of her missing arm, only just decently disguised beneath the surgical sheet.

And all the time I concentrated on how to avoid having my knees jammed in the groove where the two parts of the trolley joined.

'Sign this.'

A slip of paper slid beneath my face. I raised my head to read it, but the Sister pushed it back down. So I took aim and signed, hoping it was my consent to the operation I was giving. It could have been anything.

I was amazingly calm, totally at peace, certain that an unseen hand was protecting the little life inside me. Even when I came round some time later feeling as if I'd been run over by a double-decker bus, with a nurse saying, 'Make her look at her baby in case she thinks it's dead,' and Peter shouting excitedly in my ear, 'It's a girl, it's a girl, she's all right, she's alive, look at her,' all I could manage was a feeble, 'Get me the morphine.'

It was some days later that the trauma really caught up with us. Delayed shock suddenly struck with a ferocity which took our breath away. We were suddenly two quivering heaps of jelly. We simply needed time together as a family. But Peter, by some strange irony, was in the midst of a training placement with the hospital chaplain which required long hours of work experience on the wards – in another hospital. His day started at seven, and ended long after any possibility of visiting. He asked the chaplain for compassionate leave, and was refused. Joel, only a little chap, was shipped from bed to bed and house to house, until he broke down and howled under the stress. With no husband around and no parents nearby to coo over their new grandchild, I howled too. We were all at breaking point.

Finally, word got back to Peter's college tutor and the placement was cancelled at once. But I've long since wondered how a hospital chaplain, finely tuned to the slightest needs and intimations of the patient, could fail to apply the same criteria to a trainee. But then isn't there a danger for all caring professionals, and especially those in the church, reared on the Protestant work ethic, to be so overpowered by the magnitude of human need, so committed to the job, that they fail to appreciate the needs of those nearest to us? This is why the Jews so strictly observe seasons of rest and festival, a time to work and a time to stop. Outside of that culture, statutory paternity leave has been the only way to ensure that families are given the chance to welcome the new little life into their midst.

For all we know, those first few days may be the most important in our whole existence. I knew all there was to know about 'bonding', that special relationship the psychologists tell us must develop between mother and child, and had been determined that this time I would breastfeed from the moment of birth. A non-elective caesarian section seemed to have robbed me of that. In those vital first hours my baby was left alone in a cot, while I lay in a heavy drug-induced stupor. What if this little life had been scarred already by emotional deprivation and neglect?

Now that truly was faithless. The first day I held her, balanced on top of the pillow which protected my raw and tender stomach, I fell madly in love with the sloe-eyed, dark lashed little bundle. A daughter. That thought tapped into immense reserves of ferocity and protectiveness I never consciously knew were inside me. I was barely aware of the fight to secure a better world for women. But as I held my daughter, and wonder of all wonders, she snuggled up and fed from me, on and on and on, I knew in my heart that I wanted this girl-child to inherit a world where she was equal to any man, where she could stand side by side with her brother.

At least we didn't have to face the dilemma of whether or not to have circumcision, or how to do so, as we did with Joel. In the end we opted to have him circumcised because we wanted him to grow up comfortable enough in the Jewish community to use the Gents in the synagogue. Through Joel, our line in the Guinness family chart and pedigree would continue, as daughters are simply marked without issue and the branch stops. But through a daughter, the racial and cultural heritage of our family, handed on through the mother, was secure.

Mercifully, theological college made no attempt to 'Anglicanise' me, but then, I wasn't the trainee vicar, only the spare tyre in the boot.

It was in fact an extraordinarily liberating time – a chance to identify what was vital for the adventure, and dispense with the extraneous burdens that were merely cultural expectations. Shortly before leaving Manchester, I had taken part in a useful Clinical Theology guided inner journey to help me discover where I was. This one involved becoming a rose bush, which took a bit of imagination, but worked despite my initial misgivings. I was horrified to see myself in autumn, blooms fully open, beginning to wilt and droop. It was clear that if I continued to try to submit to the restrictions of either Free Church conservativism or traditional Anglicanism, I would simply fade and die. St John's, Nottingham, and a host of stimulating new friendships dug some fertile, life-saving manure into the soil.

I remember just one particularly toenail curling event – a panel of mature, experienced ministers' wives set up to provide us soon-to-be-in-their-shoes little women with glimmers of wisdom to light our pathway into the daunting world ahead.

'Don't worry your husbands with minor problems about running the home and the children. He is doing God's work. Release him to fulfil his ministry,' advised the future bishop's wife, accompanied by enthusiastic nods from her fellow panel members.

I was on my feet before I knew it. 'I didn't know we were called to be parish doormats!' I heard my words resounding in the heavy, fidget-filled hush. Which of us could compete with God? And on what basis would the joyous giver of marriage be such a demanding third party in a relationship? 'I thought marriage was about each releasing the other to fulfil our God-given calling and potential.' I vaguely recall the embarrassed panel's attempt at a back pedal, but well remember the dismissive reaction of some of the other student wives.

'We always knew you were a radical and a feminist.'

A less obvious radical feminist would have been hard to find. Two years as a detached youth worker, confronted daily with the demoralizing effects of social deprivation, had left me with a fierce dislike of the diminishing of one human being's freedom at the cost of another's. Having a daughter had also raised my consciousness of unjust inequalities in the world. Otherwise, I was still the product of a fairly reactionary, well-heeled Jewish family. Shortly before our marriage, I had sat with Peter in a café in the middle of Manchester, the love-light shining from my eyes, and promised him I wouldn't go out to work. 'I will stay at home, make your meals, iron your shirts and darn your socks,' I said, and I had meant every word of it. Given the way things would turn out, we laugh about it now.

But the freedom to think for myself was obviously having a greater impact than I realized. In those heady days of the early eighties women were fighting for the right to be ordained, and though my instinctive sense of fairness placed me on their side, it was some time before I could argue the case theologically. My fairly traditional views on woman as wife were certainly in flux.

Several of the single women students thanked me for my contribution that evening. I did wonder what they were doing at a wives' meeting – to gain some insight, I suspect, into how a female curate might handle that all-powerful force, the vicar's wife. They were deeply concerned that so many of the student wives felt they had been called into the ministry as a couple, even though he, not she, would have the pay packet and inevitable predominance. If the wife saw herself as a key partner in ministry and not just in marriage, how would she cope with the arrival of a paid female assistant? In my heart I knew what my response would be. I had married Peter, not the job, and that's how it would stay.

In reality, that wouldn't necessarily alter a church's expectations. The vicar's wife fitted in. She was safe, bland, without opinions and often, without friends. Who would want their private thoughts to find their way back to the vicar? And she could hardly go to another church if she didn't enjoy the one where her husband ministered. She was stuck for life with one denomination and his sermons. There were moments when the future seemed a frightening prospect.

Chapter 11

Mining, Striking and Finding Gold

I pushed away my refusal to come to terms with my destiny for the two largely happy years at college, until we drove up the long road that led from the motorway to a little Yorkshire mining town, with a view to a first curacy. 'For better or worse', I reminded myself, as I gazed out at the endless rows of uneven, red-bricked terraced houses that flanked the road like distorted teeth in an overcrowded mouth, puffing a veil of thick yellow-black smoke into the atmosphere. And this was definitely worse, far worse. The car filled with an acrid, sulphurous smell. Peter turned down the ventilation. I looked for greenery but there was none – not a tree or a shrub, no sign of spring though March was almost past. The tiny gardens, separated from the pavement by two-foot-high walls, were muddy and bare. It would have taken a fairly determined plant to shove its way to daylight through gravy cartons, scrunched up newspaper and empty pop cans.

'Well,' Peter said, breaking the silence, as we caught sight of the pit wheel in the distance, 'Could you live here?'

'Oh, it's not so bad,' I replied, trying to rally his rapidly falling spirits. I had registered an occasional splash of colour – a brightly painted front door, fancy cladding, bottle bottom windowpanes and that ultimate symbol of hope and pride: frilly net curtains. 'It feels familiar – like Felling, as I remember it.'

'Ashton-under-Lyne,' he snorted. His memories were not nearly as positive as mine. He is nine years old again, forced to exchange a lakeside apartment in Geneva for a mausoleum of a vicarage, complete with stables and servants' quarters, when his father became vicar of drab, grey, gloomy Ashton – a trauma he never got over.

I had never expected my lot to be anywhere vaguely beautiful and thought I could cope – until I saw the curate's house. It stood at the furthest edge of the large council estate in glorious isolation on a desolate patch of wasteland, overlooked on all four sides by the local inhabitants. I wandered across the scrubland to a children's play area and sat on the one swing that hadn't been vandalized, disconsolately rocking my nine-month-old baby backwards and forwards. The ground was covered in litter, broken glass and dog mess.

'Oh God,' I whispered, 'I can't bring up my children here.'

And strangely, I thought I heard a firm reply, 'Typical! That's what your ancestors said in the wilderness. Our children will die here. But they didn't – they thrived, as yours will here. This will be the best place in the world for them.'

It wasn't until we met some of the local people that I was completely convinced. And there, deep in the earth of this depressing little town, raped and pillaged for half a century in pursuit of its black gold, we discovered real buried treasure. As we shared our stories at that first meeting, I was face to face with people who didn't hold back, who said it like it was, who took you as they found you, and didn't take themselves too seriously.

'Tell me what you do, Daisy,' I asked a shy-looking woman with bobbed hair.

'I pack for Asda,' she said. 'You know them packs of four apples you get wrapped in cling film? I'm the one who puts them together – all day every day.'

'Doesn't it get a bit monotonous?'

She nodded. 'It's a job,' she said, then added, with a grin, 'Once we got kiwis and nearly died with excitement.'

I have to admit that given the gloom that had descended on us as we had driven around the town, I wasn't in my most tactful frame of mind.

'All this smoke,' I grumbled rudely to Alan, a tall, striking-looking former miner, with a winning smile and wicked sense of humour, 'Has no one heard of the Clean Air Act round here?'

He surveyed me with a quizzical expression that seemed to say, 'What have they sent us this time?' then seemed to remember we were foreigners after all.

'If yer work fert Coal Board, yer get it free.'

'Don't they give them anthracite?'

'They do – but half as much. And who can afford to be finicky? Besides, it's the only perk to working down pit.' He weighed me up for a while, then added, 'And anyway, if yer think Normanton's bad, you want to see Castleford on other side of motorway. If this country were a human body, Castleford would be the haemorrhoids.'

Everyone laughed uproariously at a goal scored against their nearest neighbour, and the evening came to an end.

As she got up to go, Daisy turned to us and said, 'Tonight's been special. If you don't come back, you won't forget us, will you, because we won't forget you.'

How could we not go back?

Peter was ordained in Wakefield Cathedral in June 1982. I thought three-year-old Joel had a right to be there, but failed to check the playthings in the little suitcase he had so carefully packed to take with him. Five minutes into the service, sitting in the front row, he tipped its entire contents – around fifty big Lego bricks – onto the pew. The almighty clatter was drowned, instantly, by a volley of angry ssssshhhhh from every part of the cathedral. Joel was worryingly silent for the next twenty minutes or so, totally absorbed in his building project. And then, during the prayers, he stood up on the pew, turned and faced the congregation with his creation – a large shotgun – and with the appropriate noises, killed them all stone dead. So much for trying to teach our child non-violent games.

As Peter publicly swore his allegiance to Church and Queen, as he vowed to pastor and teach his flock, the enormity and folly of what we were doing hit me like a bullet in the brow. We had given up Peter's secure teaching job with prospects, a reasonable salary, a home of our own and the friends we loved... for what? A crazy job with no prospects, unspecified commitment, unlimited hours, a six-day week, minimal pay and life on a council desert island. Yet already, as I caught sight on the other side of the cathedral of the warm, encouraging faces of the people we had already met, I was ready to face the future, and willing to commit myself, not to some vague noble vocation, but to Normanton, a town that would always manage to touch the fierce maternal emotions in the deepest recesses of my being. Spurned by the metropolitan borough when it handed out the goodies, abused by a nation that only wanted it for coal, it reminded me of a much neglected child, with tear-stained cheeks and runny nose, too proud to admit its hurt and need.

'Miners?' my mother had said, when, hesitantly, we told her where we were headed. 'You'll be fine. They're wonderful. They'll look after you.'

That was an understatement. We arrived to find the lurid blue walls of the curate's house had gone. Alan had apparently spent hours up a ladder covering it with white paint, moaning all the while.

'If you can't do it in the right spirit, don't do it at all,' his long-suffering wife, Sally, had eventually called to him.

He had obviously found the grace he needed as the place was light and airy, floorboards scrubbed, kitchen sparkling like a detergent ad, and on the counter, filling a double bench, the largest food hamper I had ever seen, stuffed with tins of steak, chicken, salmon, strawberries and pineapple. There were packets of soups and sauces, jars of jam and pickles, a basket of fresh fruit, a bouquet of flowers, home-baked cakes and flans, a bottle of wine and a card that read, 'With love from your new family'.

I could barely speak for the lump in my throat.

'Goodness,' Peter exclaimed, 'this must have cost some of them a week's housekeeping.'

Despite my mother's protests that she would never stay in a vicarage, my parents were soon on our doorstep, but we had nowhere else to put them other than in a tiny annexe to the kitchen that was supposed to be a dining room. It was hardly conducive. My father's health had been slowly deteriorating. He had had a series of ischemic attacks, each one longer and more devastating in its consequences than the last. As the leaks of blood encroached on his brain, the dedicated doctor and loving father retreated further and further into his own little world where we could no longer reach him. It was heartbreaking to have to witness the slow, sad destruction of so many fine faculties, especially for my mother who was his main carer. The church generously decided to sell our goldfish bowl of a house and buy us a bigger one.

One night, we left them babysitting.

'I've sold your house,' my mother announced triumphantly, as we walked back in. We looked blank.

'A couple called at the door on spec,' she explained. 'I showed them round, did a hard sell, and they're going to make an offer.'

And then, while we still stood open-mouthed, she added, 'Even the Church of England has to send for the Jews when they want to sell anything.'

It was a major miracle in 1984, the year the housing market ground to a halt, as the fated miners' strike slowly drove the people to near destitution. Despite the desperate situation, no community could have surrounded us with greater love and generosity. Although we were on family income supplement with free school milk and dinners, we were rich by comparison, yet they would still have given us their last allotment-grown potato if they thought we needed it. When the news of the Ethiopian famine broke in the middle of the strike, miners' wives who sat by the Co-op checkout begging for food tins for miners' families, also acquired charity boxes for Ethiopia, and the charity boxes were always heavier than any in the richer cities of the south, because the locals knew what hunger was.

This was a town where special needs children and senile parents were cared for at home, because they belonged to the entire community. If demented Gladys wandered through the streets, there was always someone to take her in and make her a cup of tea. Doors were left open. Neighbours walked into each others' homes, settled elderly folk down for the night, made sure the fire was no longer burning, the house was warm, the lights turned off, and then, the next morning, that the milk was taken in. This was the way of life they were fighting for, but in the no-such-thing-as-society Thatcherism of the eighties, it was doomed to extinction. The men were not prepared simply to doff their caps and capitulate when it was threatened. And nor were their feisty wives, who organized soup runs and stood shoulder to shoulder with their men on the picket line. I'd never seen a picket line before, and the naked aggression, played out in front of my very eyes, particularly of the police, armed to the hilt against a bunch of nakedly defenceless human beings, was truly frightening.

My heart ached for the town as it fought for its life, bruised, battered, weary and confused. The locals cared little for Arthur Scargill, the hot-headed leader of the National Union of Miners, and suspected him of self-interest. But no one would break the picket line and risk the stigma of being called a 'scab'. There was no greater shame to pass on to your children. It wasn't very different from the Jewish community's attitude to one of their own becoming a Christian.

McGregor, the foreigner brought in by the government to kill the Coal Board, could be trusted even less. Managers had always been hard, vindictive and insensitive, moving men heartlessly from pit to pit, without any concern for their personal circumstances. That Mr McGregor was the name of the nasty farmer who persecuted Peter Rabbit for stealing his vegetables, meant that Joel's favourite bedtime story took on a whole new meaning.

Who should the locals believe? They were helpless – pulled one way by lifelong loyalties and another by cold, hunger and the threat of the bailiffs. They were pawns in a political game of power, and they knew it, but couldn't simply stand back and watch the dissolution of the tight bonds that bound them together, born of a history of shared tragedy, pain and loss in one mining disaster after another. No one cared much about the job itself. Lying on your back, in a narrow, confined, airless tunnel, hacking coal out of a seam above your head was filthy, choking, health-destroying labour. But there was an unbeatable camaraderie in the shared drudgery of it all. 'Woe betide' any daughter who misbehaved herself. Her misdemeanours would be all the talk in the showers.

Separated from their flesh and blood families, our children grew up with countless surrogate grandparents, aunts, uncles and cousins, who treated them as if they were their own. They understood that not everyone had their advantages and opportunities, saw first-hand what it was like to go to bed cold and with an empty belly, thrived in an environment where there was acceptance, affection and laughter, and grew up with a healthy intolerance of middle-class cant and hypocrisy.

Nowhere are people as ruthlessly honest. I was surprised one day, delivering parish magazines door to door, to have my hand almost snatched off as I reached for the letter box.

'I only get it fer't deaths,' confessed the shrivelled, elderly woman on the doorstep, when she saw my startled expression. So much for all the creative energy that went into the writing of it. 'There's only Elsie to go, and I'll have outlived all my old friends,' she finished with triumph.

For Peter, pastoral work never went quite as he was led to expect at college. On one funeral visit the son, waxing lyrical about his late father, freely punctuated every sentence with copious 'f' words, totally undeterred by his mother beating him around the head every time he used them, with a 'Stop swearing in front of vicar.' On another, he was asked by the grieving widow whether he thought she would be reunited with her husband. He took immense care with his answer. He didn't want to compound her pain. He said he believed that Christ seemed to say that there would be no such thing as marriage in heaven.

'Thank God,' the woman sighed with relief, 'He led me such a dog's life down here, I wouldn't want any more of it up there.'

Nonetheless, the pressures of Peter's job came as quite a shock. We guessed that living over the shop would cost us our privacy, but what I hadn't grasped was how much our family time would be threatened. In one breath the church proclaims the value of family life, and in the next, undermines it. Endless evening meetings separate spouses and require a continual stream of babysitters. It got to the point where every time one of us went out, our eighteen-month-old, barely able to speak, pointed at the door and said, 'church'.

'This can't be right,' I said to Peter, 'I don't want the children to grow up seeing the church as a rival that takes their parents from them. That's sure to breed resentment. I want them to associate God with the happiest, not the most miserable, memories of childhood.'

And what about their birthright as children of a Jewish mother? After all, they would attend their cousins' *Bar Mitzvahs* and weddings. They must be able to take their place in the synagogue with confidence, not discomfort. More than that, in the event of another Third Reich, God forbid, their identity as Jews would be unquestionable. They must be able to make positive connections. After all, had Jesus himself lived in the Nazi era he too would have been rounded up and shipped to Auschwitz.

Fortunately, I married a man more convinced of the value of my Jewish heritage than I was. With his encouragement I began to reassess the traditions of my childhood, to explore which might work for us now. I rejected the complex system of Judaic laws – including the dietary laws – as too complex, too restricting and obsolete for Christians. But Friday nights – knowing my parents would always be at home for us no matter what, eating a special meal with them by candlelight – had left a vivid and lasting impression. 'The family that prays together stays together' we were told when we were married. But how? That's what they never explained. Expecting Joel to get off his little trike or switch off the TV for family prayers was like asking for a pitched battle. And anyway, why inflict an unnatural, boring ritual on them that was divorced from the rest of their daily lives? So we introduced a weekly Sabbath meal with songs, prayers, presents, candles and the simple symbols of bread and wine – bread for work, wine for rest. Praying for people who had no bread, no work and not much leisure was immensely significant for six-year-old Joel, who had really taken the Ethiopian famine disaster to heart. He prayed fervently for the people there, and for his friends whose dads were on strike and came to school with half-empty lunch boxes. In fact, his petitions went on so long that Peter and I, glancing across at each other, raised our eyebrows in despair that we would ever get to eat that night.

Sometimes the meal worked well and sometimes our children were in a mood to misbehave. Often they entertained us, and the guests we invited, with songs learned at school that were anything but holy. But what did it matter as long as faith was fun?

We reworked our Sunday too, to make it more free for the family – both the blood and church variety – holding on to traditional Sunday lunch as Peter had known it when he was a lad, growing up in a vicarage where Sundays were sacrosanct. It wasn't difficult to invite another family and cook for eight, or ten, operating on the *Yiddishkeit* principle of having everything prepared the day before, so that I could relax and enjoy the occasion, rather than spend it slaving in the kitchen. Judaism certainly taught me the value of advanced preparation. My Christmas fare is often in the freezer by the end of November. By early March my shelves are filling up with Easter cakes and biscuits. In fact, it's more habit, than organization, a vital auto-response for anyone committed to creating celebration.

In the autumn of the strike my father died. He actually died on the last day of Tabernacles. Only those very close to the heart of God – the deeply religious and orthodox – are supposed to die on such a holy day. My father was neither. But I think it quite in keeping with the divine sense of humour to aggravate the more pious members of the community by giving my bacon-loving, law-breaking, yet God-fearing Pop a special death day. So many of his non-Jewish friends came to the funeral, the rabbi resorted to reading half the service in English. He balked however at a request from the St John's Ambulance Brigade to lay their cross on the coffin.

A Jewish funeral is much more relaxed than the Christian variety. Christians have formalization, not ritual, undertakers who take over, the coffin carried by four po-faced professionals in black, expressions fixed by habit and expectation to fit the sobriety of the occasion, though they have no knowledge of the deceased whatsoever. The family walk behind, exposed, conspicuous, on show. Will they or won't they lose control? Everyone hopes they won't.

In a rather disorderly mob, we rolled Dad up to the grave on a trolley, lowered him down, then took it in turns to take up the spade and shovel earth over him. It was all very normal and natural. My presence was obviously a bit of an embarrassment to the rabbi. He couldn't be seen to condone what I had done, but nor could he slight the bereaved. In the end he maintained a gracious, albeit uncomfortable reserve. Only my great-uncle Hymie, miserable little man that he was, let the show down by trying to drag the shovel out of Peter's hands when Mike handed it to him – because Peter wasn't *kosher*. Bigotry has a way of desecrating the most sacred circumstances.

I stayed with Mike and Agi, my brother and sister-in-law, who lived within yards of my parents. There was much laughter in the house along with the sadness. My father would have enjoyed that. He would have certainly been amused by the code of practice surrounding Jewish bereavement.

'What do we do now?' we all asked my brother repeatedly. 'Can we eat this? Wear that? Watch the television?'

'Don't ask me,' he said. 'Look it up.'

So we did, in a weighty tome called *Rules for Mourners*, which was our official guide and so detailed that none of us read it from cover to cover.

We were to stay at home for the week of mourning known as *shiva*, the Hebrew word for seven, while the community came to mourn with us, and, twice a day, to pray with us. There was no problem finding a *minyan* – the ten men needed for official prayers – in the evening, when the house was packed with visitors. But in the morning, when people were at work, my poor brother had to plead, beg and borrow any men he could lay his hands on. Ironic, when so many women were already there in the house.

It was a strangely comforting experience to hear the sound of those hauntingly sad, yet beautiful words of prayer, rising softly up the stairs to my room, as I got up each morning. *Yiskedal v'yiskadosh shemay rabah*, 'May the great name of the Lord be blessed. Amen and amen... the Lord has given, the Lord has taken away.' It is a wonderful song of praise and trust, transcending all pain and sorrow, one of the most familiar prayers of the Jewish people, and one which always has the power to bring a lump to my throat because of its painful associations. Singing it at every *shiva* is the reflex that enables the participants to let down the emotional defences that human beings hold onto so tightly, enabling them to weep together and identify with each other in the common experience of loss and bewilderment. It is the trigger that says, 'Permission to cry now' – even to the men.

As the bereaved we found old pullovers to wear so that the rabbi could make a cut in them, about four inches long, on the right for a spouse, on the left for a parent, harking back to the days when people would rend their clothes in grief. It was a distinctly odd sensation to walk around for a week with your jumper hanging in shreds. It marks you out. It makes you feel conspicuous. It is a powerful external symbol of the tearing sensation inside which bereavement undoubtedly is. The world sees your pain. You don't need to explain any irrational behaviour. And that is an immense relief.

Throughout the day we sat on low stools and received our visitors. It amused me to see my mother's non-Jewish friends arriving with flowers, while her Jewish friends humped in vast tureens of chicken soup. It seemed to symbolize a major difference between the two cultures. Within the Jewish community, food is the cure for all that ails you, and in this instance, it certainly helped. We had no heart to shop or cook and were glad it was forbidden anyway, for at the end of every hectic day, filled with visitors, phone calls, letter writing and sorting out my father's affairs, it was bliss to sit down to a meal that was already prepared. Agi's freezer was full from top to bottom with fresh salmon, casseroles, pies and luscious cakes. Mike said he hadn't eaten as well since he got married, and from the look on Agi's face, I doubted he ever would again.

Sitting there on our low stools, waiting to be served, we were reduced to a kind of childish dependency on others, and bereavement is the one time in our lives when that is not only acceptable, but necessary. When a loved one dies the body seems to produce its own instant anaesthetic. The faster the numbness wears off, the sooner the real grieving process can begin, and all the Jewish rituals are designed to create the kind of environment in which that can happen. Helplessness means resting on the loving support of others. It means having time and space to attend to the inner life, without the usual physical distractions. Small children are taken off for the day to play, so that their parents have a little calm and quiet. Much as I loved my children, much as I needed the sound of their laughter and play, a wonderful symbol of life in death, I also needed a chance to mourn, and valued the tranquillity I was given.

We also appreciated the company – the visitors who sat quietly, holding my mother's hand, or who reminisced about my father, making us laugh with stories of him we had never heard before. Even those who rattled on about their own problems distracted us for a few brief moments. For life goes on.

We in the christianized West, with all our apparent belief in the afterlife, do not, on the whole, cope well with death. My sister-in-law was horrified when a non-Jewish colleague of hers returned to work the day after her mother's death.

'I must take my mind off things,' she said by way of explanation.

'On the contrary,' said Agi, 'You must keep your mind on them. You need time to grieve, so that the wound can heal properly.'

'Oh no, keeping busy is the best way.'

'It strikes me as a very dangerous way,' Agi said to me afterwards. 'Her grief is bound to catch up with her one day. That's where, I suppose, the rules and regulations work for us.'

Unlike the Jews, Christians tend to stay away from the bereaved, and justify it by saying that they need to be left in peace, when perhaps what they really need is someone to sit with them or hold them. They might, heaven forbid, want to chat about their memories of the loved one, and even worse, cry. And then what would we do? We are embarrassed about what are seen as negative emotions, and end up colluding in spinning a web of silence around those who so badly need to talk. We force them, and ourselves, into a kind of stoical, dry-eyed acceptance, which may not in fact be the healthiest way of dealing with the situation.

Now I appreciate why the Jews visit the family graves every year between New Year and the Day of Atonement, and why they light a memorial light on the anniversary of a death. Every year I have a chance to reflect on how my father's life was an inspiration to me, and how much I still miss him. There are no flowers on Jewish graves, nothing that will wilt and fade. Instead, mourners bring pebbles, smooth and polished, which will survive the elements and the passage of time, a symbol of the way their loved one will live forever in their hearts and in the tales they tell their children. I told my children how Dad used to take us to the tuck shop on the way home from school, buy the teachers cream cakes on school sports days, play cricket in the street and dance the twist when it was the latest rage.

Most important of all, it was Dad who helped me formulate an image of a kind, truly loving, father in heaven – and that was his greatest gift to me.

Going back to wounded, weary Normanton forced me out of my quiet, safe cocoon. Looking out of the kitchen window at the now familiar sight of the pithead wheel in the distance, unnaturally still and motionless, something seemed different.

'Peter,' I called, 'Was it my imagination, or did the Council put up a brand new fence around the middle school playing field just a few weeks ago?'

He came up behind me, looked over my shoulder and nodded.

'Thank heavens, I thought I was having hallucinations. Where is it?'

He grinned. 'Every morning, when I get up, a little bit more had gone. I expect it makes very good firewood – especially when you're cold.'

I had to laugh. 'Ah, well, it was only a fence after all.'

I could put the strike out of my mind for a week, but Normanton couldn't forget, not for a minute. 'When it's over...' everyone muttered, as if we were in the middle of a war. No plans were made, no dreams were dreamed, life itself was suspended as we lived a strange kind of limbo existence.

As financial constraints began to squeeze out some of the basic necessities of existence, there were amazing stories of providence. Ginny had kept her four little girls off school as they had no coats to keep out the chill.

'If God's supposed to take care of the sparrers, what about my girls?' I asked him. 'The next day there were a knock at the door. It were Dorothy with four coats in her hands that her girls had grown out of – each the right size and even the colour they'd prayed for. Don't tell me that's just coincidence.'

Pride meant that people found it hard to accept the food packages the church delivered to their door, but admitted all the same that it was nice to know someone cared. Nicky, a miner's wife with small children to feed, told me one day, 'The funny thing is that now that we've nothing, we've never been so rich. What we need arrives just as we need it. Just as I'm down to my last tin, or my last piece of coal, someone comes to the door. At least I've more than them kids in Ethiopia. I don't take basics for granted any more. So maybe this strike isn't all bad. You ask yourself whether your faith is just a delusion or real enough to cope with a genuine crisis. Now I know which it is and I don't regret the chance to find out.'

But life wasn't easy – and not just for miners on strike, but for the raft of people with small businesses affected by the fallout. Only the police on picket duty had extra money in their pockets, and since they were brothers, cousins and in-laws of miners, relationships were often strained to breaking point.

One Sunday, during the Communion service, I looked up during the administration of the bread and wine and noticed that at the altar rail, in a row, was a miner on strike, one who had left the pit in disgust and found other work, a man whose fish and chip shop had closed due to lack of business and a policeman on picket duty. And as I watched them from behind, they stretched out their arms and wrapped them around each other's shoulders. Relationships in the church were stronger than ever.

Then suddenly, after eighteen months of near starvation, Scargill capitulated and it was all over. There was little elation, no dancing in the streets. On that first morning, the men marched back to work behind their banners to the accompaniment of a full brass band. The entire town turned out to cheer them on, but they slouched home with sloping shoulders, having been given their first pay packets in advance. After deductions for debts, fuel, rent, rates, union dues and insurance, there was virtually nothing left. Hope, pride and security had gone, along with a marriage or two, and all those little nest eggs set aside for the future.

For the church, celebration became more, not less important than ever. We had already discovered before the strike that men who spend hours a day, every day, constrained in a tight, dark tunnel, are in no mood to stand rigid and unmoving on Sundays too. Party was a way of life in this close knit community, unencumbered by middle-class reserve and propriety. All ages came together to share fantastic home-made food, home-grown, brass band music and dancing that spawned many a Billy Elliott. For the week between Christmas and New Year, there were leftover parties every night. People passed each other in the street with carrier bags full of half-eaten pizzas, turkey bits, squidgy cheesecakes and half bottles of wine. 'Eyup,' they greeted each other, trudging up the road to their Nelly's or their Freda's, 'eyup, lad, eyup, lass'. Towards New Year, as the scraps ran out and the women rebaked, the food improved. It was this party spirit that made a Jewish woman feel so much at home.

This was a time for the community, not to lick its wounds, but to heal its self-esteem.

'We need to concentrate on those things that matter most to the people of this town,' suggested Derek, the gifted, ex-Salvation Army, trumpet-playing worship leader when he came round to share his vision one evening. 'Sundays should be more of a celebration for the whole community – kids and all. There should be more letting our hair down. It would create more of a bridge between town and church.'

I couldn't help but smile, remembering how one miner, unused to church, had come to an informal Communion during the strike.

Seeing the participants murmuring something to one another as they passed the cup of wine from person to person, he decided his attempt at liturgy was as good as the next man's and said, 'Get this down thee, lad, it'll do thee good.' He was right.

'A man should feel as happy at his church as he is at his club,' Derek continued, mirroring my thoughts exactly. 'It shouldn't be such a psychological leap. The test would be whether our children could sit through services. If they're bored, we've missed it. If they're not, we've cracked it.'

I was temporarily struck dumb hearing so many of my ideas on someone else's lips.

He grinned at me. 'I thought it all might sound... a bit Jewish? Oh, and something else I wanted to ask. We now worship as a family at home once a week. It seems natural to have bread and wine. Is that all right?'

'You can please yourself what you do in your own home,' Peter laughed. 'We do.'

As Derek was leaving, I reached up and took a children's *haggadah* off the bookshelf. 'Can you do anything with this?' I asked him, handing it to him. 'It's the Passover service. It's full of psalms and songs that could be set to new music.'

Derek studied it for a while, then smiled. 'Funny,' he said, 'I was going to ask you if you had any records of Jewish music you could lend me. I'd quite like to have a go at writing some of my own. Shall we have our own Passover? Can you write us one in English?'

So I did, and we held our first ever church Passover. Everyone dressed up in their best clothes and brought their best food. Joyce Sykes put her teeth in, in honour of the occasion. Some said it made a very pleasant change, others that 'it were better than a night out at club'. A vast amount of wine was consumed, people got up to dance, and no one went home until the small hours of the morning.

'We do like yer, yer know,' Annie Briggs confided in me, on her way out, 'Even though you are a Jew.'

I took it the way it was meant – as the ultimate acceptance. We had done our first Passover – and it worked.

I cried myself to sleep the night we left Normanton for Peter's first incumbency, and woke with a start at around 3 am. 'I've just had a terrible nightmare,' I muttered to Peter in my confusion, 'I dreamed we were leaving.'

'We are, darling,' Peter whispered soothingly, and as the awful consciousness seeped into my brain, I started crying all over again.

For years we went back every New Year's night for the last party of the season – because we needed to. They are still the only people who make me laugh till my sides ache. And gradually the town changed – almost beyond recognition.

The deathblow dealt by the pit closures had inflicted deeper, more invisible wounds on the little community. Many of the young felt disillusioned and alienated, despite the valiant attempt of their leaders to preserve some sense of local pride or self-worth.

'I know what we could do,' one of the councillors was once heard to cry at a council meeting, as inspiration dawned, 'We could turn our town into a tourist attraction.' His colleagues blinked. This wasn't an obvious option.

'Well,' he said in the concentrated silence, 'we could get a gondola and float it on't lake.'

The 'lake' was a large pond the size of a bowling green in the middle of the park. 'Aye, aye' agreed a colleague, not wanting to be outdone in creative thinking, 'We could that', then added, warming to his subject, 'We could get two gondolas and mate 'em'.

Not surprisingly, tourism never arrived, but a rather more unwelcome form of progress has – in the shape of 'Port Wakefield', ringing the town with endless container depots and distribution centres for incoming goods from the Channel Tunnel.

'Give us the land,' cajoled the developers, 'and we'll give you a new library, swimming pool, superbowl and other, lavish communal facilities.'

No one put up a fight. What was the point? But no one was taken in either, which was just as well, because all the locals got was a massive roundabout network at the bottom of the town, with around twenty sets of traffic lights and a whole load of extra hassle to get onto or off the motorway. For a town that had only ever had one set of traffic lights, this did seem a little like overkill.

'Road-calming measures' turned the only main road from the motorway into a hazardous snake pass, undulating around bollards and semi-circles of pavement that stick out into the path of unsuspecting cars. It continues right through the town, its entire length dissected by dozens of new little roads leading to endless, homogenous housing developments, that have devoured every green space from school playing fields to golf course. The modern boxes bear no resemblance to the original higgledy-piggledy terraced properties that boast new pebble-dash, double-glazing and a raft of unsymmetrical extensions. The dingy corner shops, brightened with a lick of paint, now offer a host of exotic wares from all over the globe. There is no personal animosity to the incomers – that isn't how the people are – but it doesn't mean that losing the familiar ways and landmarks hasn't been difficult. Loss of intimacy always is.

Two miles down the road Castleford is no longer dwarfed by the shadow of the pit, but by Xscape, a shiny new 'entertainment centre' with restaurants, shops, cinema and, most incongruous of all, a ski slope – a white mountain of snow, instead of black slag. It's hailed as one of the most successful mine regeneration projects in the country, and ex-miners and their wives find it fun to shop there, but it's a cold, heartless place by comparison with what it was – a globalized, Americanized pseudo-version of what once was a real community.

Part of me will always belong in Normanton. I rediscovered some of my childhood roots there, left undisturbed beneath the northern coalfields since my parents abandoned my father's GP practice house in Felling, under the looming shadow of the Heworth Colliery, and headed for the dull, anonymous suburbia of greater Gateshead in its pre-Metro shopping days. I found a family and community that replaced the Jewish community I had forfeited, but such is a vicar's lot that I loved them and lost them too – but left more enriched and hopeful than I ever imagined possible. Their bequest to me was a lasting and abiding belief that celebration is not only possible, it's positively life-enhancing in even the darkest times, that community does matter, and can and must be recreated in the loneliest and most alienated of places. And that belief was about to be tested to the limit.

Chapter 12

Sent to Coventry

*L*eaving Normanton was, in some senses, a very brutal end to all the securities I had lost, rediscovered, and lost again. I set out reluctantly, uncertainly, like Sarah in the Old Testament, several steps behind her husband Abraham, who strode out, full of faith, focused on his unknown future, while she, probably convinced he had lost his senses, kept saying to herself, 'I only hope he knows what he's doing.'

We were being sent to Coventry, Peter said confidently. His hotline to the Almighty always functioned better than mine. All I felt was a profound emotional chill. Coventry was an unengaging city robbed of its past by Hitler's bombs and then by its 1950s planners. When it came to architecture, post-war Great Britain was anything but great. If only we had resorted to rebuilding the beauty that was bombed. But no, the fashion for a stark Le Corbusier modernism didn't do any town any favours. It lumbered Coventry with gloomy concrete walls and characterless dual carriageways, that gave way to vast industrial landscapes as barren as the West Yorkshire coalfields, dominated not by pitheads, but by the monoliths of the new wealth that manufactured Jaguars, Austins and Rovers.

The people had come from the far flung parts of the United Kingdom, from the empty clang of the coal house, steel factory, or boatyard door as it slammed shut in their faces. They came to make money, not relationships. The emotional landscape could be as bleak as its physical counterpart. The Christmas carol singing round the parish, so appreciated in Normanton, was greeted by silent, empty streets and firmly closed doors. Only the slightest waver of a net curtain at a window let us know that our best efforts were not going entirely unnoticed, as we trudged from cul-de-sac to cul-de-sac and sang our hearts out to the accompaniment of a valiant accordion.

I couldn't get used to living in a 1960s box on a main road to nowhere. It was a biggish, stand-alone box, admittedly, but still a rectangle with straight lines and uninteresting proportions, several inches from the fifty-foot brick wall of the church, which filled the landing window. The kitchen was tiny – no room for a table, so no room for children doing homework as I pottered – and the dining room, without any furniture other than the table, only seated six people holding their breath. We couldn't extend our dining room table to its full length. It wouldn't even take the small wool rug we had so lovingly bought with every last penny we had when we first got married. When my father-in-law died, my mother-in-law came to live around the corner. Had she needed to live with us, it would have been impossible. A vicarage family may not have those kinds of choices. As it was, squeezing us all in for lunch on Sunday was an acrobatic feat. Inviting another family was out of the question, unless we ate buffet style. It was a terrible denial of the Jewish Mama hospitality gene, let alone the New Testament hospitality command. The concept of the extended family was manifestly unknown to Church of England architects. This was the new, streamlined, cheap-to-run, Lego vicarage for the new, strapped-for-cash, stereotypical clergy family, who manifestly shut themselves off from the parish, and didn't bother with aging parents.

'The clergy don't want big houses nowadays,' said our diocesan surveyor, when I harangued him on the matter. Here was an uncontested expert in the particular foibles and preferences of clergy spouses. 'Can't afford to run them.'

Fair point. The letters page in the *Church Times* from clergy families, unable to heat their vast barns on a pittance, appeared to support his view – but couldn't there be a happy medium, a place large enough to encompass friends and extended family, if not half the parish? And did the newer vicarages have to look so obviously public service, so police house, announcing to the world that it was not and would never be ours?

I drew the line at the mustard cupboard fronts he sent for the kitchen, without consultation.

'I am surprised,' he said mildly, as he surveyed the flat packs left stacked on the floor. 'All the other clergy wives seem to like them.'

None, it was abundantly clear, were as difficult as this one. But then, there was always one! His look said it all.

The fact that Peter's study was big enough to seat a dozen round a large table and still find room for a dresser or sideboard, his desk and bookshelves, only added to my frustration. I thought of switching the rooms around, but the study had been built next to the front door, opposite a visitor's toilet, and both were safely separated by a further glass door from the rest of the living quarters. The boundary between work and play was carefully set out. A vicar's wife, I presumed, needed the freedom to flit to the bathroom, in the altogether, if she so chose.

One of Peter's first jobs was to get himself onto the diocesan parsonages committee – and from that moment, vicars' wives chose their own kitchen cupboard fronts. To be fair to our diocesan surveyor, even Peter was surprised at the issues they had to deal with. Some clergy wanted jaccuzis or whirlpool spas, some had endless problems with pollution in the pond in the back garden, while others left more behind than just a job vacancy – their vicarages needed fumigating.

Church fabric has always obsessed my mate, graduate mechanical engineer that he is, and his congregations come to appreciate it in the end. Asceticism within the Christian tradition tends to lead to hang-ups about warming our churches. In most countries where temperatures fall to sub-zero the inhabitants work with the climate, not against it. But even when the world is an ice rink or there's three feet of snow on the ground, Anglo-Saxons refuse to run dilapidated church central heating systems for longer than the customary one or two hours.

My husband tells me (to the accompaniment of our children, playing a melancholic lament on imaginary violins – their usual response to their father's hard-luck childhood tales), that when he was a lad at boarding school, he had to crack the ice in the basin first thing every morning before he could wash. Then he dressed in ten seconds, holding his breath, and ate a vast breakfast of rib-clagging porridge to warm the body from the inside. Things could have been worse. The tradition for ice cold showers in boys' boarding schools had just been abandoned at his school. Presumably the powers-that-be realized there might be more effective ways of transforming a horde of unbridled infidels into the Christian leaders of the future.

He did leave the school with his faith reinforced, but that had little to do with surviving in almost sub-zero temperatures, and a great deal more to do with the friendships he formed. In fact those years filled him with an abiding intolerance of cold places. Expending all one's inner energy on keeping warm, rather than on creative projects and relationships, always seemed a futile waste of time and resources. He carries a radiator key in his pocket permanently, bleeding thousands of non-functioning radiators wherever they fail to keep the nation warm. Why human beings allow air locks to accumulate in their pipes is for him one of life's greatest sources of puzzlement and dismay. The theological college we attended was permanently cold – a source of misery in lectures, until Peter arrived with his key. Wherever he went, blood-thawing, marrow-warming gurgles and rattlings followed him. They called him the 'College Bleeder', and blessed him for it.

When we were weighing up the pros and cons of going to Coventry, we rang a close friend for his wisdom.

'Does the church in question need a new boiler?' he asked.

'Why?'

'Because if it does, I should take it as a clear sign of God's guidance.'

It didn't, we moved, and soon discovered that the boiler needed replacing after all.

Peter's intolerance of cold churches isn't simply a matter of personal preference. A cold church will, almost inevitably, be socially and spiritually cold. It says, 'We are merely tolerating, not welcoming your presence. Keep your coats and parkas on, stay muffled in your bonnets and scarves. Wrap yourself up in your own little world and don't attempt to reach out into anyone else's.' When human beings take off their coats, they make themselves at home. They relax. They meet each other.

I have never been cold in a synagogue. Coats are removed as people come in and are left in the cloakroom. In a temperature which make the Sahara seem pleasantly cool, the congregation, possibly there for several hours, unwinds, enjoys the environment and the company and inevitably falls asleep. The whole building is warm, light, comfortable and inviting.

I often wonder what impression our churches make on visitors, whether they see the hard, unwelcoming face of an alien culture, or the warmth of true belief. Peeling paintwork, bare walls, crumbling cement, rotten woodwork, dusty banners and even a jumbled mass of yellowing pictures and notices, which would be gladly received by the local museum, don't announce to the world that the inhabitants of this building love being here and are comfortable and creative in it. And often, since most visitors to the church are attending a wedding or a funeral, the building is all they see of us, all they know of our faith.

So there is more to a church boiler than first meets the eye. I have had a love-hate relationship with many in my time. Arch-rivals in my husband's affections, they have still become for me a symbol of the way the practical and the spiritual must be integrated. It also means that callers are more likely to ask the vicar to pop round because their central heating, not their marriage, has broken down.

'If you had the same effect on people as you have on engines and machines, you'd have a reputation as a miracle worker,' I tease him.

'Just as well I don't then,' he counters.

St James' in Coventry, built in the thirties, had a decidedly Calvinist look about it. Inside, despite an open-plan seating arrangement which lent itself to dance, drama, and other, attractive ways of worship, vast expanses of bare brick wall gave a rather cold, austere feel to the building. Peter was informed that he would be expected to wear a cassock alb, a long, white, monkish hooded tunic, when he was leading services. Self-conscious at the best of times, he didn't even like what he calls the 'medieval angel kit' of cassock and surplice. He thought uniforms tended to make a man pompous, and that particular uniforms created an unhelpful separation of people from the priest.

'What do you think of it?' he said to me, in his monk's robe, surveying his reflection in the mirror. He's a very tall, fairly slender man.

'Well, if you want my honest opinion,' I said to him, 'All you need is a yellow bobble hat, and you'll look like a walking candle.'

That did a great deal to allay his awkwardness.

It has always been a mystery to me why some people enjoy dressing up their minister more than their building. I have to admit that there was plenty of this particular human maypole to decorate, but there was a great deal more of the wall. The first little number he was given to wear was some woman's converted wedding dress. The row of pin marks where the bust darts had been were a bit of a giveaway.

Eventually, to his relief, it was replaced with a new cloak, and a set of lovingly embroidered scarves in colours that matched a dazzling array of altar fronts, coverlets and banners, made to reflect the seasons in the church's year. It was a delight to walk into the building on festivals and see a mass of purple at Advent and Lent, crimson at Pentecost and white and gold at Easter. It created a gentle whirring sensation within me, the reminder that today was different from any other day. 'Why is this night different from all other nights?' asks the youngest child at the Passover table, at the sight of so many specialities that appear only once a year. Every festival is distinctive. Every festival is unique.

Until we moved to Coventry, I always felt Easter was a bit of a damp squib. No one, looking on, would have guessed that Christians were a people of resurrection hope. St James's however, had a prototype for the occasion, imbibed from various historic, para-Catholic influences, honed to a fine art. Meditations day and night during Holy Week prepared the entire congregation for a truly celebratory Easter Day. They had mastered the art of the slow build-up.

One favourite Holy Week tradition was the daily breakfast, which everyone ate together in what was known as the 'narthex', the no-man's land between the church porch and its entrance. It must have befuddled the neighbourhood to open their curtains early in the morning and see, through the glass doors, about two dozen people sitting round tables, tucking into their cornflakes.

I couldn't understand the great attraction for my children. Why did they leap out of bed, during school holidays, in what I can only describe as the middle of the night, for quiet meditation? Neither had ever shown such piety before.

'Prayer?' asked Joel, in response to my enquiry about how they were coping with such a long stint in church. 'We don't go for that, do we Abby? We go for the breakfast.'

'It's still very early for breakfast when you could have it here.'

'But,' said his little sister, 'You won't let us have white toast or cornflakes because they're not wholemeal and not good for us.'

How could I object to this sacrifice of roughage for a week, when they were made so welcome, and obviously enjoyed being part of a wider family?

The St James' Easter package was so effective that it was only with the greatest trepidation we dared suggest any alterations. After all, each church has its own traditions, and they can be harder to tinker with than the traditions of the Jews. Creatures of habit that we are, we find any change profoundly disturbing, and would rather miss out on potential benefits than risk an adventure. But for me Easter could not now be complete without a communal Passover. Celebrating it at home on our own simply wasn't the same. I wanted people to see how, at the last supper, Jesus had applied the rich symbolism to the Easter events, so that for years to come, long after he had gone, the disciples would never be able to experience the Passover without making the connections.

We suggested a *Seder*, a Passover service night, on Maundy Thursday, instead of the traditional Communion.

'Sounds great,' said the enthusiasts.

'It might be interesting,' said the careful.

'It's a dreadful idea,' declared a small minority. 'A party! On one of the holiest days in the church's calendar? When we should be having a Eucharist befitting the occasion?'

It was customary, after the Eucharist, to 'strip the altar', an old tradition which involved removing every decoration from the front of church – flowers, tapestries, banners, any gold or silver ornaments – until all that remained, for the night-long vigil into Good Friday, was a solitary wooden cross. It was an important tradition, but we felt that it told only half the story. If Jesus had been expecting the last supper to be a lugubrious, morbid sort of affair, why did he

Chosen

tell the disciples he was really looking forward to it? That
didn't make sense. Most people, knowing their death was
imminent, would want their last moments with loved ones
to be memorable, even happy, so that the bereaved weren't
left utterly bewildered.

So we came to a compromise. St James' was a truly
monstrous building, whose ceiling was so high that many
years earlier, a floor had been hung halfway up, creating a
spacious hall above the body of the church, known as 'the
upper room'. It lent itself to a last supper re-enactment. While
I was chopping apples and walnuts and wine, concocting
charoset, symbolizing the mortar the Israelite slaves had
used while building walls in Egypt, some contemporary
slaves, their forced labour imposed by the minister, were
manhandling trestle tables up six flights of stairs, groaning
loudly as men do when they're enjoying themselves. Each
table was covered with a white cloth, and decorated with a
posy of flowers and a '*seder* dish', of unleavened bread, bitter
herbs, and 'mortar'. Enough space was left between them
for the hardy to get up and do a quick hora when the mood
took them.

When I arrived after work, children and adults had
changed into party gear, and the atmosphere was charged.
The churchwardens, armed with corkscrews, were attacking
a crateful of red wine, ready for everyone to have their
statutory four glasses. A series of low, full-throttled plopping
sounds, and the scent of wine mingled with the already
intoxicating smell of cinnamon and horseradish that
pervaded the room.

I laid out my grandmother's best silver on the top table,
the candlesticks lit on every important occasion, the bowl
of salt water, symbolizing the Red Sea or the tears shed by

my ancestors in their captivity, the jug to be used in the ritual hand-washing ceremony, probably the moment in the evening when Jesus insisted on washing Peter's feet. The silver and satin, dozens of expectant faces, the entire room, glowed in the soft light shining down from dozens of tiny spots, hidden under the heavy wooden arches.

We explained that apart from on a kibbutz in Israel, the *Seder*, or Service, was usually celebrated at home. It was a bit like Christmas, in that several families joined together, but better than Christmas, because this was so much more than a meal, and people didn't get time to fall out with each other. The service is contained in the *haggadah*, 'the recital' or 'narration', which recounts, in full, the escape of the children of Israel out of Egypt, through the Red Sea, into the desert. They do not, as far as the *haggadah* is concerned, ever make it to the Promised Land, but then the service already takes almost as long as the first year in the wilderness. Thirty-nine more might have made the narration a little excessive.

'Tonight,' began my husband, 'Abandon any preconceived ideas you may have about 'holding a service.' Forget reverent silence. The atmosphere will be the same as in a Jewish home. No distinction will be made between storytelling, singing, praying, eating or chatting. If you want to hold a conversation with your neighbour, make a joke, go to the toilet, or even doze off, as Michele's grandfather used to do, that's entirely up to you. I'll try not to nod off, and I certainly won't be waiting for you. If you miss something, tough! I won't repeat it and you may have to wait until next year to catch it. This is the great freedom festival, celebrating the redemption of the Jewish people from the tyranny of Pharaoh – the liberation of God's people from the tyranny of evil. How you choose to celebrate that freedom is entirely up to you.'

I lit the festival candles, and celebrate we did – with such gusto that there were times when the precariously hung floor began to sway and I feared we might all end up in the church below.

It never ceases to amaze me how easily Christians enter into the spirit of the occasion. For the church, the whole evening was a series of new sensations. Alternate groans at some of the strange tastes, and murmurs of appreciation reached us at the top table. The children coughed, spluttered and screwed up their faces as they took their first sip of wine or tried to chew a piece of horseradish. Some tables left their bowls of *charoset* untouched; others scavenged for second helpings. Some people scrunched their way through entire boxes of matzah. Others thought it tasted like sawdust. They really wondered what I was doing when we produced sliced hard-boiled eggs in salt water for the hors d'oeuvre, and explained that the sliced egg was supposed to represent the eyes of the Israelites, the salt water their tears. 'Gruesome,' they said. The poor egg, traditionally enjoyed in every home at teatime, lightly boiled with toast fingers, suddenly found itself blackballed. It's all a matter of association.

No one's appetite suffered in any noticeable way. A massive buffet disappeared beneath a contemporary plague of locusts. While the adults were drinking their coffee the children scrambled under tables, into corners, up the walls, hunting for the *afikomen*. The middle of the three *matzot*, kept in a coverlet on the top table, represents the Passover lamb, and is broken in half and hidden during the meal. We actually hid about thirty pieces, wrapped in serviettes. It means a great deal of cleaning up later, because *matzah* has a habit of disintegrating, especially when sat on, but the alternative was two dozen disappointed children – a far greater ordeal. Peter ransomed all the pieces back with a small Easter egg. The egg is a symbol of mourning for the Jew, and of new life for the Christian. The whole game is a wonderful picture of the Passover lamb hidden for three days, then rising to life.

Then, as the Jews do, immediately after the meal, Peter broke the pieces of *afikomen* and distributed them to the entire gathering. 'On the night Jesus was betrayed, he took unleavened bread, gave thanks to God and broke it, saying, "This is my body which is for you."'

The *afikomen* is followed by the third cup of wine, traditionally known as the cup of blessing, accompanied as it is by prayers that bless God for his endless mercy and love. 'After supper he took the cup and said, "This cup is God's new covenant, sealed with my blood. When you drink it, remember me."'

We used only two or three cups on this occasion, and sang quietly as the cup was passed from person to person, from child to adult. 'It is a cup of blessing we now drink,' said the Apostle Paul in his letter to the Christians in Corinth, not the fourth and final cup, known as the cup of wrath, that appeals to God to bring justice on those who abuse their neighbours.

The clock ticked on. Outside the huge arched window behind the top table, darkness fell. We sang our way through dozens of psalms, and we danced. We poured a cup of wine for Elijah, opened the door and waited, with bated breath, for him to announce the coming of the Messiah. He never arrived. Nor, thankfully, did any of our gentlemen of the road, looking for shelter. It would have been their lucky night.

Then came the moment that belonged uniquely to St James'. Just as Jesus went out from that great feast of joy into Gethsemane, we asked people to leave the upper room in silence, then walk down several flights of stairs in single file into a darkened church. There, a solitary, rough-hewn cross was illuminated by a single candle. Bleary-eyed children, who, a moment earlier, lay slouched with sleeping-sickness in their chairs, walked up to it, and knelt, wide-eyed, as if they were seeing it for the first time. Adults sat motionless in the pews. The intense, profound silence, after so much noise and celebration, drove home, as nothing ever had before, the overwhelming desolation of Jesus in the garden, having said goodbye to his loved ones, now facing the unbearable, alone. No one wanted to leave the building. Never was any Maundy Thursday vigil so compelling. 'You've danced and sung and laughed with me, now won't you stay with me a while in my sorrow?'

It was the small hours of the morning, and even then with reluctance, before the last few people trickled home and Peter managed to lock up the church and go to bed.

That Easter I learned an important lesson. When two great traditions appear to clash, it doesn't necessarily mean one is right and the other wrong. Each may have an insight the other lacks. Put the two together, and a far richer picture is painted. What began as compromise became revelation.

However tired the children had been the night before, there was little evidence of it the next morning, when they arrived, lunch boxes in hand, for a Good Friday workshop. While they made unleavened bread, their parents had a three-hour meditation, culminating at 3pm precisely with everyone together in church for the snuffing out of the paschal candle.

'Ooooh', I heard one child gasp in wonder, 'Is he dead then?'

Mother nodded, resolutely refusing to break the silence that hung over the church for the rest of the day, and the whole of Saturday, waiting for an explosion of praise on Easter Sunday morning.

In 1991, the year of the Gulf War, we kept a candle burning in the church throughout the conflict. It shone through the glass doors out into the neighbourhood. Parents of lads who were out with the armed services would come and go, and sit for a while in the quiet. Sometimes I sat with them. Living only two metres away from the church became a privilege rather than an imposition. For most of the time I was presenting a current affairs programme on local radio, living, breathing and sleeping the misery and worry of it all. I remember driving into work one morning thinking, 'Oh God, let this be over by Easter. Let it be over for the season of hope, joy and resurrection.' And it was. That year it felt as if life was beginning all over again. Just as well I couldn't read the future.

It was in Coventry that I first started collecting Easter decorations for our home, determined the festival should be every bit as good as Christmas, if not better. We developed a family Easter ritual. My friend Rose from Normanton and her family joined us for the weekend. They arrived on Good Friday, just in time for tea and hot cross buns. On Easter Saturday, after the children were in bed, cracking endless egg jokes, the adults filled the house with streamers, miniature chickens, rabbits, chocolate eggs, twigs, branches and armfuls of flowers. On Easter Sunday morning everyone was awakened to the 'Hallelujah Chorus', blasted through the house from the hi-fi system, and came down to a magical world, full of treats and surprises. After church and a lunch of roast lamb and Easter-egg trifle, we held a chocolate bunny hunt in the garden.

'Joel, have you had a look up your back passage?' I heard Rose's daughter Kate shout one year, pointing to our back alleyway. Another year, the hamster died on cue. She had a

wonderful funeral, led by Joel, who, at eleven, preached on
the resurrection of the body to a glorious afterlife.

Though the church loved our children, the local schools
did not. They found them far too individual and imaginative.
Joel was bullied. I asked him whether it was because he was
a vicar's son.

'Not so much for that,' he said reflectively.

'Then for what?' I asked him.

'For being a Jew.'

'Everything is all right,' he said, 'until the teacher begins
to talk about the Holocaust. And then they laugh. The whole
class laughs. I try and explain, but they just laugh more.
Why, why, why?'

It is hard, at eleven, to understand that laughter may be
the only possible response to horror on such a scale. 'Kill 600
Jews,' Goebbels is supposed to have said to Hitler, 'and that
will go down in history as a tragedy. Kill 6 million and they
will be a mere statistic.'

Joel must have been no more than nine or ten when he
asked me the inevitable question. He was sitting in front
of the television watching a programme about the Nazi
invasion of Europe. He turned to me quite suddenly and
asked, 'What would have happened to me if I had been
living in Germany or Poland or Holland during the nineteen
forties?'

It was the moment I had waited, for and dreaded, never
anticipating it would come so soon – that moment when
you have to try to explain to your child that for many people
he would have been of less value than dog mess. You try to
make it easy. If not acceptable, then comprehensible. But
you look into the face of innocence and see, 'Why me? What
did I do to deserve that?' and know that there is, and cannot
ever be, any adequate explanation.

St James' provided a totally unexpected moment of healing. Twinned with a church in Hamburg, as part of the cathedral's policy to build bridges and bring reconciliation between the two cities after the war, we enjoyed several exchange trips. On one occasion we invited all thirty of our German visitors for Friday evening supper. It seemed both natural and right for me to light my Sabbath candles, and for them to share in our *kiddush* of bread and wine. Squeezed into our home, sitting on the stairs and in every available space, they watched me intently and in silence. I had no means of knowing whether their expressions reflected sadness for past history or interest in a now unfamiliar culture, but it didn't matter. I sensed they found the whole experience as moving as I did and some unspoken restoration undoubtedly took place. Together, Christians must be able to confront the past and lay it to rest.

There was a great surprise in store for all her children, when my mother announced her decision to marry again. Lively and attractive as she was, the thought had never crossed my mind that she would. But the Jewish community had other ideas. She was invited, by cousins, to meet an 'eligible' widower.

'No strings attached,' she said, when she rang me to tell me about the introduction.

'Of course, not,' I replied.

'I've no intention of getting married. But meeting someone can't do any harm.'

'It can't. It may even be a good idea.'

And then it was, 'We're just having dinner out together. Nothing more. Pleasant company, that's all I want.'

I thought the lady was beginning to protest too much.

Within days a coy, wheedling, little voice asked down the telephone whether I would mind if she married again. Mind?

I was overjoyed that someone was prepared to take her off our hands.

'Since when have you ever asked our permission for anything you want to do?' I asked her. She had said it to me often enough. 'Go for it.'

'Does he know what he's letting himself in for?' my brother asked me anxiously.

Surely, I thought. A Jewish widower in his late sixties must know how the game is played.

Boris, her intended, was very London Jewish, and a surprisingly humorous and accommodating man, given his chequered history. His father, an itinerant businessman in the early years of the twentieth century, had settled his wife in Shanghai, where she died giving birth to their only son. Boris was raised in a Roman Catholic orphanage by Sisters who refused to give him up without a court battle when his father remarried and returned to claim him – inexplicably, some three years later. His new stepmother was systematically cruel to the child, who grew up to be the only one of her three children who bothered to care for her in her old age.

The highlight of his existence, the only years he spoke of with any real enthusiasm, were spent in the British Army during the Second World War. One of his favourite stories took place just after it ended, when German prisoners waited on the occupying forces. Every morning, outside his room, he found his boots polished to mirror-like perfection – the only Private in the British Army who did. He found the German responsible and asked him why he bothered polishing the boots of a mere Private.

'You have heard about the camps, what we did to your people?' the young prisoner replied, unable to look Boris in the face. 'I don't know how else to say sorry.'

Within months of their first meeting, the family gathered in the home of a cousin to watch Mother exceptionally elegant in silver grey and rose, take smiling, unsuspecting Boris, as the second martyr to the perfect Jewish home. They were married in the traditional way, under a *chuppah*, supported on poles held by my brother, and Boris' three antique-dealer sons.

'Rings?' demanded the rabbi.

Boris handed them over.

'Are they paid for?'

The extraordinary mixture of dignified ceremonial and farce was almost too much to bear.

'This young... er, this couple,' began the rabbi, and the *chuppah* began to shake. Mike swallowed hard and forced down the corners of his mouth. The *ketubbah*, or marriage contract, the Jewish alternative to vows, was read aloud, and signed. Failure to observe the contract is a serious matter and can lead to divorce. Mum always claimed she never heard it the first time round. She listened to her rights carefully this time. Then the groom, according to custom, wrapped a glass in cloth and smashed it underfoot. It is supposed to be a moment of sober, quiet reflection on the destruction of the Temple. Instead it has now become a signal for generalized chaos. The room erupted into shouts of *mazeltov*, and much kissing and hugging. Hats slid sideways over their owners' eyes or fell to the floor. Mother was a wife again, and looked very pleased about it. Until the rabbi announced that the young... er, the couple would now retire for *yihud*.

Yihud, the Hebrew word for seclusion, a compulsory opportunity for the couple to retire in private together, gave a young bridegroom the chance to check out the dues stated in the contract, if he so chose. And presumably, if there was any question about his partner's virginity, now was the chance to complain and get his money back.

'But I don't know what to do,' Boris protested loudly.

'So you'll think of something,' said the rabbi, ushering the reluctant couple into a bedroom.

It was just as well they didn't. They had barely had the time to open some of their presents when there was a short knock on the door and the rabbi wheeled in a trolley laden with tea and cakes.

Yihud, in fact, now simply gives the couple a chance, immediately after their wedding, to have a few moments of space together, to say whatever they want to say to each other, in private. Food is often wheeled in, in case they have been fasting as a sign of repentance of past wrongdoings, and preparation for their life together.

Meanwhile their guests don't miss the couple at all. They are having a wonderful time. Musical instruments, forbidden in the synagogue, are compulsory at a wedding reception. So is dancing. Even the Song of Songs talks about a dance of two companies, possibly referring to an old tradition where the men and women danced separately, the bride brandishing a sword in her right hand, defending herself against all suitors other than her chosen. Mum and Boris opted for something a little more sedate, given their riper years.

Midway through the proceedings, the *shammus*, the verger of the synagogue, sidled up to Boris, and nodding and winking, whispered in his ear, 'I've said *chay v'rachmin*, prayers for your dead.'

'Thank you,' said Boris, genuinely moved, until he realized, from the verger's continued crowding of his space, that he was waiting for something. Boris handed him a ten pound note.

Jewish tradition maintains that charity should be dispensed whenever you remember your departed loved ones, for God may be more disposed to forgive them their sins. But the *shammus* didn't move. Observing the bewilderment on Boris' face, he said, waving the note, 'That's enough for your father, but you are an orphan.'

Boris dug into his pocket, temporarily aggravated with a mother who had been inconsiderate enough to leave her child so unprotected in the world, and was about to hand over another note, when his new wife intercepted it with a deft snatch of the hand.

'Enough,' she said.

'Phew', muttered the *shammus*, 'The ink's not dry in the register and look who's the boss already.'

Boris turned out to be a lover of pranks – usually against my mother, a master of nonsense language, and a dab hand at *Kaluki*, which made him a great step-grandfather. He only really protested with his lot in life when my mother colour-coded the shirts in his wardrobe.

Chapter 13

Of Work, Womanhood, Sex and Sensuality

A career finally caught up with me. Abby had been at school full-time for a month when the phone rang, and I was offered a job as a researcher and presenter in Religion and Education at Central Television in Birmingham. Despite doing an increasing amount of freelance work for the media, I had never intended working full-time outside the home. Besides, I had started writing up the mammoth amount of research I had been doing into my husband's extraordinary ancestors.

'How will we manage?' I asked Peter. 'Who will look after the children after school?'

'I can be at home doing administration,' he reassured me, 'and if I can't, there's always someone in a church willing to help out.'

There were, it seemed, hitherto unknown perks in being married to a minister. Sadly, having my own study wasn't one of them, so writing the Guinness saga was relegated to the small hours of the morning, at a computer installed in our bedroom, while Peter taught himself to sleep to the constant tap-tapping of the keyboard.

I sat at an empty desk on my first morning at Central Television, terrified out of my wits. For the past seven years I had pushed a pram around. Now it was a blank piece of paper on an empty desk. Despite an academic education, rated highly for Jewish daughters, any job I had done until I met Peter had simply been filling in time as I waited for my prince to ride up on his charger and sweep me off into the distant sunset. But the romantic dream of being a stay-at-home mum in a gingerbread cottage with honeysuckle growing up the wall, and sweet-smelling nappies pegged out on a line in the garden faded with the reality of inner city Manchester, the Yorkshire coalfields and Coventry car factories. In fact, the baby and toddler years were my wilderness years. I thought I ought to enjoy having babies, but instead, felt bored and demoralized.

If just one person had told me I might make a better mother of teenagers than babies, it would have alleviated the guilt. But no one ever does. In fact, most say, 'Just wait till they're teenagers, it gets worse.' 'It' never did, I have to say. The hard work was done when they were little. They grew into adults I like and enjoy – despite the fact that I was catapulted into the workplace when they were still quite small.

'The allergies may well come from your side of the family,' I say to my husband, as we gaze at them fondly, 'but the neuroses are from mine.'

But when the Central TV job turned up, unsought and unexpected, that world beyond my limited horizons was a terrifying place. I knew only baby talk, how to make dungarees, butterfly cakes, flour paste and sandcastles. I shunned confrontation, trembled if a shopkeeper was shirty, was a doormat at the doctor's and a walkover when a workman did a lousy job. I was scared to death of making a decision, deferring far too readily to my all-knowing husband.

That hard-won confidence, for which my parents made so many sacrifices, had been eroded by the continual drip-drip of depreciation. It is a sad reality that running a home and raising children, which require such energy, such creative ingenuity, are so undervalued. Going to work was as good as a rest. No wonder men had hidden this little gem of truth from the female of the species for as long as they could. My mother had never had an opportunity like this. 'Next time I'm coming back as a man!' she used to say to my father, as she plonked his lunch on the table in front of him. She had no actual belief in reincarnation. And even if she had, I don't suppose she would have ever really opted to be a man, any more than the rest of the female population, who out of sheer frustration, have probably said something similar. She simply wanted him to understand how hard it was to be a woman.

For Jewish women of my mother's generation, grumbling was part of an elaborate game they played with their men. They pretended their gender was the ultimate snub, that upon this slightly inferior specimen the Almighty had conferred the dregs of the physiological processes – periods, pregnancy, childbirth and the dreaded menopause. That's why the male thanked God in his morning prayers that he was neither a Gentile, nor a woman. But beneath the obsequious facade was the belief that the male of the species was actually weaker and malleable – the inferior model. Apart from one, necessary, biological function – in those pre-IVF days – he was, in fact, utterly dispensable. The aim of the game was that he must never find out. He must go on believing that he was the master and centre of the universe. The slightest suspicion that he wasn't could dramatically affect the fundamental balance of nature, bringing an abrupt end to matriarchal civilization as they knew it. I often wondered, in my childhood days, what havoc would have been unleashed if one Jewish man had taught himself to cook.

The moment the Jewish male crosses the threshold of his own home, he is a subordinate in the woman's kingdom. Her power is sacrosanct, inviolable. Those who accuse Judaism of paternalism because men lead the prayers, have never had close contact with a real Jewish Mama.

'Why don't you put your foot down?' my Mother said to me, when Peter and I were discussing the decor of the Coventry vicarage.

'What about?' I asked her.

'Well, the colour of the carpets and curtains are none of his business. Since when has a man good taste? Tell him to stick to his responsibilities. And you stick to yours.'

My mother couldn't quite work out whether Peter didn't know the rules, or played deliberately foul. Being non-Jewish as he was, and a clergyman as he became, she gave him the benefit of the doubt. It was evident to her that taking on a Gentile, untrained, unfettered, loose canon as he evidently was, was quite an undertaking. It would take a very firm hand to force him into any kind of reasonable shape.

'And in whose name is the house?' she asked when we first married.

'His,' I said sheepishly.

'His? His? You must be mad. And if he goes bankrupt? Has an affair with a dolly bird? Throws you out, so that he can install her? Don't come running to me if you have no roof over your head.'

In the area of women's rights, Judaism has been centuries ahead of most of the Christian cultures in which its people lived. When a woman brought property into a marriage, it remained hers. Her husband could not touch her capital. He was entitled to a share in any profit it might make, only if he had promised in the *ketubah*, the marriage contract, to be responsible for her maintenance. If she had decided to support herself, he was not eligible for any of the profit, since he had done nothing to deserve it. In the event of a divorce, she took back everything she had brought into the marriage. If she had no property, she could claim the sum of money he had been forced to put in her name when they married. In most countries of the world, women do not have that level of independence and financial protection even today.

Jewish parents have learned through bitter experience the waywardness of human nature. A daughter must be protected from that potential little heap of wanton destructiveness she is marrying. She must have security. She must have property. The home must be in her name alone. In the event of bankruptcy no one can take it from her. In the event of his unfaithfulness, he could come home to find his belongings stacked in the garden. Jewish men think very hard before they commit an infidelity. It could be a costly business.

'And you must have your own bank account too,' Mum told me, once I had started earning, 'A little something put away that he can't lay his hands on. You have one, don't you?'

I hadn't.

'So you know what he'll do if anything happens to you? He'll marry again faster than he can clear your clothes out of the wardrobe. All that you earn, the money you sweat and sacrifice for, that you put away for your children... hers will get the lot.'

'Oh no, Mam,' I said, 'Peter would never do a thing like that.'

She shook her head in despair. Was I naive or was I naive? 'A man obsessed,' she confided all-knowingly, 'is a man possessed. There's no knowing what nonsense he won't get up to.'

I have lost count of the times I have been forced to admit that my mother's outlook on life, with thousands of years of Jewish experience to back it, has proved to be the voice of wisdom. I made a documentary for Central Television called *Great Expectations*, on the strains and stresses facing the couple in the manse, and discovered that when their marriage broke up, often because of the man's adultery, many clergy wives found themselves abandoned and destitute.

'It's these young ones today,' my mother-in-law, a retired clergy wife herself, said to me, knowingly. 'They don't want the role any more. They want to go out to work.'

She was wrong. Most of the divorced clergy wives I met, as I researched the programme, had sacrificed their all for the job, played the part of minister's wife with gusto, given their best for the church, and had no career to fall back on. Since the house did not belong to them, there was no home to split. While he got himself a new living, she was left with the children, homeless and penniless. Only when Frank Field MP raised the scandal in parliament and a support organization called *Broken Rites* was formed, was the church shamed into taking care of them. On the whole Jewish women have been spared that kind of trauma.

Discovering that I could create television programmes, and ultimately winning a national award for one of them, was one of the most exciting and affirming experiences of my life. As my self-confidence was restored, I rearranged the cutlery drawer at home. Most of our belongings were sorted according to what Peter defined as 'logic' – usually the way his mother had arranged them.

Watching smugly on, my mother whispered to my father, 'The worm has finally turned.'

No Jewish woman ever says she is 'just a housewife'. The home is a miniature version of the temple. Her job is to ensure that festivals begin smoothly at sundown, and that the whole extended family relaxes into celebration. It involves choosing the right food, how the table looks, inviting the elderly and the lonely. It means instilling in your children a love for Jewish festivals, so that they will grow up to carry on the traditions of their ancestors. Upon her shoulders rests the very survival of the Jewish people. Not for her the role of second fiddle, like so many Christian leaders' wives who, I discovered, were often backup for their husbands, one step behind him on any platform, but largely running the home and the kids so that he was free to rush out to his ministry with a warm heart and a full stomach.

By the 1990s, however, even Jewish women were refusing to be fobbed off with the promise of power in the home. My niece, at twelve, celebrated her *Bat chayil*, or 'Blessing of the Daughter', with ten of her friends. It was not, the rabbi was at pains to explain, the female equivalent of a *Bar Mitzvah*. Reform Jewry may well have submitted to that particular social pressure, but not the orthodox. This was a graduation from Hebrew classes. Each of the girls read out a piece she had prepared about her favourite Jewish heroine. Some were biblical, some medieval, some contemporary. Each had changed the world in which she lived. The girls sat down and the rabbi, with barely a glance in their direction, got up to give his address. His students, he claimed, had been well prepared by their female teachers to fulfil that high calling of every Jewish woman – to be a wife and mother. The girls were manifestly unimpressed, as the brightly coloured bubbles of their aspirations were so summarily burst.

Sitting along the row from me was my cousin whose only son had been killed recently in a car crash. What did the rabbi's words make her feel, I wondered? What sort of a mockery was made of her life if the young man she had just buried was her only reason for existence? The women whose lives the girls had just described were women in their own right, valued for who they were, not in relation to anyone else, not for what their bodies produced.

Jewish women have shaped the destiny of their people. Adam, Abraham, and Jacob, Jewish men everywhere have always listened to their wives. 'Women persuade men to good as well as evil, but they always persuade', says the old Jewish saying. Miriam, the sister of Moses, was a prophetess in her own right, Deborah was a wise and much loved leader, Huldah was consulted on matters of state, and Esther, Ruth, Hannah, Abigail and Bathsheba all had major roles to play. Even race and religion are handed on through the mother's line. This is why there are two different genealogies for Jesus in the Gospels, one showing his priestly descent through Joseph's line. The other, through Mary, proves beyond doubt that he was a genuine Jewish boy.

Evidence from excavated inscriptions in Israel now suggests that at the time of Christ and for some time after, women served as council members, and even as leaders, of local synagogues. They participated in services. They even sat beside the men. Centuries would pass before rabbinic edict, under the influence of Islam, banished women to an upstairs gallery. Even then, some became chasidic rabbis – Perele of Kozienice, Malkele the Triskerin and Hannah Rachel, the Maid of Ludomir. But on the whole, being the rabbi's wife was power enough. 'He who has no wife,' said one eminent rabbi, 'lives without good or help or joy or blessing or atonement.' The Yiddish writer Isaac Bashevis Singer tells the story of the sage who was about to perform an exorcism on a dead chicken, which kept sighing loudly every time its purchaser put it on the table to prepare it for the Sabbath lunch. In came his wife, who promptly removed its oesophagus, and solved the problem.

The Hebraic tradition of woman as earthy, practical and the salvation of her people, is a far cry from the portrait painted by the early church fathers. From their jaded perspective, based on Aristotle, Socrates and Plato, she had no real contribution to make to intellectual or religious life, and was a sexual snare to the male. Augustine felt that 'nothing so casts down the manly mind from its height as the fondling of women and those bodily contacts which belong to the married state.' Abstinence from all sexual contact was the only route to spiritual purity. And never in the Christian West did woman really manage to regain the status in home or church which belonged to her Jewish neighbours.

I finally began to understand that this historic negativity also contributed to the ambivalence many Christian women felt about their body and its desires, and explained the unattractive clothing they often used to cover themselves up – a real mystery for a Jewish girl. Even as a child I was surprised at how non-Jews opted for beige and grey. In my early days in the church some girls thought that to be spiritual enough to get a man meant resorting to 'mish' dressing. 'Mish', was short for 'missionary' – a stereotype in dowdy, post-war, tweed suit and brogues, with hair scraped back in a bun. Apart from skirt lengths, I couldn't see why 1940s fashion was so much godlier than the 1960s variety.

At a conference I shared a bedroom with two young women who worked for a Jewish missionary society and who, to my mind, were quite shockingly mish. Both looked middle-aged in their twenties. At night one of them took the pins out of her bun and let masses of glorious chestnut hair cascade over her shoulders.

'Wow,' I gasped, as she sat at the dressing table, brushing her mane, 'You really are stunning. Why don't you leave it down like that?'

I saw her blush in the mirror.

'Oh, I couldn't,' she said, in her lovely Scottish lilt.

I detected a faint hint of wistfulness.

'Why not? You look so much younger.'

Smiling, she surveyed her reflection in the mirror, moved her head from side to side, then sighed and put down the brush. 'It wouldn't be... seemly.'

I wasn't sure what she meant, but it struck me that she was seeking to please her society's bosses, rather than fulfil her calling.

'Look girls,' I said to them, in exasperation one night, 'Didn't the Apostle Paul say something clever about being a Jew amongst Jews and a Gentile to the Gentiles? Do you want to get to know younger members of the Jewish community or not? Because if you do, you're going to have to dress very differently. You're never going to relate to any Jewish woman looking like a hillbilly granny in the Waltons.'

I could see they knew the truth of it. They looked sheepish – or rather, muttonish – and I gave up. After all, I knew what a powerful pull conforming to accepted standards could be.

It wasn't just women who weren't at ease in their own skin, and tried to hide it or repress its immense capacity for sensual enjoyment. In nature the male of the species wears bold colours, prances and preens and makes a spectacle of himself to attract the female. Throughout history men have worn bows and breeches, velvet and brocade, powdered wigs and painted beauty spots. But unlike the rabbi or imam with their upstanding gait, some of the Christian men I met shuffled round with sloping shoulders in unflattering puce and puke colours, afraid of standing out in a crowd, of expressing individuality or sensuality, ashamed of their very masculinity. Apart from church dignitaries in certain denominations, who robe in scarlet and purple, men are as condemned as women to a rather dull existence, unless they have the courage to break free.

Walking to the synagogue on the Sabbath, the Jewish community is a heaving mass of rainbow-bright colours. Flamboyance is part of the culture. The women perched on the synagogue balcony look, and sound, like canaries in an aviary. There's a favourite story about Hymie Cohen who is walking down the street one day when a flying saucer lands in front of him and a Martian climbs out, dressed in a wonderful lurex outfit.

'Love the suit,' says Hymie, approaching the Martian slowly. 'Does everyone wear that kind of thing on Mars?'

'No,' says the Martian, 'only we Jews.'

Though there may well be more than just a fair smattering of designer gear in the synagogue, wearing bright and interesting clothes doesn't necessarily mean a bulging wallet. The Jews refer disparagingly to the cheaper items in their wardrobe as *schmatters*, or rags. My vicar's-wife wardrobe was full of them. And I must say that the clothes which were most admired, which gave me most satisfaction, were always my own creations, usually something several sizes too big found in a charity shop, unpicked and recut. They were unique. There weren't thousands like them hanging on pegs in department stores up and down the country. They were truly 'me'. No one else would have worn them, that's for sure. Once I went out to work I could afford to buy them, and though today I am an inveterate bargain hunter, hardly ever prepared to pay full price for anything, I don't have half the pleasure which using my own creative imagination gave me.

Generations of pious churchwomen have been inhibited by the Apostle Peter's admonition not to plait the hair, wear gold or dress up in fine clothing. Instead, he said, put on the inner jewellery of a 'quiet and gentle spirit'. Modesty and piety became equated with drabness. The great Spanish Carmelite and mystic, Teresa of Avila, writing about her mother in the sixteenth century, said she was a very virtuous woman. 'Though extremely beautiful, she was never known to give any reason for supposing that she made the slightest account of her beauty; and though she died at thirty-three, her dress was already that of a person advanced in years.' How unutterably depressing to think that looking old before one's time could ever be a sign of virtue. In fact, Teresa of Avila's mother had twelve children before she was thirty-three. That was why she looked like a shrivelled old prune.

The Apostle Peter lived in a culture heavily divided by wealth and status, and what he deplored was showing off. I soon discovered that in professional life, a world largely dominated by men, a woman has to do a certain amount of 'power dressing'. What she wears may hold the key to what she achieves. Peter's words didn't condemn me to dreariness. They were a reminder that it's what we are inside that counts – a vital truth in a world dominated by superficial judgments.

There is no doubt that in the sixties, many Christians feared the unleashed, uncontrollable flood of sexual awareness. I was bowled over by a book by missionary doctor Anne Townsend called *Faith Without Pretending*, where she told the story of her attempt to take her own life and the painful rebuilding process which followed. It echoed so much of what I had seen around me in the past twenty years. Instead of liberating her, Christianity had frozen the real woman inside. Gradually, as the thawing, healing process progressed, her senses reawakened. She gave herself time to lie on the grass and feel the warmth of the sun on her body, to inhale the scent of lavender, let the sparrows peck her arms and listen to the gentle buzzing of the bees. She walked by the sea, revelling in the taste of salt on her lips and the wind whipping her hair. She began to discover what it meant to be truly alive. As her dormant sexuality gently awakened she bought jeans for the first time, watched the sort of television programmes she would have once switched off in case she was caught watching them, and was tickled by delicious new stirrings within her own burgeoning femininity. To her amazement, God came to her in a new, tangible way, putting his arms around her, holding her in a warm and loving embrace, leading her by the hand out into a world which shone and sparkled, as if she were seeing it for the first time.

If being 'born again' means anything, it must make a person feel doubly, not less, alive. 'Heaven above is brighter blue, earth around is richer green', said the hymn-writer, and that was certainly my experience. The world, as I had never seen it before, dazzled me. Every sensation was sharper, every colour more vivid. Then, over the next months and years, I was encouraged to mistrust my senses and use my poor brain instead – even though it seemed unnatural to switch them off, like a mobile phone, at the church door.

In Hebraic thought, mind, body and spirit cannot be divided in that kind of arbitrary way. The senses are not a poor second to the intellect, as they were in the Greek-Roman philosophy that had influenced the early church. 'Shalom' or 'wholeness', requires a total integration, or integrity, of the human persona. My childhood was infused with the taste and smell of freshly baked *chollah* and crisp, crunchy, unleavened bread, with pungent, slightly acrid herbs like horseradish, and sweeter symbols like apples, almonds and cinnamon; with the burgundy glow of wine in a silver cup, and twinkling candles; with the silky feel of the satin of a prayer shawl or bread coverlet, and smooth, shiny pebbles; with the haunting rise and fall of human voices chanting, and the shrill blast of the ram's horn. Judaism is an accessible religion. It can be touched, felt, smelt, heard and tasted. It created a thousand subconscious impressions in my childhood mind, associations which have never left me and well up, unbidden, at the most surprising moments. One whiff of the familiar smell of oil of cloves used to line our cavities at the dentist, and instead of lying in the chair with my mouth wide open like a dying goldfish, I am transported to some joyful Jewish festival.

The Catholic Church has known the value of the senses for centuries, positively encouraging its followers to sublimate sexual feelings into religious ecstasy. The more non-conformist the church becomes, the more ill-at-ease with sensuality of any kind. Out with the candles, with colour, with smells and bells, with all but absolutely unavoidable symbols. Both traditions have moved a long way away from their Jewish roots. For the Jew a symbol is only a symbol. The horseradish used at the Passover has no magical qualities. We used to grow it in our back garden in Coventry, near the dustbins, only because it wasn't available on that one occasion when we needed it. It's a tenacious weed. Fortunately we moved house before it took over, but our successor wasn't best pleased. In the service it represents the bitterness of the Jewish people in captivity. Leftovers can be thrown on the compost heap. No such irreverent treatment for any symbol in the Catholic Church. It is elevated out of everyday life and placed in a special building or receptacle. You may see and hear and smell, but only the initiated may touch or feel. On the other hand, the low-church tradition is so afraid that the people might invest it with special powers and worship it, that the poor symbol is thrown out of the window altogether.

Peter came back from a retreat in Wales with a gnarled branch he had found when he was out walking. He stuck it on the dresser in the dining room among the china ornaments.

'Take that filthy thing out of my dining room,' I shouted in true Jewish Mama fashion. It looked to me like just another walking-stick he had collected, the way men do, when they graduate from stamps, stones and toy soldiers.

'But I like it there,' he said. 'It spoke to me.'

I looked at it with new eyes. My husband isn't given to conversing with inanimate objects.

'What did it say?' I asked him carefully.

'Well, it speaks to me of the beauty of the natural order. I like carving wood, creating something out of raw material. This piece doesn't need carving. It's already beautiful, as if God had worked on it himself.'

'And it wouldn't be telling you by any chance, that it would rather go out in the garden, where it belongs?'

He looked hurt, so I left it where it was, planning to remove it after a few days. But the branch grew on me. I began to love its knobbly old shape too, and to appreciate it as the work of a master craftsman. Like Anne Townsend, I had to learn to open the doors of my mind to my senses again, to appreciate the world of potential symbols in my orbit, and as I did so, I felt I became a little more integrated, a little more whole again.

Repressing our sensuality inevitably leads to ambivalence about our sexual feelings too. The Greek-Roman culture that so influenced the church was suspicious of the body with its needs and pleasures. Our spiritual father Augustine's view of 'the shame which attends all sexual intercourse' certainly doesn't reflect Hebraic thought. In fact, one of the Jewish holy books says that after creation was finished, the last thing God did was watch Adam and Eve enjoying sexual intercourse. That prompted him to say that his work was 'very good'. In other words, 'That idea of mine has certainly gone down well.'

When an angel tells Sarah that she and Abraham will have a son, she laughs at the idea, not, according to my Bible, because she's ninety and too old to have a baby. What she actually says is, 'At our age, can Abraham and I have pleasure together?' The entire spiritual destiny of human beings hangs in the balance, and what is Sarah thinking about? Sex. Can Abraham actually manage it? But surprise, surprise, there is obviously life in the old boy yet. Most men smile for a fortnight when my husband tells them his father was born when his grandfather was seventy-two.

Sex, for the Jew, is sacred. The Hebrew word for marriage, *kiddushim*, comes from *kaddosh*, the word for 'holy'. But 'holy' for the Jew does not mean, 'put on a pedestal', removed from everyday life. It means it is a special gift, to be enjoyed and appreciated to the full. Unlike the Christian view of chastity, chastity in Judaism is not the avoidance of all sex, but of illicit sex. Within marriage it is to be experienced whenever possible, as often as possible, and is all but compulsory on festivals. The Law says a man must give his wife pleasure on the Sabbath. Nowhere does it say that he himself is entitled to it. Hundreds of years before the Christian world woke up to the female orgasm, Jewish men knew their duty. And since duty isn't always enough to ensure wifely satisfaction, the rabbi often gives preparation courses, providing the necessary, vital information.

For most married couples, no matter how loving, sex can be an act of profound spiritual and emotional oneness on one occasion, then simply be a means of gratifying a craving the next. Like food, it can be taken thoughtfully and prayerfully, fully conscious of the richness of its symbolism. Or it can simply satisfy the appetite. And, says Judaism, the two different approaches divide human beings from animals. Only humans are made in the image of God. It is the way an act is performed, and the intention behind it, which determines whether it is holy, a special gift or not.

Never is there any suggestion that procreation is the only justification for the sex act. Nor is contraception prohibited, except among the fundamentalists. Some whisper that they only make love through a hole in a sheet, but it is a myth perpetrated by the less orthodox, who find it hard to imagine that anyone walking around with side-curls and top hat by day, can abandon themselves to unbridled eroticism at night. The only real restriction is during menstruation. Many Jewish women argue that they rather like that guaranteed little rest from time to time, a monthly chance of a few early nights and a good book. Self-denial for a few days can add a certain sparkle to the resumption of the relationship. Anticipation is a vital part of pleasure.

A 'Judaeo-Christian' tradition in sexual matters is almost an oxymoron – a contradiction in terms. The religion which gave birth to one of the most erotic love poems ever written is light years away from one dogged by the idea that sex was the most unfortunate mistake God ever made. It is no coincidence that in my Jewish prayer book is the Song of Songs in its entirety – the only book of the Bible to be included there in full. I have rarely seen a short quotation in any Christian prayer book. Nor is it often the subject of sermons. But then, being full of breasts and belly buttons, that might be a little difficult.

Sex at its best can be a spiritual experience, the ultimate communion between two human beings, the visible symbol of God's union with his people. At its worst it can be a disaster. It is inevitable, in some way, that such a great gift should be so easily abused. Its graphic portrayal on our television screens, when every couple manage wild, total and simultaneous ecstasy in thirty seconds flat has done everyone a great disservice. It hardly inspires the idea that the sex relationship, like any sport, may require years of training and practice. And occasional outside advice. For if the church does not talk about the immense joy of married sex, nor does it talk about the immense sense of failure or frustration it can cause when it goes wrong. Despite our so-called 'openness' on the subject, sex is more of a taboo than it ever was, and the same web of silence we weave around death, is woven about this vital part of our lives. We dare not ask for help without a sense of shame, when it could, and perhaps should, be the most natural thing in the world.

At around fifteen years into our marriage, Peter and I both decided that our relationship was feeling a little 'same-ish' and dull. Neither said anything to the other, because we couldn't quite work out what the problem was. Peter went away on his own to study for ten days. And while we were apart, as couples do in enforced absence, we thought a great deal about our sex life. Both of us realized, separately, that it felt as if we had been eating minced beef all the time, when chilli con carne, or curry, lasagne and moussaka were all on the menu. Without conferring, we decided to do something about it once we were together again, and prayed for a renewed sense of being God's gift to each other, which we had felt so strongly at the beginning.

His return was a second honeymoon, though much better than the first, because we were more sure of each other, safer, more confident. We spent an extraordinary week. It was a journey of discovery, each learning what the other had imagined in their wildest dreams, each learning to give, as well as receive, in a new way. The Hebrew word for intercourse is *yada*, from the verb 'to know'. God gives human beings the opportunity to know and delight in the hidden recesses of every part of mind and body of their spouse. And though, sadly, because of work and children, we couldn't sustain the pace for longer, the raptures of those few days have never really died away.

God's special relationship with Israel, Christ with his church, no other relationship is as elevated as marriage. No other relationship is as vulnerable therefore. Promiscuity and adultery are not frowned upon because the Almighty is a killjoy who finds sex distasteful and wishes he hadn't created it, but because he deeply loves those who will be appallingly hurt by its misuse. Jewish law maintains that the marriage relationship must be characterized, above all, by mutual respect and loyalty. When that breaks down, as in the case of Michal, wife of King David, who mocked her husband for dancing for joy before the ark of the covenant, something in the relationship withers. Michal never had children...

possibly because she and her husband never had sex again. He certainly began to take other wives. But when loyalty, respect, trust, and humour remain alive and well, sex is one of God's unbeatable jokes.

Chapter 14

Auntie Beeb, the Blitz and Being in the Money

orking in an office for the first time opened my eyes to a micro-environment I never knew existed. All over the country there are thousands of miniature kingdoms with their own language, legislation, culture and politics, each with their own intrigue, in-jokes and power struggles. I loved the banter, the teasing, the easy camaraderie. I loathed the groaning, griping, and back-stabbing. It can be a very creative environment when positive ideas are bounced like balls from one to another. It can be immensely destructive when the balls land on the floor and people fall over them. The best democratic system can be destroyed by petty arguments and grudging resentment. But most offices opt for dictatorship rather than democracy, and the thirst for power does the oddest things to the nicest people. It makes them manipulative and underhanded. I sometimes came home feeling sad and tainted.

I learned very quickly that the one who wielded the greatest power was she who shared the boss' bed – in our case, the production secretary. The producer's every judgment of his team's character, every decision on programming, was based on the sweet nothings she whispered in his ears *in delecto flagrante*. And that taught me an invaluable lesson about being married to the minister.

At a conference a dear little elderly nun insisted on asking me repeatedly what my function was as the minister's wife. Eventually I understood what she was driving at.

'I am a member of the congregation like any other, a lay person with no special favours or influence.'

'Right,' she said, and skipped away, happy at last.

But she was wrong. I had a special hotline to the vicar. The workplace had shown me that I could modify his sterner judgments, or aggravate an already difficult situation. I suddenly realized that unless I consciously recognized the power I had, I would never use it carefully, wisely, generously or fairly.

Not everyone appreciated the benefits I was reaping from the workplace. My gem of a mother-in-law, who often cared for the children after school when the vicar was off on a mission, implied obliquely that her son and grandchildren were not being cared for adequately. One or two church members let me know that they would have preferred a minister's wife who was there for them. Others hinted darkly at the long-term emotional damage to children of working mothers. One turned up one day and told me in no uncertain terms that the church could have understood my doing a caring job like nursing or teaching, acceptable professions for a minister's wife, but not an unproductive, glamorous job in the media. If she could have only seen me chasing lighting and sound engineers across fields in my anorak and wellies.

Within two years everyone knew exactly what I was doing and even what I was saying – and they were much the happier for it. I was invited to front the three-hour daily lunchtime programme on the new BBC Radio Coventry and Warwickshire station, combining it with some ongoing presenting for Central TV. But if the church enjoyed my new role as radio presenter, I did not. I hated being cooped up in a studio like a battery hen without daylight for several hours a day. The sound desk, which was like a flight deck on an aeroplane, resisted all my attempts to master it. And with twelve live guests a programme, not to mention the half-dead ones that were hard to interview, it was inevitable that the same spokespeople were rolled into the studio day after day. I found myself stifling the yawns, despite knowing that the support staff watching my performance through the glass would have killed for my job.

Salvation came in the form of the fiftieth anniversary of the blitz of Coventry. In 1942 this centre for arms manufacturing had all but been razed to the ground by the German airforce. Thousands of ordinary civilians were killed. It had subsequently emerged that Churchill might well have known of the planned attack, but could do nothing to save the city for fear of giving away the fact that the allies had cracked Enigma, the secret German code. Fifty years of commemoration and celebration rubbed shoulders, for as we remembered those who lost their lives, we also celebrated the resilience of the human spirit rising above devastation and despair, to build a new life for future generations.

The anniversary had an extraordinary, unforeseen impact. Older members of our congregation began to share the pain they had buried with their loved ones so long ago and never spoken of again.

'How could we cry?' Dorothy explained to me. 'Everyone had lost someone. About half the class of children I taught were killed. The school was in a poor part of the city. They had no air raid shelters. And then my fiancé was shot down on active service. But why should I be entitled to my grief any more than anyone else? We put a brave face on. We all had to be strong for each other.'

On a programme I was making for Radio 4, I asked her to describe the blitz. She said that the following morning she had tried to cross the city to collect her sister from hospital, because even the hospital had been bombed and could only handle urgent cases.

'I set off, picking my way through the rubble, then began to feel frightened. I hadn't a clue where I was. All the familiar landmarks had gone. It left me with a feeling of total disorientation. At last I found the cathedral, or what was left of it. I'll never forget the sense of utter desolation I felt when I first saw what had happened to it... the place where I loved to worship every week. Among the debris, the Provost had found two charred beams. He formed them into a cross, and we met around it, as usual, the following Sunday, in one of the crypts. And perhaps our worship meant more to us that morning than it had ever done, as we sat, stripped of all man-made trimmings, thankful for the very gift of existence.'

The cathedral ruins were left where they stood. It is a rather wild and desolate spot, despite being right in the centre of the city. The wind whips around the stark, jagged pieces of stonework, and in one corner is the charred cross, above it the words, 'Father, forgive'. The modern cathedral, adjacent to it, is a visible symbol of resurrection, the new structure rising like a phoenix out of the ashes.

A gracious Queen Mother, who had come to the city in the wake of the disaster to comfort the people, attended the commemoration service there to what the Nazis had called, 'Operation Moonlight'. As a grand piano picked out the haunting chords of Beethoven's 'Moonlight Sonata', thousands of leaves, one for each person who had died, swished softly down from the ceiling to the floor, like a gentle waterfall. Some, who had never been free to weep before, wept at last.

In the evening, as crowds filled the city for the great procession, the atmosphere became more like a carnival. Sitting on the BBC Radio float, waiting to move off, I couldn't shake off the interview I had recorded that afternoon with one of the many special visitors to the city, a Czech woman who had been forced to watch the Nazis round up and kill every man and boy in her town.

'We were left,' she said in a soft, lilting voice, 'a town of grieving women. But we survived.' There was no bitterness in her gentle face. With a fond, proud smile, she introduced me to her companion, a gracious man in his mid forties, the first male child born in Lidice after the war. Hard-nosed journalist that I was, I cried all the way through the city centre back to the radio studio, clutching my precious tape. I wept for Lidice, for a world which still hadn't learned its lesson from their tragedy, and for my own shallowness in the face of such grace and courage.

Initially, sitting on a float in a procession seemed a superficial way to acknowledge such immense human pain and courage. And then all the city lights were switched off, and in complete darkness a deep silence fell for two minutes, broken only when, unaccompanied, through the loudspeakers, Dame Vera Lynn's voice, as powerful as ever, resounded through all the streets with, 'When the Lights Go on Again All Over the World'.

I was transported in time to a world I only dimly knew through the moving recollections of my mother-in-law. My father-in-law had been a prisoner of war for four years, living in a hell he could never speak about once he was free.

'When Paul was released and rang me for the first time, he knew I wouldn't be able to cope, so he told me he would ring again later and hung up. And then, there he was, at the station, pale and bloated, too weak to lift his empty suitcase. But he was home. Life could begin again.'

It was a story I made my mother-in-law tell me over and over again, and she never tired of telling it. For him, the starvation, isolation and humiliation. For her, the separation, dodging bombs in London and torpedoes in the Atlantic, protecting her babies and bringing them up alone. They survived, their love and faith intact and stronger than ever. But post-war life wasn't easy. Paul hadn't seen their little daughter for four years. He had never seen their son. So much rebuilding. The commemoration day, procession and all, was a fitting tribute. It convinced me of the importance of pageants, fête days, carnivals, all manner of public and communal reminiscence and celebration.

One apparent benefit of my going out to work was that for the first time in our lives we were no longer so stretched financially. And then discovered that having more than just enough money caused a great deal of extra work and heart-searching. I had begun to grow very weary of our hand-to-mouth existence as we tried to survive on a single stipend. Before I went out to work, I had been doing some public speaking, but extracting even expenses could resemble a surgical procedure. An honorarium, other than a bouquet, was rare. But flowers, nice as they are, didn't pay National Insurance or food and fuel bills. They, presumably, were paid by the Great Banker in the Sky – without a thought that human beings might be his designated paymasters. And I was too nice to ask – or just too inhibited.

Where did the inhibitions come from? Not from my background, that's for sure. There's an old joke about a Jewish man knocked down by a car.

'Are you comfortable?' asks a bystander who has wrapped him in his coat.

'I make a living,' comes the reply.

Jews will never admit to being anything more than 'comfortable', in case God is playing a little game with them – so don't tempt fate. Dying is not the worst thing a Jewish man can do to his wife. Dying and not providing for her is the ultimate failure. Husbands after all are replaceable – often to be found on Mediterranean cruises. That's why the widow needs the legacy – to afford the cruise.

It is hardly surprising, after centuries of grinding poverty, of exclusion from professional life, of insecurity and persecution, that the Jews should develop an obsession with survival. And money helps. It provides opportunities and choices, a sense of personal worth and value. It opens doors. The lack of it ensnares the poor in a stranglehold of powerlessness and rejection.

Unfortunately the attitude of the Jews to money, their openness on the subject, is often regarded by outsiders as crass. The money-grabbing caricature, carved in the national consciousness by Shakespeare's Shylock, when the means to make it was limited to money-lending, dies slowly. Nationals often resent the wealth of immigrants. Money has a way of making us greedy, grasping and jealous. And it's such a relief to project our covetousness onto its victims. But like any other people Jews can be immensely mean, or immensely generous. Whichever, they rarely do things by half.

Many Christian organizations pay their workers just above the breadline. When my husband was a deacon in the

Free Church in Manchester the elders were invited to the home of one of the trustees to discuss the new minister's salary. They arrived at an expensive, gracious detached house, set in its own spacious grounds, a BMW parked at the top of a sweeping drive, and were shown into a large, lavish sitting room, filled with expensive furniture.

'The man we're inviting to be our pastor,' said the church leaders, sunk so deeply into their armchairs they could barely balance the plates of dainty sandwiches in their hands, 'is at the top of his profession and is leaving it for us. We plan to pay him the equivalent of a top teacher's salary.'

The honourable trustee all but choked into his teacup.

'That seems more than just a little extravagant,' he said.

'Why?' they asked.

'Well... I'm a solicitor and I'm paid a solicitor's salary. A pastor should be paid a pastor's salary.'

'Which,' they replied triumphantly, 'if we're going to follow the New Testament to the letter, should be double your pay.'

Many pastors and ministers are forced to live on such a small income that they cannot afford a basic annual holiday or a home in retirement, while most of their congregation would balk at such a hair-shirt existence. It seems as if those who serve the church are expected to live a holy life, unspoilt by too much luxury, on behalf of its punters. And it is yet another example of how detrimental it can be when the spiritual and practical, idealism and reality, are kept in different compartments.

As a Christian I quickly learned to acquire verbal inhibitions on the subject of my earnings and what I did with them, lest I became a caricature of my Jewish self. I am a bit of a squirrel and it came as a nasty shock to discover what percentage of his salary my fiancé had been giving away and intended to go on giving away after our marriage. If I gave up my job, and lived off my man like a regular Jewish matron, how could we repair, decorate and furnish our new home? 'I don't see why I should change the habit of a lifetime, just because I'm marrying you,' he said.

There then ensued the first of many heated discussions on a subject that has never ceased, throughout our married life, to provoke lively debate. Jack Dominion, the marriage counsellor, claims that money is the single greatest cause of marriage breakdown. If couples cannot be totally open in this area of their lives, how will they trust each other in any other? Peter and I called an uneasy truce. He still gives away more of his salary than I give away of mine. He must have more faith, and he is usually vindicated. To this day I have no idea how we managed to spend two years at theological college without any regular income – though, admittedly, we never had any shoes repaired.

But come to my home, and in the great Jewish tradition I would kill the fatted calf. There would be a joint with all the trimmings, even if the family had to starve for the rest of the week, and Peter, if he knew what I had spent, would probably have a nervous breakdown. I also find it much easier to give away extraneous things than he does, on the basis that if my fellow can use and enjoy something more than I do, they ought to have it. Giving appears in many different disguises.

So does taking – in the niggling attitude of some churches, so obsessed with offerings and finances that visitors feel unwelcome; in the penny-pinching refusal of churches to pay their workers what they are worth; in the rampant materialism of the richer churches, paying unnecessary fortunes for the latest tricks and technologies, blissfully unaware of the struggles of their more deprived, 'have-not' neighbours.

Of course Jesus said our right hand shouldn't know what our left hand was doing, but he didn't mean that we should keep both hands well beneath the pew. The sound of small change clinking on the collection plate never ceases to amaze me. It means that the congregation is emptying its purse and pockets of its spare change, an amount which will barely heat the small square foot in which they stand. It means that there has been no forethought about how much to give. It means some poor committee spending hours of nervous energy wondering how and whether to find the resources to satisfy the endless demands of the monster of a building handed down to us from previous generations.

Whatever happened to the Old Testament principle of the tithe, giving away ten per cent of one's income? The Jews don't risk waiting for it to arrive voluntarily. They extract it. Once a year a bill from the local Hebrew Congregation lands on the doormat. The charge is for a seat in the synagogue and access to all associated facilities, including burial. My father objected violently every year when the bill from the orthodox congregation arrived. The problem was that he had started to attend the Reform Synagogue and they sent him a bill too. Why should he buy shares in two opposing companies, when he wasn't even sure he was familiar with the Chief Executive? And then my mother would remind him that if he wanted to have an eternal resting place next to her, then he must contribute towards the plot in the proper place, the orthodox cemetery, which was where she would lie. He always conceded, driven, I suspect, by the necessity of peace with her in this world, rather than the next.

Every year the dues were greater, to keep pace with the cost of heating, lighting, decorating, repairs, the rabbi's salary and expenses. There are many advantages in having such a system. It is a reminder of the practical responsibilities involved in being part of a community. It targets the members rather than the visitors. On the other hand, and herein lies its major disadvantage, it does necessitate being well-off. Rich and poor pay the same, whatever your ability to pay. If you're having a hard time, why should everyone else have to suffer for it? And I suspect that under this system the rabbi rests more easily in his bed than his Christian counterpart. No fundraising problems disturb his beauty sleep.

Never has my husband preached about giving away a minimum 10 per cent of one's income without provoking a ripple of panic. 'How can anyone, in these difficult times, give away such an amount? It's irresponsible. Madness.' Peter understands their sense of confusion. He was unemployed for several months, struggled with his tithe then and on many other occasions since. He always replies that he would love to be able to make it easier for people, but wasn't responsible for laying down the basic guidance.

The problem is that money has a way of worming itself into the very heart of our being, until it is embedded so deeply that it cannot be removed without major surgery. It exercises such control over our thinking that inadvertently, our values become topsy-turvy. The main road outside our home in Coventry was a major accident zone. One Friday night a visitor to a conference at our church was killed instantaneously. The following week there was yet another car crash. Neither driver was hurt, but one of them, a young woman, kept lamenting the state of her car over and over again.

'Last week a woman was killed. You're alive, thank God,' I said to her, 'No one is hurt. The car is only a heap of metal, only money. It's replaceable. You're not.'

But I appeared to be speaking another language. The inanimate box was more important to her than the person in it.

A friend of ours who is a university lecturer receives regular visits from what he refers to as 'men in macs', checking out the records of students who have applied to join the civil or intelligence services. One day his curiosity got the better of him and he asked the visitor, 'In what areas are the people you recruit most vulnerable, most likely to be at risk?'

'In their twenties, it's alcohol,' came the reply, 'In their thirties and forties, it's money. Sex doesn't rear its ugly head until they reach their fifties.'

It's at the age when we rear our families, worry about their education, fall foul of the mid-life crisis and the haunting spectre of not being successful, that money exercises its greatest allure.

We are victims of our alienated society. With little community support we cannot simply give our extraneous income away. We have to 'put a little by', but we dare not let it become our only security, we dare not let money dominate and manipulate us.

This was a lesson Peter and I learned the hard way, but now, looking back, I am glad we did. We didn't know what to do with our first savings. We had altruistic visions of one day buying a cottage for the use of all the poor church ministers who couldn't afford a holiday – and for us, of course. In the end, as a temporary measure, we approached a financial advisor, who advertised in several reputable Christian magazines. He invested our money in a company called Barlow Clowes. And our problem was solved overnight. Mr Clowes needed our money to fund his luxury lifestyle.

One night the television informed us that all our savings had disappeared somewhere between Cheshire and Gibraltar. Worse, the press intimated that those who had been foolish enough to invest in such a company did so out of greed and deserved their lot.

It cushioned the blow when we reminded ourselves that our losses were as nothing compared to the elderly and retired who were divested of lump redundancy sums, pensions, the very means of survival. But we felt sheepish, ashamed to admit that we had lost our savings. On the whole friends were very supportive. As we suspected, one or two, perhaps to the more left of centre, wondered, tactfully of course, whether we ought to have had investments. Ought we to have a mortgage? A car loan? Ought we to own dish washers, washing machines, DVDs, all the paraphernalia of a materialistic age which is supposed to make our lives so much easier and more pleasurable? I do. But I admire my friends who will not be pushed into it, and think carefully before they purchase.

During the months which followed we had bouts of telling ourselves that all we had lost was money, and bouts of real depression as we came to terms with what felt like a bereavement. Our treasure, surgically removed, had left us with a deep, inner wound. Fortunately the manipulation of the knife was so swift we hardly had time to fight or squeal. And when, some years later, the government decided to make good much of what we had lost, it was a welcome surprise, though not a desperate necessity. 'Don't store up treasure which the thief can steal.' Theft, fraud and burglary happened to other people, not to us, not until Barlow Clowes. And it could happen again. We survived, without being tempted to leap off any high buildings, as some did after the Wall Street crash, though we took a bit of a tumble nonetheless. We learned the hard way to hold our purses, bank accounts and credit cards on the open palms of our hands. Hopefully we haven't closed our fists again, for our complex world monetary systems could rob us of all we have overnight. Economic recession hovers like a giant bird of prey over rich and poor alike. And when it strikes, the rich, not the poor, have the most to lose.

The secret is to receive all we have as a loan. There's a story in the Talmud of a woman whose son dies while her husband is away. She doesn't know how to break the news to him when he gets back, and then suddenly an idea occurs to her.

'I borrowed a necklace,' she tells him, 'And while you were away the owner came and asked for it back.'

'And you gave it back, of course,' her husband says to her.

'Well,' she says, 'it was a very valuable necklace. I liked it a lot. I didn't want to part with it.'

'You have no choice, my dear. It doesn't belong to you.'

And at that point she takes her husband by the hand and leads him to the room where their son lies dead.

The story of course has great theological problems. It takes no account of the evils of illness and death, but the principle remains that all that we have comes from God's hands, and he has the right to do with it exactly as he pleases. 'Don't let me have too little lest I curse you, or too much in case I forget you', pleads the Psalmist. It is ironic that the subject we find such a taboo should be the one that Jesus spoke about almost more than any other. But then he was a Jew! And he knew that here was the real test of how much we loved him.

Our financial security was once again put to the test in 1992. The station manager who had employed me moved on to higher things, and was replaced with a new manager who had instructions from the BBC in the Midlands to move in presenters who were still under contract, from another, defunct BBC radio station. I was one of many staff to be asked how soon I could leave. It was an enormous blow to my pride. But I quickly realized that I had two choices – to blame the source of my pain, rant and rage about him behind his back and inflict on him as much damage as my tongue was capable of doing, or, to button up my lips, and accept what had happened as part of some invisible, as yet unknown, plan for my life and take my leave, with dignity, in silence. I opted for the latter – and it half killed me. I virtually had to clamp my tongue between my thumb and first finger, but a few weeks after I took my leave, my former PA rang me.

'It's like a battlefield in here,' she whispered, 'corpses everywhere as the sackings continue, screaming and crying in the corridors and blood on the wall. You didn't make a fuss,' she said reflectively, 'we've all commented on it. Did that have something to do with your faith?'

It was then that Peter saw an advert for a job back up north that seemed to fit the mental identikit we had of where we felt we should be. I wanted to go to a community where the children would flourish, and had ended my long list of requirements with an, 'Oh by the way, God, the seaside would be nice too.'

The mudflats of Morecambe were not exactly what I had in mind – but near enough to the old holiday haunt of Blackpool. And now we were free to go, liberated from the pressure of having to decide whose job was the more important, and which of the two of us would follow the other. The doors to working in the media never opened in quite the same way again, but an unexpected new career opportunity arose.

And the new station manager dropped dead in the work car park one day after he had bicycled in from home. Manifestly his stress was greater than mine.

Chapter 15

In Red Rose County

*W*e were flying down the fast lane of the motorway in her plush, maroon Jaguar, my boss and I, returning to the office after the funeral of one of our much-loved little six-year-olds. 'Do you believe in all that?' she suddenly asked me.

'In what?'

'In heaven. In God. In his having a place for little Jenny?'

When we moved to Lancaster, a city at some distance from any major TV or radio centre, I had suspected it might be time for a career change. I was getting to that age when women presenters have a wrinkle and a sag too many, and besides, I wanted to do something more useful with my skills. A friend at Central Television, who worked part-time as a press officer for the children's hospice in Birmingham, discovered that funds were being raised for a similar hospice in Lancashire, and passed my name on. I found myself with a job I really loved, that confronted me with the difficult issues of life and death in a way nothing had ever quite done before.

'Yes, I do,' I said, eying the speedometer needle, wondering whether that belief was about to become a reality.

'Hmmmmmm...' said the Chairman of the trustees, thoughtfully.

I admired her enormously. What had begun with nursing an elderly aunt had ended with a string of nursing homes, making her one of the wealthiest businesswomen in the area. Despite her success, an inner hole remained, and she was now dedicating most of her time and a great deal of money to building a respite care centre for terminally sick children.

'I'd like to think there was an afterlife, but I'm not sure. It always seems real to me when I go to church. But then, on a Monday morning with a business and a charity to run, it seems remote, and irrelevant somehow. But if faith is only real in church, surely it's a bit of a sham?'

I found myself telling her about my own struggle to live Christianity the Jewish way, to disentangle God from the building and become more in tune with him through life's ordinary events – in food, festivals, and in finding symbols. She listened with interest. 'Why are we never told this? Why aren't we given any guidance?'

That was my question precisely. As the century rolled swiftly to its close, and church attendance was being decimated by the power of post-modern thinking with its rejection of institutions, authority, rationalism, and traditional morality, it became ever more urgent to explore new ways of living out our faith. The Jew in me still kicked me in the guts – often at Communion. The services seemed such a rigid formalization of the warm, happy, homey Sabbath occasions I remembered, that I had to stop myself shouting out, 'What have you done to our *kiddush*?' Jesus never said, 'I want you to have a special service once a week, where you say the right words, form an orderly queue, take a cube of bread on your palm, swallow it with minimal fleshly contact and go back to your seat looking holy and chastened.' He only said, 'When you eat bread and wine, remember me.'

But such thoughts were only symptoms of my indigestible past, I told myself. Regular doses of ecclesiastical antacid would settle it down one day.

I only realized how Jewish I was when I found myself cut off from all that was familiar from childhood. The church just didn't seem able to shake itself out of the Greek-Roman culture in which it grew. In the fourth century, when Emperor Constantine made Christianity the official religion of the Roman Empire, worship moved into a setting that owed more to the amphitheatre than the intimacy of the accessible, daily-ritual setting of home. The Sabbath was officially moved from Saturday to the pagan Sun Day, and Easter was to coincide with the pagan festival of Oester, removing any possible connection to the Passover. Observing a Jewish festival was punishable with excommunication. And so the church was deliberately cut off from any sense of its Jewish roots.

'That was very nice, thank you,' a man said at the door, as he left a Passover service Peter and I had led at a church in Yorkshire. 'I didn't know the Jews use our psalms.'

Only my husband's firm grip on my arm saved the poor innocent from a throttling. But how could he know any better? Human beings who don't know their roots have a sense of disorientation. An adopted child often needs to find its birth parents. Christians without any feel for Judaism flounder in the entirely Hebraic world of the Bible.

It was the colourful traditions and celebrations that preserved the unique, separate identity of the Jewish people, despite centuries of persecution. Their communities have been scattered, their synagogues destroyed, but the faith preserved because it didn't need a building, or even a rabbi, to ensure its survival – just one Jewish home. Like the Greek philosopher Aristotle, Christians uphold family life as the key to a well-ordered society. Jews uphold family life as the key to the survival of Judaism. That is its secret.

The family, in whatever format, cannot survive alone. At no time has commitment to community been more vital than in our alienated, fragmented, self-sufficient Western society, where economics has meant an end to having granny or aunty next door. The Department of Health did a survey into what people wanted from social services. Second on the list was 'company in my loneliness'. Professionals cannot fill a hole like that. But the church could. There is no shortage of surrogate grandparents, aunts and uncles to 'adopt' one-parent families, lone individuals, and the aged. The Apostle Paul tells a largely Gentile, Roman church that they are called 'to make the Jew jealous'. That's a high standard of community to beat.

For the Jew there is no such thing as private religion. His entire existence, from birth to death, is bound up in his community. No man's business is his own affair.

My grandfather's greatest pleasure was to sit on a public bench overlooking the sea on the cliffs at Roker.

'Well, what sort of a day, Dad?' my mother would ask him on the way home.

'Bah! No one even sat next to me,' he would say, some days, with bitter disappointment. But on others, his whole face would be alive with excitement. 'Do you know who I met? Such an interesting man, a plumber with six children. Do you know how much he can earn in a week? But he has no pension, of course.'

All men were his friends. Hours whiled away at the synagogue had taught him to make people his hobby. Where else but in church will two people who have already seen each other on several occasions sit side by side and even share a hymn book, whilst barely saying hello, let alone discover which football team they each support?

What the Jews see as duty, Christians call, 'having someone for a meal'. The latter is optional, despite the command to practise hospitality. The former is not. There must be room at every meal table for the widow, orphan, or stranger, the single person and the student from out of town. My brother will do a detour of sixty miles to give a widowed great aunt a lift to a bridge party. He'll moan about it, but still do what is expected of him. But try to find a volunteer to do a four-mile round trip to bring an elderly person to church every week, and it may well be a problem. We simply do not have that sense of responsibility for our 'relatives'. Yet the church is an institution revolving around the life and sayings of a Jew, founded by Jews, based on a book written by Jews for Jews. It should, in theory, it seems, be just a little bit Jewish. Sitting in my pew, still feeling alienated on occasions, even as the minister's wife, it occurred to me to wonder that if Jesus walked in now, would he know what this was? Would he feel any more at home than I did? Or would he be bemused – a quantum leap for him as much as for me – at how far the church had diverged from its colourful Jewish beginnings?

I longed to be part of a community where joy and sadness, pleasure and regret, blessing and sorrow were fully shared, and drove the pain of isolation away – a community open-minded and accommodating enough to experiment with symbolism, story-telling and celebration. And we found it at St Thomas's in Lancaster. Here was a rare church, secure, adventurous and flexible enough not just to be ecclesiastical guinea pigs, but to throw themselves wholeheartedly into the rather untraditional services Peter and I wanted to try. Many churches had begun to have Passovers in some disguise or other, but few had yet attempted a harvest festival Tabernacles-style. St Tees gave us permission to try.

In an urban society a harvest festival can seem woefully anachronistic. Most of us don't 'plough the fields and scatter'. We nip down to the local supermarket. The ingratitude for the produce we distributed at Normanton, pre and post-strike, finished off any sympathy for the service I ever had.

'He won't eat cauliflower. It gives him wind.'

'What did you say they were, cor-jets? I don't know what to do with them.'

Sukkot, or Tabernacles, not only looked back at God's provision over the past year, but also thanked God for his protection in the present, and looked forward to a messianic age. And that seemed much more all-encompassing and relevant. Jesus himself went up to Jerusalem every year for a week's holiday, to celebrate *Sukkot*, 'The season of our joy'. It was on the seventh day, *Hashanah Rabbah*, the Day of the Great Hosanna, that he spoke some of his most wonderful words.

The children, hoisted onto their fathers' shoulders so that they can watch the Levite choir, wave palm branches. The whole congregation joins in the singing which rises to a crescendo of messianic fervour. There is a long blast on the ram's horn and the priest pours water from the Pool of Siloam over the altar. It flows through the elaborate drainage system in the Temple out into Jerusalem and on into the Dead Sea, while the people cry out, '*Hosheanu*, Lord, save us, send us the Messiah.' In the midst of this unchurch-like hullabaloo of waving, singing, splashing, and trumpeting, Jesus walks to the *bimah* or podium and quietly declares, 'If anyone is thirsty let them come to me and drink. Whoever believes in me, streams of living water will flow from within them.'

So many men complain they have two left feet, but at Tabernacles it's the men who dance – frenetically and all night for seven nights. So at St Thomas' we began the celebration with a ceilidh the evening before. All night for even one night was too much for our men! We built a large tabernacle, made out of the Potter family's tent frame covered in sweet-smelling greenery. With the other traditional symbols of seeds, light, palm branches, water, and trumpet, we tried to recreate the excitement of the original celebration. We may not have succeeded completely, but as services go, it was huge fun, and got better as the years went by and familiarity enabled people to enter more fully into the experience.

'What is it about sitting in that tabernacle?' someone asked me every year. 'It's only the Potters' frame tent they take on holiday.' I didn't expect it to feel any different from the rest of the building, but whether it's the scent of the pine or what, there's a coolness, a tranquillity in there that I can't explain.

According to the New Testament, our 'earthly tabernacle', our physical body, is as fragile and temporary as a *sukkah*. Everything we have and are will disintegrate into dust. We have no permanent home here on earth; we are waiting for one to come. As a minister's wife, forced, because of my man's calling, to move around more often than I might want, I have taken great comfort from those words. A home-loving girl at heart who likes to put her roots down deep, I whither when I'm uprooted. Whenever the going gets rough I long for home, to be where I belong, with the people who know and love me. The problem is, after so many moves, I don't know where home is any more. And I'm grateful to a wise monk who suggested that my condition might be spiritual, rather than geographical.

Since a Tabernacles harvest festival worked so well at St Thomas', we decided to have a go at celebrating Pentecost, the birthday of the church. It's Hebraic precursor *Shavuot* was a spring harvest festival, but has come to be associated with the giving of the ten commandments on Mount Sinai. *Shavuot*, like the word Pentecost, means fifty. The children of Israel arrived at the Dead Sea. The Egyptians gave chase but the waters parted and they walked on into freedom. Apparently, it took exactly fifty days from crossing the Dead Sea to arrive at Mount Sinai. But what were they free for? To do as they pleased? Sadly, humans have a tendency to abuse each other with their individual freedom. *Liberté, égalité, fraternité* is the French motto, but for many of the French, *liberté* is what matters most. The problem is that the rights of the individual have a tendency to supercede *égalité* and *fraternité*. Like a river, freedom needs banks to prevent it from becoming an unleashed, destructive force.

Torah means 'direction', rather than law, guidance for communal living rather than a harsh and rigid set of regulations The ten commandments were intended to protect the people from a great deal of unnecessary hurt and pain. The idea was that such would be their quality of life that the whole world would want to know the secret of their happiness. That was what constituted being a 'chosen people'. There's an old Jewish joke that goes: God went to the Egyptians and asked them if they would like a commandment. 'What sort of a commandment?' they asked. 'Well, something like "thou shall not commit adultery,"' replied God. The Egyptians thought about it, then said, 'No thanks, that would ruin our weekends.' So God went to the Assyrians and asked them if they would like a commandment. 'Like what?' they also asked.' 'Well,' God said, 'Like "thou shalt not steal."' The Assyrians immediately replied, 'No thanks. That would ruin our economy.' So finally God went to the Jews and asked them if they wanted a commandment. 'How much would it cost?' 'They're free,' said God. And the Jews said, 'Great! We'll take ten!'

Such is human nature that it's almost impossible to keep all ten, community-building as they are. The forbidden so often appears the most attractive fruit. Out of utter heart-break the prophet Ezekiel promised that one day God would have only one solution, and write his directions on his people's hearts, not on tablets of stone.

Year by year the Jews count down the days from the barley harvest (which happened to be resurrection Sunday) to *Shavuot*, the wheat harvest. 49, 48, 47... 10, 9, 8, 7... It must have provided a wonderful build up to the festival. And after the resurrection the disciples would have been waiting like everyone else, though that particular Pentecost unable to say exactly what they were waiting for. 'Power from on high' was what the Master had promised. They had no clear idea what that meant – until the day itself, when three thousand are baptized in the *mikvaot*, the ritual baths, which alone could process three thousand immersions in fifteen minutes. Just as the giving of the Law on Mount Sinai was the birthday of the Jewish community, this is the birthday of the Christian community known as the church.

At St Tees we introduced a large, fifty-day calendar on Easter Day, scratching out seven days on every Sunday for seven weeks. Since red – speaking of fire, power and glory – is the official liturgical colour for Pentecost, and since the Jews of old used to mark the first fruits of their harvest by tying a red thread around them, we decorated the church with twigs, branches, and red silk flowers, held together in clusters with big red bows. Everyone was encouraged to wear something red, and my engineer husband designed two wind machines that blew red chiffon flames into the air. We re-enacted the first Pentecost story with the traditional Temple readings, drum rolls, trumpet blasts, and various other sound effects, ending in a more reflective frame of mind as we committed ourselves to receiving enough power from on high to live as the followers we professed to be. Integrating a Hebraic and Christian spirituality is not without its critics.

'Aren't you just trying to be Jewish?' one of our rather earnest university students suggested. 'And haven't we superceded all of that?'

Superceded what – colour, fun, joy, celebration, a spirituality that touches the heart and not merely the head?

I must say I have learnt at last to appreciate the great wealth of history and rich tradition in which the Church of England is steeped, and though the Anglican prayer book will possibly never call from me the same emotional response as the *shema*, the *kiddush*, or even *yiskedal*, the prayers of mourning, yet I have come to value its liturgies and prayers. Its gentle, usually unobtrusive, authority structure has created a very secure, safe and open place, where I could inflict myself on some very gracious congregations, experiment, innovate, make mistakes, learn, develop and grow.

Being married to a minister has its compensations and privileges, and not just a parking space near the church. Working like a pit horse to subsidize my husband's stipend wasn't easy, and at times I resented the assumption that, if we wanted family holidays, a university education for our children, and a home of our own one day, that I would have to provide it. On the other hand, a career turned out to be immensely and surprisingly satisfying. With the children's hospice up and running, and just as I was wondering what next, I was introduced to Carolyn Johnson, a barrister who was exchanging the law for a job as chair of the board of the brand new Preston Hospitals Trust in Lancashire. She invited me to be her press officer, which was scary, since I knew so little about the NHS, but I would be the first in Lancashire – so no comparisons could be made. Carolyn was a dream to work with – dynamic, caring, imaginative, and innovative. To the horror of the traditionalists who seemed to think no one should feel happy in a hospital, she turned a typical, anonymous Dickensian waiting room into a shopping mall, and introduced soft furnishing and soft music to some of the clinics. But sadly, a change of government brought a change of chair, so I moved on to the Blackpool Community Trust, traipsing up and down the prom as I had when I was a child on holiday at the Norbreck Castle, only now, instead of a bucket and spade, I had a pen and notepad as I drove from one community hospital to another gathering stories for the press. Then, yet another government re-shuffle of the NHS brought in a supervisory tier of organization called 'strategic health authorities', and I ended up supporting and supervising around thirty communications managers when I inadvertently became Head of Communications for the whole of the NHS in Cumbria and Lancashire.

Peter had pushed me into an interview for a job I never thought I stood a chance of getting, and wasn't sure I wanted. 'And how will you encourage the staff to communicate better?' the chair of the strategic health authority asked me. With nothing to lose, I answered, 'I'll tell them Alan Bennett's story of when he went to a London hospital for an X-ray and asked the receptionist for directions. 'Second floor,' she said, without looking up from her magazine. He wanted to shake her until her teeth rattled and say to her, 'You have the power, as much as any consultant in this hospital, to make your patients feel better simply by being nice, so be nice – you cow.' The genial chair smiled broadly, and my heart sank. 'Blow it, I've got the job.'

It turned out to be one of the biggest learning curves of my whole life. I had never planned on becoming a political animal, delivering the government's health agenda, or even playing she-who-must-be-obeyed. For four years I felt out of my depth and challenged, frustrated and fulfilled, exhausted and exhilarated – and so glad to have been given the chance. I learnt the art of looking knowledgeable, while being completely ignorant, praying continuously for wisdom. And miraculously, skills I never consciously knew I had were there when I most needed them. Or perhaps they simply fell from heaven at the right moment like a ripened fruit. My greatest sorrow was that my father hadn't lived to see how health care would become a vital part of my life, as it had in his, and as he always hoped it would.

Chapter 16

Let Children Be the Barometer

When Israel stood on Mount Sinai ready to receive the Law, so the old Jewish legend goes, God said to them, 'I don't know whether it's worth giving you the Torah or not. First, bring me some sort of guarantee that you will keep it.'

'King of the Universe,' they said, 'Our ancestors are our guarantee.'

But God said, 'Your ancestors would never have kept it. You'd better bring me a better guarantee than that.'

'Our prophets will be our guarantee then,' they replied.

'Your prophets are as bad,' God said, 'Can't you do better than that?'

Eventually Israel said, 'Our children will be our guarantee.'

And God said, 'You're right. They are the best guarantee. For your children's sake, I will give you the Law.'

There's a tendency in individualistic Christianity not to see beyond our own three score years and ten to the potential of our children. 'God has no grandchildren,' said the Dutch preacher, Corrie Ten Boom, who spent years in Ravensbruck for hiding Jews during the Second World War. She was right, in that unlike Judaism, faith and redemption are matters of will, not birth. If the Talmud sees children as a divine trust, how much more should those of us who believe that their future is by no means guaranteed by their parenting?

Neither Peter nor I will ever forget that extraordinary moment when we held our first baby in our arms. All of five minutes old, he looked like a little old man, with wrinkled walnut skin, and fine, fluffy hair, but he was ours, and we thought he was beautiful. In the face of such an extraordinary miracle there seemed little else to do but dedicate him, there and then, to his creator. Despite enough visits to the local casualty department to entitle us to shares in the hospital, that commitment has never really been put to the test. I know from friends who have been where Abraham stood with his beloved Isaac, that it is the most desolate place in the whole world. Nothing is so terrible, so sad, as losing a child. When Martin, my uncle, though only four years older, died at twenty-seven, my grandmother lost her hopes, her dreams, her future. The family line had been cut off, and all the years of mothering and worrying seemed a futile waste of time.

Only after two years as press officer for Derian House Children's Hospice appeal did I fully appreciate how precious a life is. Some of the children were severely disabled, brain damaged by the progressive ravages of their disease, but no smile ever had the ability to give me the pleasure that theirs did. The very fact that a child had a life-shortening illness made me stop and listen to them, treasuring each moment in a way we tend not to do, not even with our own children. And because I gave a more intense quality of attention, I became aware of all kinds of responses I never normally noticed, a deep throaty chuckle, a twinkle of merriment in the eyes, a moment of pensive wistfulness. That innate wisdom which is the birthright of every child, but we so often fail to encourage, because we're too busy, too distracted, or simply too deaf, is finely honed when every second counts.

'I want to die in the hospice, and not at home,' one little boy whispered to me one day, 'My mum is on her own. I want someone to be there to look after her when it happens because she will be so sad.'

They had no fear of death, only concern for those they left behind. What I received from them far outweighed anything I could ever give them. In their short lives they made their mark on the world more than one grouchy old codger Peter buried who beat his wife, berated the kids, kicked the cat and lived to ninety. In the fullness of time, since all our lives are over faster than a blink, whether we have seven years or seventy is an irrelevance in the light of eternity.

Bringing up children may well be a privilege, but it is also the hardest task any of us have to face. And are they grateful for all our hard work, sweat and enforced labour?

'Mum, why are there no decent yogurts in the fridge?'

'Mum, why isn't my football shirt washed?'

'Do we have to have sausages for tea again today?'

I used to look at my two sometimes, particularly in bed in the morning, when I have just been assaulted by a volley of complaints, and wonder whether they were a good idea after all. Don't they realize that their father and I decided to have them, that without us they would never have existed? What makes them think they are entitled to a mind of their own? How did that beautiful little bundle nestling in our arms become this six-foot, answering-back, opinionated adolescent? Who, I had to admit, was really just as enjoyable. Probably more so, once he stopped bringing back most of his food.

I was no expert at child rearing, my children will tell you that, but when it came to passing on spiritual values we tried a Hebraic approach, based on the notion that children learn with their hearts, as well as their heads. Judaism, tactile, sensual and accessible, revolving around the home, enables a child to experience, not simply hear about, the spiritual life. The church has tended to offer a more intellectual diet. Just as the Jews offer their children an indefinable feel for a 'Jewish way of life', a conducive environment in which faith can grow, we experimented with creating more of an emotional feel for a 'Christian way of life', in the hope that whatever their choices, wherever they went, they would always associate their Christian upbringing with the happiest, not the most boring, moments of their lives.

And that meant putting real meaning and vibrancy back into the Christian festivals. I have friends who stalwartly refuse to celebrate Christmas because of its pagan connections. And what they miss! I suspect Jesus may have been born at Tabernacles in a late September heatwave. But that shouldn't spoil Christmas. Luke, with his meticulous attention to medical details, records that it's while he's doing his priestly duty in the Temple that Zechariah is told by an angel that his wife, Elizabeth, will have a child. Zechariah is of the division of Abijah, which has the eighth lot of duty each year – around August time. Luke also tells us that it's in the sixth month of Elizabeth's pregnancy that Mary goes to see her cousin to tell her about her own pregnancy. That would take us to January. So it's the conception that takes place at the end of December. And after all, there was nothing miraculous about Jesus' birth. Fortunately, it was perfectly straightforward – no suggestion of forceps, ventouse, episiotomy or stitches. It was the conception that made him unique.

Putting the festivals into their context can restore that missing confidence in their value, especially at a time of unbridled consumer exploitation. Having been denied a decent Christmas for so many years, I sweat blood and tears to make it memorable and special for my children – without the presents. I felt it was imperative to make the occasion more in a child's mind than the opportunity for rampant, unleashed greed and self-acquisition.

One Christmas, when Peter was a student at theological college and money was scarce, I had found, in a jumble sale, a bag full of second-hand Dinky toys, the perfect stocking-fillers for four-year-old Joel. We cleaned each car, tractor and bus carefully and lovingly, wrapped them in coloured tissue paper and placed the stocking-full at the foot of his bed in the house we were sharing with another family with four children.

At six o'clock on Christmas morning everyone was awakened by loud whoops and screams of delight from Joel, who tore from room to room like a miniature tornado, throwing the parcels from his stocking onto the beds of the other children, shouting, 'He's been, he's been. Father Christmas has been. And he's brought me a present, and one for you, and one for you, and one for you.' Then he sat down on our bedroom floor to open the one present he had kept for himself, and gasped with delight and gratitude when he pulled off the paper and saw the very battered, second-hand lorry.

Peter and I went round the bedrooms taking back his other presents, brought them to him and put them beside him on the floor. He looked at us in bewilderment.

'All for me?' he asked slowly, and there was no pleasure on his face.

With a sinking heart I knew that we had destroyed something very precious. The little lorry had lost its lustre. One cream cake is a treat. Several eaten in a single sitting make you feel sick. Materialism had sated our son and spoiled his pleasure. Jews give their children one present a night for the eight nights of *Hanukkah*, the Festival of Lights. Now I saw the sense of it. Joel had discovered instinctively that it was more satisfying to give than to receive. We had turned those values upside down.

'I hate that story about me,' my frighteningly materialistic adult son says now. 'I was so stupid.'

'On the contrary,' I say to him, 'You were right. It's we who were stupid.'

The early Jewish Christians made a definite association between the Feast of the Dedication of the Temple, or Winter Festival, *Hanukkah*, and the coming of the Messiah. *Hanukkah* celebrates, not the dedication of Solomon's original Temple, but an event which took place a great while later, in the time of Nehemiah's second Temple. In 164 BC Antiochus IV, King of Syria, pillaged Jerusalem and polluted the Temple. He showed his utter contempt for the God of the Jews by sacrificing a pig to the god Zeus on its sacred altar.

Three years later, in true Hollywood fashion, onto the scene swept guerilla leader Judas the Maccabean, who succeeded in driving the Syrians out of Jerusalem itself. Before the people could give thanks for their deliverance, the Temple had to be cleansed. A single phial of holy oil was found hidden behind a stone in a wall, barely enough to keep the holy flame flickering for a day, but miracle of miracles, it lasted eight days, just long enough for the priests to consecrate a new altar. The Temple was finally rededicated with huge rejoicing – on the 25th December. Strange, isn't it, that it's the very day Christians celebrate the coming of the Temple incarnate, the Light of the World?

There is a danger that Christmas is so familiar and so busy that it's passed in a zombified haze, any spirit of anticipation long-since drowned in a surfeit of shopping, cooking, carol-singing, cards, and family quarrels. Wonder and awe have been preempted by too many nativity plays and too much hype. Each organization, every school has had its own, individual Christmas event, each the exact replica of the other. We succumb to Christmas-fatigue and one of the greatest festivals in the church's year seems more like an endurance test than a cause for delight and thankfulness.

One Christmas Day Peter came up with an ingenious way of creating a quiet atmosphere for the service – no small feat when half the congregation are still opening their stockings and the other half are worrying about the food in the oven. He gave the volunteer on the sound desk a CD of a well-known cathedral choir singing carols. 'Play that as people come in,' he said, 'It will put them in the right frame of mind.'

The problem arose later, as the congregation went forward to take Communion, and our hardy volunteer, following the dubious principle that what worked well once would work even better a second time, decided to put the CD on again. Out from the speakers blasted, 'We all want figgy pudding, we all want figgy pudding, so bring some in here'. I walked out to take Communion accompanied by, 'And we won't go till we've had some, we won't go, no we won't go...'

Small wonder that the child kneeling at the altar next to me whispered to her mother who had just taken the bread, 'What are they giving us today?'

I was in a state of near hysteria, but as I looked around, no one else appeared to have noticed, or if they had, didn't even manage a smile or a titter.

Because Peter's parents lived abroad, and having both had years of spending Christmas without family, we were determined it should be a high spot in our calendar, a genuine festival of thanksgiving for the greatest gift of all – God with us. Christmas Eve – after a 5pm candlelit carol service at church and as the city centre shops were closing – became a time for friends, games, charades, playing musical instruments, and a huge casserole bubbling on the stove. We read the children Christmas stories like 'Baboushka', 'The Little Cobbler', or 'The Spider's Web', stories handed down through the generations with their own lessons about love and generosity.

On Christmas Day the two families who have shared Christmas with us since we were at college in Nottingham arrive for the week. Lunch is dips and cheeses, pâtés and nibbles, as we never know what time the vicar might bring himself home and I don't want to be like my mother on the Sabbath, willing my father to finish work. In the afternoon we walk, talk, listen to music, read, then, in the evening, when the atmosphere has mellowed into a contented, tongue-loosening tranquillity, we eat our Christmas dinner. I've tried to experiment with the decorations, filling my dining-room with crimson, gold and emerald, sweet-smelling spices, poinsettias, candles and fairy lights, in an attempt to convey something of the kingly majesty of the special guest, who shares his birthday (or conception) with us.

Christmas is not my mother's favourite time of year. 'I can't touch a mince pie without thinking of Martin's death. You remember how many we made that afternoon he died?

And then of course there's your father's birthday, God rest his soul.' All the sad memories keep flooding back, and she asks whether it isn't the same for me. It isn't. Not that I don't remember. It's simply that they have been supplanted by the joy of the occasion, and by a rather special, once-and-for-all, Christmas gift from above which still fills me with thankfulness to this day. My husband is and will always be one of the best Christmas presents I ever received. I often ruminate on the fact as I wash his bristles from the washbasin and help his dirty socks on their journey from the bedroom floor to the laundry basket, or, in those wakeful hours of the night when I wish I could switch off the roaring motorbike on the other side of the bed. 'You, my darling,' I whisper in his ear, 'are the ultimate in God's generosity to me.' Marriage was for me a very special healing of the memories of so many miserable Christmases past, so that I could begin to celebrate the festival with the exuberance it deserved.

Peter and I usually try to find a bit of time alone together on the 23rd, to recapture some of the romance of our special day, so many years ago now. And it's a principle I try to apply to Christmas itself. I find a secluded spot, or use time when I'm doing one of those brain-deadening chores, like peeling chestnuts, to ease my spirit into its proper gear, to try to recapture the real sparkle of the special season.

There are so many other, minor Christian festivals that need an injection of imagination and innovation – Mothering Sunday, All Saints Day, Shrove Tuesday, Ash Wednesday and Ascension. All are passed over, barely acknowledged, compared to *Purim*, the Feast of Esther. Far be it from me to suggest that churches should set aside a day to remember that great Jewish heroine, Esther, but the principle of interactive storytelling, fancy dress and carnival could well enliven some of our more neglected, potentially fun days. All Saints Day lends itself to dressing up as famous saints, dead or alive, past or contemporary. Mothering Sunday is a time for the stories of great mothers – of children, projects or nations. We have so little appreciation of our heritage, but it is imperative that we create situations where we can recount the history of our people, the legends of its saints – Augustine, Ambrose, Teresa of Avila, Wycliffe, Thomas More, Thomas Cranmer or Josephine Butler, to name but a few – primarily around our dining room tables. As we share our food in extended families and home groups we need to tell our children the great tales of bravery, sacrifice and redemption that have given us the freedoms we enjoy and the principles we value. They must be handed down from one generation to the next – lest we forget.

I'm not really a 'peep out from behind my curtains' person, but when I do (it must be my age), I sometimes see the young man who lives in the first floor flat across the road, probably a student, sitting in front of the TV, shovelling food down his gullet. Sometimes, he's so entranced with what's on the box in front of him that he can't find his mouth with his fork. If all the nutrients he needed could have been supplied by a pill, or even osmosis, I think he would have welcomed it. For him, a meal is not an occasion. He has no concept of fellowship, family, communion or community. What an unprecedented opportunity to model it in small groups and extended families, before our society disintegrates altogether.

Our children are our greatest treasure, our future. We know it in our heads, but we are still, generally, a child-hating nation. We would rather they were neither heard, nor seen having fun. They can so easily feel as if they are only in the church under sufferance. We hush and shush them, tell them to sit still, stop fidgeting and end up making them self-conscious, not God-conscious. Then, we heave a sigh of relief when they are banished to their own classes. Small wonder they feel in the way, not following the way. And if we don't lose the battle for their hearts when they're children, we lose it when they reach their early teens, and realize that only adults are allowed any real respect or responsibility, or have access to the decision-making processes.

Whatever his degree of maturity, a Jewish boy becomes a man at thirteen, when he has his *Bar Mitzvah* (the Blessing of a Son). In the old days, like my brother, the poor youngster used to be the ungrateful recipient of endless suitcases, sports hold-alls and alarm clocks, but now a '*Bar Mitzvah* list', like a wedding list, eradicates the problem of multiple, unwanted gifts, making the whole occasion less of an ordeal. After all, it is stressful enough having to stand up in the synagogue on the Sabbath before your entire family and the local community, sing several portions of the Torah solo, your parents willing you to get it note perfect, without having to appear grateful afterwards for a set of disappointing presents.

The whole day focuses on the child. There are now equivalent ceremonies for daughters, as this is a recognized important ritual transition from puberty to adulthood. From that moment they are deemed old enough to know the difference between right and wrong. They must exercise self-control, and are accountable for their own behaviour. They are full members of the community, and can be called upon to read the Torah, lead prayers, or be elected to the synagogue council. Sadly, the church has no real equivalent.

Some denominations have confirmation. Some have adult baptism. Neither is a 'coming-of-age' ceremony in the truest sense, for they do not necessarily confer eligibility for what are regarded as strictly adult roles. I have heard few teenage confirmation or baptism candidates preaching or leading prayers at their own service, let alone being invited to join the church council.

Today fewer children than ever walk through the church's door – though most have to at some point in their lives. If all we do is berate or banish them, if all we offer them is a cerebral exercise, and if – probably the greatest sin of all – we bore them half to death, we can hardly be surprised when they want none of us, and none of our God.

One of the saddest aspects of humanity is that we forget so quickly what it feels like to be a child. I remember hearing one child say on the way back from Communion, 'You get patted on the head, then ignored.' Patronized is how they feel.

After years of having *kiddush* in our home on Friday nights, Joel bitterly resented being unable to take Communion in church.

'Why can't I have bread and wine?' he asked. He was only six at the time.

'You're not old enough to appreciate what it means,' I explained. That was the official argument.

'Are you?' he asked.

A reply escaped me. Thankfully, many churches are waking up to the anomaly of it and are now allowing children to take Communion, a sign that we take their spirituality seriously.

The problem for adults is that we have tended to see children as those we do something to, not as those who have something to give to us. We fail to respect their integrity and wisdom. I discovered at St Tees the dividends of expecting to receive from them. At Tabernacles one year, two eight-year-olds came out spontaneously, took the jugs from Peter and me, and started pouring water, gently and sensitively, over people's hands. At Pentecost, uninvited, half a dozen ten-year-olds joined the prayer tunnel, their arms held up over the adults until they ached, and prayed for the congregation as they passed through. It is incredibly moving to watch.

Children are only obstreperous if they are bored. In fact, where church is concerned, they're excellent quality assurance monitors. If they are caught up in the whole experience, if their senses are fully engaged and they have a part to play, they are far less likely to end up somersaulting over the pews. In both Coventry and Lancaster, the children would often sit together in an open space at the front of the church. In Coventry one or two of them would climb onto Peter's lap, or play at his feet, while he was leading the service. Some liked to be in his arms at the very end, so that they could help him with the final blessing. Others, when the mood took them, and it often did, would get up, spontaneously, and dance. Visitors always commented on it. Nothing is as potentially liberating as the example of children at home in their church.

There are times, inevitably, when they simply haven't the concentration power, but the alternatives should be equally creative and imaginative. In Coventry my children had their own home group, and developed a spiritual wisdom I barely imagined possible for children of their age. Their faith was boundless, often making me feel totally inadequate.

It is her grandchildren that have enabled my mother to mellow and engage in conversations that once were unthinkable for a Jewish Mama.

'Let me tell you about Jesus,' Joel said to her one day, sitting in the back of the car. He was about six at the time.

'No, Joel, tell me about Moses,' she said, from the front.

'Moses,' he said, after a short time of reflection, 'was Jesus' daddy.'

But in recent years it is they who have been there for her when she has been ill, they who have brought her encouragement and hope, saying the familiar psalms and prayers with her.

These days, she even enjoys the shock benefits of being mother-in-law to a vicar – especially at the bridge club.

'What does your son-in-law do for a living?'

'Oy, don't ask,' she replies, shaking her head, the sufferings of Job negligible compared to hers. 'You'll never guess.'

And then, with minimal prompting, they force it out of her, because she can't resist seeing the expression on their faces.

She sometimes says loudly, 'I won't be around for a game next week. I'm staying with my daughter – at the manse!'

'Never mind,' says a sympathetic partner, patting her hand, 'my son-in-law has an alcohol problem. We all have our crosses to bear.'

When we moved to Lancaster, Abby, then aged ten, chose to come with me to the adult evening service. When she had had enough, she used to slip out and sit chatting with her friends in an upstairs lounge, or, if they weren't there, with any grown-up who would listen. Watching her appear and disappear, like the Cheshire cat in Alice in Wonderland, reminded me of how I used to dip in and out of services at the synagogue when I was a child. In for a song or two, out for long prayers, in for a dramatic moment, out for the sermon, running up and down from my father to my grandmother and great-aunts in the gallery. Three hours was a long time. No one ever told us to sit still. In fact, many of the adults, looking for light relief themselves, would stop us for a chat as we rushed past. Yet how many children in church are ignored when it comes to sharing the Peace?

In my childhood no religious ritual excluded children – not even the Day of Atonement. From the age of twelve I was expected to fast for a full twenty-four hours. It made me feel grown-up. So did reflecting on my failures. Whenever I had pestered them with my endless questions about the existence of life after death, my Hebrew teachers had explained the system of *mitzvot* I needed to perform – the good deeds which would balance out my debits, hopefully swinging the scales in my favour. I knew what I was like inside, and wasn't so sure that I wouldn't spend eternity emptying the bedpans of the world's greatest villains.

Some years ago, my brother, feeling that his childhood instruction in the faith was woefully scant, decided to take part in a teaching programme set up by the ultra orthodox Jews of Gateshead, seriously concerned for their more worldly, law-breaking brethren on the other side of the River Tyne.

'What sort of things are they teaching you?' I asked him with interest.

'I'm learning about *mitzvot*, good deeds,' he said, 'so that I can be a better Jew.'

I said that since my good deeds were somewhat erratic, I thought it was an altogether happier arrangement to receive the free forgiveness Christ had organized on the cross. Belief versus behave, but belief was simpler, surely?

'What a cop out,' he replied. 'Trust Christians to want the soft option. Keeping the Law requires effort.'

'And so you're now keeping it?' I asked him. 'Pardon me, but I can't say I've noticed a radical change.'

'Ah,' he said, thoughtfully, 'Ah, well. Not exactly. But my teacher says that it's a *mitzvah* just to know what I should do...'

'Even if you don't do it?'

He nodded a little sheepishly, and I could almost here the cerebral cogs registering, 'Really must try harder in future.'

'Now that,' I said to him, 'sounds to me like the ultimate cop-out.'

It's a wonderfully liberating, purging experience to have a grand, communal, public confession like the Day of Atonement, every year. Our spirits need both solemnity and laughter, reverence and euphoria, times of fasting and times of feasting. We in the West no longer live simply with the weight of our own failures. The media has ensured that we are sated every day with the injustices of the world. Poverty, abuse, exploitation, rape, pillage and plunder assault our minds almost before we have had the time to digest our first cup of coffee in the morning. My husband is a real saint. He not only brings me coffee in bed, he then reheats it in the microwave when the Sleeping Beauty who shares his bed has failed to respond to his first efforts to awaken her. And by the time he has made two trips to the kitchen the radio has alerted him to all the worst news of the day. In fact, we have a 'no discuss' and 'no moan' policy operating until after breakfast, or the chances are that I wouldn't get up at all.

What do we do with our outrage, our anger, our profound sense of indignation, sadness and helplessness at the sort of world in which we live, and will, one day, bequeath to our children? What do we do with our own personal and national collusion in creating it? I can of course absolve myself from all responsibility, or find someone to blame, or even sue! But passing the buck and litigation cannot heal a wounded spirit or a guilty conscience.

Acknowledging our failures is so much more powerful when we do it communally. For without some ritualized expression of them, what do we do with the disappointment of not living up to our standards at work or at home, our profound disappointment with government and leaders, our tendency towards hate, discrimination and racism, our abuses of nations trapped in the cages of our materialism? Most churches have a weekly 'Confession' of some kind. But the words roll over us before we can capture and absorb them.

There is a Christian tradition of penitence – largely in the more Catholic wing of the church, but far from exclusively so – at Lent, and to a certain extent, at Advent. But while the Jews, in their Days of Awe between the New Year and the Day of Atonement, look for positive ways of putting wrong relationships right, Christians look for what they can give up, highlighting an essential difference between the two. Healing relationships benefits the community. Mortifying the body benefits the individual. There's nothing wrong with encouraging children to give up sweets for Lent, as long as it isn't a substitute for treating family and friends with consideration. Real fasting, said the prophet Isaiah, is about actively fighting injustice, caring for the poor, and behaving with integrity – all qualities that appeal to children.

Catherine Booth, wife of the founder of the Salvation Army, became a well-known speaker when women preachers were something of a joke. She also managed to find the time to have eight children, all of whom grew up to play a leading part in the life of the church. Here was no traditional, stay-at-home mother. A succession of nannies supervised the domestic front. But she passionately believed that children ought not be sheltered from the harsh realities of life. They needed to see immense poverty to appreciate how rich they were. They needed to see despair to understand what, by the grace of God, they had been saved from. Nor were they the church of tomorrow. They were the church here and now, from the moment they were born, when they could barely walk or talk. So she took them wherever she went, and they handed out food and clothing to the poor, helped clean up filthy accommodation, washed brand new babies, laid out the dead, played their musical instruments, sang, prayed, and preached. She practised the Jewish idea of encouraging her children to learn by doing, sharing her work so that they knew, from experience, what being a disciple meant. And when they grew up it was perfectly natural to go on doing what they had always done.

Children respond positively to a rhythm of life. In a Jewish home Sabbath lasts from sundown to sundown. Holy days may move, but always occur roughly at the same time of the year, heralding the arrival of autumn, or the imminence of spring. There are times for feasting and times for fasting, a time to light candles and a time for darkness, a time for singing and a time for silence, a time for kissing and a time for having a good cry. For grandma and grandpa life goes on just as it did when they were the grandchildren around the family table – same food and festivals, same stories, same jokes, except that time has moved on and another loved one is missing, another child old enough to join in the family arguments and answer back. The very familiarity of this way of life is its charm.

When he was at university, our Joel carried on the Sabbath eve tradition in his own room in college, using beer when he had no wine, lemonade when he had no beer, and biscuits when he had no bread. It became an important community ritual for many of his fellow students, with some faith or none – a gateway to the weekend, a herald of rest, a reminder of home.

Chapter 17

The Years Roll By

I am in what may well be the winter of my life – though I am loathe to admit it, and have no idea how I got here so fast. These days, it's with a sudden shock that I recognize the face looking back at me in shop or car windows. It is almost a caricature of the one I knew. The lines are more deeply set, the bags under the eyes more pronounced, the jaw sagging, and the nose more prominent. And as for the body – bits have gone south, click, twang, ache, or are missing altogether. Had I known what obstacles awaited me in my gynaecological pilgrimage I would have asked the consultant to install a zip when Abby was born. Buying a bra is almost an engineering feat now that gravity has taken over. Being fitted in any lingerie department is such a convoluted process that it would be quicker for the fitter to bring me her choice and let me have plastic surgery to fit. Despite having half a dozen pairs of reading glasses, I can never remember where I put any of them, or their cases for that matter, and can't see to find them. And even though I promised myself it would never happen, I have to sit down to put on my leggings lest I fall over.

I've never been particularly fond of winter. I suppose there is a beauty in it – the ice-bespeckled garden on a freezing morning, the glistening pavements in the evening after the rain clears, the stark tree branches outlined black against a purplish sky – but there's a loss to it too. In the dank and dreary mornings, and the dim, dark evenings, I lament the long, lazy, golden days of summer – a distant memory now. No more shorts and sandals, t-shirts and sun cream. Out with the thermals and tights, the woollies and coats – less freeing, if more forgiving, for a woman of my riper years. So much death and decay without the comforting signs of life to come. And winter for me heralds yet another birthday, another year passed into the annals of history. It's a challenge now to be grateful for every new year, to see it as another year of opportunity, not a farewell to those long-engulfed in the passage of time.

The children used to bake me a cake. Like cardinals choosing a new pope they would closet themselves in the kitchen concocting a grand surprise. All was well until my husband joined them, throwing the weight of his opinion into the melting pot. Then the sound of raised voices would reverberate around the house, reaching me in my attic haven, whence I had retired to write. I wasn't allowed to emerge until the long-awaited smoke signal told me the whole process had come to a satisfactory conclusion. Now they are grown and gone and the birthday cakes are for their little ones, not the aged folk. Just as well – it would only stick more firmly in the gullet as the years go by.

All those years when I longed for time 'just for me', to eat what I wanted, to go out where I wanted, to bathe in peace when I wanted, to write all night if I wanted. Perhaps I always knew that when it came, I would yearn to have the demands, the frustrations, the sacrifices of family life all over again. But no matter how much I tried to hold on to the joys of every developmental stage, through babyhood, childhood, adolescence and teens, the years still slipped through my fingers like sand through an egg-timer.

'But why do you not like winter so much when it happens every year and you can't stop it?' Joel wants to know, waxing lyrical about the delightful, distinctive features of the season – brisk walks on cold, crisp days when pale grey clouds glow pink around the edges and the ground crunches beneath your feet, then coming home to a bowl of something hot around the fire. He's so right – but doesn't yet realize how much more some of us can see and do in daylight.

It isn't easy to welcome the slow fading of the body, even though faith says that it is moving us ever closer to the ultimate triumph over human decay. British society venerates youth and has little regard for maturity and experience. But why submit to ageist pressure? A friend of mine, kicking seventy and a mere youth, recently went out for a walk, slipped and sprained her ankle jumping over a stream. The general consensus was that she deserved it. 'At your age,' people said to her, 'you should know better than to go leaping over streams.'

God preserve us from becoming sedate, cautious, fearful or dull at any stage of however many years we may be given. Let me go on leaping over streams and stiles and all the obstacles in my path. And let me grow old like my mother-in-law, who read books and newspapers, commented on world affairs, beat her grandchildren at scrabble, listened and loved, was wise, interested, and interesting to the very end. And like my mother with her bridge, her parties, and her love life.

Jewish Mamas simply become more powerful as they age. Their sphere of potential influence widens. Not only their children, but now their children's children look up to them, listen to them, and hang on their words of wisdom. They still have more than their fair share of living, loving and manipulating to do. No one has told them that the fashion industry has finished with them, that good looks, glamour, and even sexual passion, are reserved for the young. At eighty-nine, my mother is more contented than she has ever been in a very supportive care home where she is as looked after as she had always hoped to be. Great-grandmother of eight, she has become the quintessential matriarch. For all three generations, her wish is our command. She still puts on the earrings and lipstick every morning, and after two husbands and a long term boyfriend, she can't resist a little flashing of the eyes at one or two of her male companions.

Let me be the Jewish Mama to the last, providing the younger generations with a positive, joyful, colourful and vibrant impression of later life, rather than a miserable picture of a disappointed, drab and dreary old age, waiting in God's anteroom for the final summons.

I don't seem to have my mother's flair for a quasi-totalitarian authority, but am still determined to go out, as Edith Joy Scovell's wonderful poem 'Death of Flowers' describes – not like an iris 'drawing in' in 'a clenched sadness', but like tulips, recklessly going from one perfect stage to another, 'Til wrecked, flamboyant, strayed beyond recall / Like flakes of fire they piecemeal fall'.

To enable me to flash to my end like a meteor, my favoured weapon is the bicycle – be it on the country roads of France, or in a dismal cellar in England. 'Why do I do it?' I ask myself, as my limbs creak and groan. My mother says at my age I should be taking care of myself. But if that means being able to squeeze a sagging bottom into tight jeans, then I am.

How to stave off dowdiness and stay contemporary without being mutton dressed as lamb, somewhat inappropriately for a minister's wife? A few years ago, on a city shopping trip, a friend and I saw a pair of swinging smock-like tunics in Miss Selfridge's window. They were burnt orange and frilly, and very like a certain little number we had worn in our teeny-bop days back in the sixties. Nostalgia rolled over us both in one enormous wave. Silently, reverently, like a pair of choirgirls in a cathedral, we took two down from the rack, sighing at the change in size since those halcyon, golden days, and tiptoed stealthily towards the fitting room.

Wonder of all wonders it was empty. No leggy sylphs to sneer at our wrinkles, protrusions and varicose veins, no just-out-of-school staff to stare at the older generation in wide-eyed disbelief or even panic, as if to say, 'What are you doing here? And must we all come to this?' I always want to shout back, 'Yes! I never thought I'd reach this age either. But since I have, give me a break. I've as much right to shop here as you.'

We put on the smocks and stood for some time in an orange glow, surveying ourselves in triplicate, studying the effect. Then we took hold of the hem between our first fingers and thumbs, twizzled and turned, and remembered the dances we danced and the songs we sang. And we laughed as the years fell away and we recalled what it was like to backcomb our hair into a monstrous beehive, whiten our lips, and blacken our eyelashes with solid mascara in a box, softened by our spit. For once we forgot the grind of wage-earning, our responsibilities as sensible, middle aged wives and mothers, and the weight of the years that stifle our spirits if we let them. Reverently, we took off the smocks, walked sedately out of the fitting-room and put them back on the rail where they belonged. Then we left the shop with a sigh and a giggle, feeling surprisingly refreshed and renewed by our magical trip in search of a long-forgotten part of our fun-loving selves. What a relief to discover that it was as alive and well as it had ever been behind the aging facades. And though it's a bit sad that it makes my day when a pharmacist asks why I'm entitled to free prescriptions, a train guard doubts that I have senior rail card, or a practice nurse asks why I'm eligible for a flu jab, it makes the point that age is, after all, just a number.

I've been fortunate compared with a man, with time off for child-rearing, and then, when the time came to return to a career, finding myself one of those eighties phenomena known as 'a woman returner' – she who brought the wealth of accumulated wisdom and managerial expertise gained through the nappy-bucket and supermarket trolley into the great British work-place. I started my career late, and promotion to senior management when I least expected it provided so many new challenges there wasn't time for a mid-life crisis. And after all, we more mature ladies are now being told by some media voices that, thanks to sex icons like Helen Mirren, the sixties are the new forties, and there is an attraction to having life's rich experience etched on our faces. But men, I read recently, reach an age when they're forced to face the fact they're never going to be the managing director of the company, or a world-professional footballer, or marry Raquel Welch. 'Look on the bright side,' I said to my husband, as he bemoaned his hair loss and ever-expanding waistline, 'You're managing director of the company, you never wanted to be a world-class sportsman, and you're married to a Raquel Welch lookalike.' For some reason, he didn't seem convinced.

After seventeen years in Lancaster, Peter began to contemplate possible moves, or an early retirement so that we could fulfil a long-cherished dream and try to find a property in France. He, raised in Geneva, and I, with my French degree, had both been drawn to the country since our marriage, but no neon arrows in the sky had ever pointed us towards the heathen across the Channel. 'If we're to move,' Peter said, 'I think I'll need a surprise invitation and soon, because we're getting a little beyond taking on a new church.' And so it was that the church administrator walked into his office one morning with a curious expression and said, 'I have an archdeacon from the Diocese of Europe on the phone for you.'

It was obviously archdeacon season, as the invitation to a popular coastal town in southern France was followed a few days later by yet another, this time asking us to consider St Mark's Gillingham. A major French seaside town with a three-bedroomed flat one hundred metres from the sea, or a depressed little town in north Kent with high unemployment since the docks closed? Well there was really no competition.

'We're moving,' we told the administrator and his wife before it was announced in the church, as they had been such loyal supporters and friends.

'Well, of course you are, to France,' he smiled knowingly.

'No,' we said, 'to Gillingham.'

The smile dissolved rapidly. But we had always said we would move back to a more deprived part of the inner city when the children left home, and this was our last chance to be true to our word. More than that, St Mark's had been the first Anglican church in the country to become charismatic, under the leadership of John Collins, who went on to drag Holy Trinity Brompton out of the doldrums, so it had an impressive past, even if the demographics mitigated against its present. It also had two churchwardens, infectious in their hope and vision for the future. And Gillingham was much nearer the Channel, even if retirement would have to wait five more years or so.

Those five years were five wonderful gift years, in a church so loving and appreciative that it broke our hearts to leave. Except by then, marvel of marvels and after so many years of waiting and wondering, we had managed to acquire a house in France, where we now live for around six months of the year.

I remember so vividly now how Peter's father would say of his Ibiza home, 'this is my launching pad to heaven'. And so it became one day. I understood then only too well why he would never want to leave such a paradise. Standing on one of the terraces overlooking the vast expanse of sparkling, marcasite-tipped waves, watching the mass of tiny white sails bob-bobbing merrily towards the horizon, inhaling the pure scent of the pines, listening to the gracious swish-swishing of their branches stirred by the occasional breeze, feeling its gentle caress on my naked skin, I used to wonder if I leapt over the railings down into the depths of the forest, might I, like some disembodied sylph, be allowed to wander and play in this magical fairyland forever? This really was the nearest thing to heaven I knew. But leave heaven in the hands of humankind and it soon loses its lustre.

My Great Aunt Rae – one of Grandfather Abe's three sisters, whose only son, the impersonator Eddie Arnold who appeared regularly throughout the sixties on ITV's *Sunday Night at the London Palladium* and who died of a brain tumour while still in his thirties – used to remind us oppressively at every joyous event, 'Nothing lasts forever'.

She was half right. Not in this life, it doesn't. We took all the family back to the Ibiza house, now owned by Peter's brother, for our fortieth wedding anniversary. It was far from the paradise it had once been. The island had been robbed of its calm by the criss-crossing of noisy dual carriageways, mass high-rise developments and heaving supermarkets, by the raucous sound of barking dogs, revving motor bikes, and loud music ricocheting from one rocky hillside to another by all the mindless blare of a humanity which cannot bear to confront itself in silence for fear of the emptiness it might find. This was certainly not heaven, for humans had blasted their way in and polluted gracious, tranquil creation with their effluence and debris, their booze and lust. We too had played our part in abusing it, washing in its ever-decreasing artesian wells, converting its balmy, sea-salt air into choking, black, hire car fumes. The sea, heaving with jellyfish, looked like semolina.

No, Ibiza wasn't heaven. And nor is retirement in our little French paradise, where I can pretend I am indeed ageing graciously as I bike into the village for the croissants and baguettes every day, walk for miles with friends across our unknown, unspoilt countryside, garden despite the aches and pains (before the day comes when I can't get back up off my knees again), lounge with a good book, bake to my heart's content for a continual stream of visitors, and thoroughly indulge my new role as Grandma to five. I have roots at last, but it worries me slightly. I only hope they don't hold me so fast to the here and now, that it will be a very much harder pull and tug to uproot me when the time comes to leave, as it must one day. Perhaps it's just as well we have recently acquired wind turbines at five hundred metres from our house, towering over our lovely peaceful view, filling the air with their constant drone, to remind us of Great Aunt Rae's warning that all we have here is subject to loss and decay and that the countryside isn't as unspoilt as we had hoped it would stay. One of God's 'severe mercies' – a hard-to-bear test designed only to benefit us and lessen the pain in the end.

Last year Peter suddenly developed strange symptoms – burning skin from the waist down, an inability to walk or use the loo. Fortunately, a far-sighted GP with the ability to diagnose recognized that this was a rare, but very serious post-viral illness that needed immediate treatment in hospital. There was a question mark over whether Peter would ever walk again, which would make managing our five acres something of an impossibility. In fact, he made a full recovery apart from some loss of sight in one eye. In the end I was surprised to discover that the loss I would have most lamented was not our home, but rather our many new and lovely friends. Nonetheless, it seems we must forever hold our beloved French home in an open hand.

Many, many times have I had cause to wonder how and why, with my background, I ended up where I am. 'The apple never falls far from the tree', the saying goes. It certainly hasn't been true in my case. But high risk as God's strategies often are, there is never a mistake, and as I look back I'm beginning to see that, all along, someone else has been wielding the pen, or working the word processor, and that I am a part of his story, and not the other way round. We are all chosen – tiny patches of gold or red or green or silver in a huge cosmic tapestry. It would be nice to have a glimpse of the full picture on the right side, and not just the messy knots on the wrong side, but that will come one day. I've learnt that it's not a case of what God wants with my little life, but what he wants for all eternity and all I need to know is how to play my tiny part in it. Let me do and be what I am meant to do and be. And it may not be what others have expected.

Peter's father always hoped that when he died Peter would pick up the baton and work to enhance Christian and Jewish relations in the Middle East. Our calling has been much closer to home, fed by a passion to see the church liberated from the historic Greek-Roman mindset that stifled its warmth, imagination and freedoms, a calling to restore a sense of the Hebraic roots that were integral to Jesus' outlook on life. And if we have succeeded, albeit a tiny bit, it is because we have been privileged and fortunate enough to have been involved in church communities that have affirmed, loved, supported and encouraged us, that have been willing to address cultural change, modernize and grow.

Now that all gainful employment has come to an end, we seem to be as busy as we ever were – only now we have the choice. Sometimes I'm tempted to look back and say, 'I'd loved to have been a doctor, or a policewoman, or run a tea-room. Shame it's too late.' My eleven-year-old nephew came home from school with a great quote from the American cartoonist Bil Keane, 'Yesterday's the past, tomorrow's the future, but today is a gift. That's why it's called the present.'

Many Jews criticize Christians for what they see as their unhealthy absorption with the next life. Why fasten on the future, says Jewish thinking, when life has so much to offer today? But they also concede that 'if you have your health you have everything'. And so often when trials come we think, 'If only I'd known how happy I was before.' Thankfully, the future has been graciously and wisely hidden from us. The great mystic Jean Pierre de Caussade said, 'The present moment is always full of infinite treasure. It contains far more than you can possibly grasp. Faith is the measure of its riches: what you find in the present moment is according to the measure of your faith. Love also is the measure: the more the heart loves, the more it rejoices in what God provides.'

It is essential to grasp hold of every precious moment, no matter how sensational or trivial, for life moves inexorably on, and the days and years of our existence and the world as it currently is speed forward, like the pages of a good book being flicked at an ever increasing rate to its ultimate denouement.

We shall not cease from exploration and the end of all our exploring will be to arrive where we started and to know the place for the first time.

T. S. Eliot

Some Favourite Traditional Recipes

Chicken Soup

Make at least one day before serving, because the flavour is better on the second day.

1 chicken, including giblets (or cheat by using giblets, feet, wings and 2 stock cubes)
3 pints of water
1 whole onion
2 carrots, peeled
3 celery stalks
1 whole leek
1 whole parsnip
Salt, pepper

Put the bird, salt and pepper into a large soup pan. Cover with the water and bring to the boil. Skim any froth with a spoon. Add all the remaining ingredients, skim again and simmer for at least three hours. Remove the bird and the vegetables and refrigerate the soup overnight. (The chicken can now be removed from the bone, eaten cold with salad, or served with a sauce. Discard the vegetables.) The next day remove any fat from the surface and re-heat the soup, adding a few fine egg noodles if desired. Strengthen the flavour with an extra stock cube if necessary.

Chopped Liver

Originally invented as a way of using up the giblets to make a cheap and tasty starter to the Sabbath meal.

Serves 6–8
> 200g (8oz) chicken livers
> 1 medium onion
> 3 hard-boiled eggs, finely chopped with a fork
> 50g (2oz) good quality margarine or chicken fat
> Salt, black pepper

Fry the onion in the fat until golden, then add the liver. Cook until tender, then pass the contents through a mincer or food processor. Turn the mixture into a bowl and stir in the finely chopped hard-boiled eggs, reserving some for decoration. Season to taste.

Sabbath

To ensure that the Sabbath is truly a day of rest, sufficient food must be prepared on Friday morning for the whole 24-hour Sabbath period – from sundown to sundown. This tasty one-pot casserole would go into the oven on a Friday afternoon and be served at lunch the next day!

Cholent

Serves 6

>2kg/2–3lb boneless brisket joint, or joint for pot roasting
>500g/1lb dried butter or lima beans or 250g/8oz pearl
>>barley, soaked overnight
>3 chopped onions
>6 potatoes, peeled and chopped
>2 tbsp oil or margarine
>1 tbsp plain flour
>Salt, pepper
>1 tsp each paprika, ginger and garlic
>1 bay leaf

Rub the joint with all the seasonings and flour, then brown in the oil and remove to a large casserole. Fry the onions gently until golden and add to the casserole, then cover with chopped potatoes and beans or barley. Add enough boiling water barely to cover, and seal with a tight-fitting lid. Bake very slowly (Gas No $^{1}/_{2}$, 120ºC) for several hours. Add a little extra water if necessary.

Chollah

The plaited Sabbath loaf is based on a 3000-year-old recipe from the Persian Empire. It is plaited so that it looks as if its arms are folded, and at rest. To make one large plaited loaf.

500g/1lb strong white flour
15g/¹/₂oz fresh yeast
2 eggs
2 tsp salt
3 tsp caster sugar
2 tbsp oil
200ml/8fl oz warm water

Heat the water until warm, not hot, place in a mixing bowl and add one third of the flour, the sugar and the yeast. Mix until smooth, cover with a tea towel, then leave about 20 minutes, until frothy. Add all the remaining ingredients, and knead by hand or in a mixing machine with a dough hook until smooth. Place the ball of dough in a greased polythene bag and leave in the fridge for between 12–24 hours.

Take the risen dough from the fridge and leave half an hour at room temperature, then divide it into three pieces and roll the pieces into long sausage shapes. Press all three strands firmly together at one end, then plait firmly, and place on a greased tray.

Leave the loaf to rise in a warm place for about half an hour, then brush it with egg yolk. Scatter with poppy seeds if desired, then place in the oven and bake for 15 minutes (Gas No 7, 220°C) then turn down the oven (Gas No 5, 190°C), for a further 30–45 minutes.

Hanukkah

Stuffed Cabbage Leaves (Holishkes)

An adaptation of stuffed vine leaves.

Serves 4

It is traditional to symbolize the richness of the festival of *Hanukkah* by eating stuffed foods, for example peppers or aubergines stuffed with a minced beef filling, or baked apples stuffed with cinnamon and raisins. All kinds of melons are served in the tabernacle too, and can be filled with chopped citrus fruits.

1 firm head of a large winter cabbage
The filling:

1 onion finely chopped

500g/1lb minced beef

100g/4oz long-grain rice

2 tbsp olive oil

1 pint beef stock (make with two stock cubes)

Salt, pepper

The sweet and sour sauce:

One large tin of chopped tomatoes

4 tbsp soft brown sugar

Juice of a large lemon

A few sprinkles of Worcestershire sauce

Chop off the tough stalk end of the cabbage, then blanch the whole head by boiling it for five minutes, then plunging it into cold water. Carefully peel off 12 large leaves.

Fry the onion in the olive oil until tender, then add the rice and cook for a further three minutes until opaque. Add the stock and cook until it is absorbed into the rice. (Add a little more water if the rice isn't fully cooked.) Then mix the rice with the raw meat and seasonings. Divide the filling into twelve, then spoon on a cabbage leaf, fold like a parcel, and place, in rows, in a casserole. Mix all the sauce ingredients together in a food processor and pour over the bundles. Cook for around 90 minutes at Gas No 2, 150°C, then uncover, turn the oven up slightly and brown.

Potato Latkes

It is traditional to eat food fried in oil at *Hanukkah*, such as doughnuts or fritters, as a reminder of the holy oil in the Temple which lasted eight days. We make our own doughnuts and serve them warm with ice cream. Just as good, and more savoury, are potato latkes, a kind of fritter, made originally with cream cheese to celebrate the famous cheese and wine party thrown by Judith in honour of the Greek general, Holofernes. Russian Jews first began to make them with potatoes. They're scrumptious served hot instead of chips. We once found our Joel, aged eighteen months, hiding behind an armchair, stuffing himself with three cold latkes in an empty cornflakes box he had retrieved from the rubbish bin.

Serves 4–6

    6 large potatoes

    2 beaten eggs

    4 tbsp S.R. flour (or plain four with 1 tsp baking powder)

    1 tsp salt

    Pinch of white pepper

Grate the potatoes finely and place in a colander. Pour boiling water from the kettle over them and leave to drain for ten minutes. (The potato may go a little brown.) Place the grated potato in a bowl and add the other ingredients. Heat 1 cm depth of oil in a heavy frying pan and when hot put in tablespoonfuls of the mixture, flattening each latke with the back of the spoon. Cook at a steady temperature for about 5 minutes on each side until a rich brown colour. Then drain on kitchen paper and serve at once.

New Year

It is traditional to eat sweet food at New Year as a way of wishing one another a sweet and happy year to come.

Tsimmes

An easy sweet, cheap and cheerful stew, also served at Passover, often with a selection of cold meats, or chicken pieces.

Serves 6
    1kg carrots, chopped into small squares
    700g potatoes, peeled and chopped into slightly larger
                    cubes
    A beef brisket joint (about 1kg in weight)
    4 tbsp golden (corn) syrup
    1 tbsp cornflour
    2 tsp salt
    Pepper

Trim the fat off the meat and cut into cubes. Put the meat and carrots, with 2 tablespoons of the syrup, salt and pepper into a large casserole. Barely cover with hot water, bring to the boil and simmer, or slow cook for two hours. Allow to chill and when cold skim off any fat. Dissolve the cornflour in a little of the cold stock, then add to the stock in the casserole. Arrange the potatoes on top, and add a little water until they are just submerged. Pour over the remaining syrup and a little more salt. Cover and cook very slowly for as long as possible – at least another four hours! Your stew should be a deep golden colour. If not, uncover and cook for a further half hour.

Optional: Add your favourite dumplings to the pot, about an hour before serving.

Lekach (Honey Cake)

This traditional, sweet New Year cake needs to mature for a week, wrapped in foil, in an airtight tin.

200g/8oz plain flour

150g/6oz caster sugar

250g/10oz clear honey

100ml/4fl oz cooking oil

2 eggs

1 tsp bicarbonate of soda dissolved in 100ml/4 fl oz of orange juice or strong coffee, depending on preferred flavour

1 tsp mixed spice

1 tsp cinnamon

$\frac{1}{2}$ tsp salt

Optional: 50g/2oz chopped nuts

Mix together all the dry ingredients, then add the honey, oil and eggs and beat well until smooth. Dissolve the bicarbonate of soda in the orange juice or coffee, and add to the mixture. Pour into a parchment-lined loaf tin and bake for about 1 hour 15 minutes, until firm. This cake improves with keeping, and can be iced with coffee or orange icing just prior to serving.

Passover

Coconut Haystacks

Egg is the only raising agent allowed during Passover, so with no flour available, Jewish Mamas have to be creative with cake and biscuit making, and these are a great favourite. Passover is a wonderful time for anyone with a wheat intolerance!

  2 eggs
  100g (4oz) caster sugar
  200g (8oz) dessicated coconut

Beat the eggs with the sugar until thick and creamy, then stir in the coconut. Put spoonfuls of the mixture onto a greased baking tray and make into pyramids with a wet fork. Bake on gas No 4/180°C for around 10 minutes until golden. Leave to cool.

Shavuot/Pentecost

A Pentecost meal may consist of all your favourite, fur-lining, artery-warming dairy goodies. Or you can be boringly good and substitute the cream with low-fat alternatives, as suggested here.

Dips (Serve with crudités, or a selection of potato crisps)
    1lb (500g) low fat cream cheese
    $^1/_2$lb (250g) low fat fromage frais or 5fl oz yogurt
    Salt, pepper

Mix together until smooth, then add one of either ground garlic, or chopped chives, or drained, crushed pineapple, or a little curry powder, or a little chilli powder.

Cheese Blintzes

The glory of the Jewish kitchen, a blintze is a paper-thin pancake, fried on one side only, filled, and fried again on its unbrowned side. Use your traditional pancake batter. Fry the pancake until the top side is dry, remove from the pan and place bottom or brown-side up on a board. Cover with a tablespoonful of the filling (250gms/$^1/_2$lb cream or curd or blended cottage cheese, mixed with 1 tbsp sugar, and a little cinnamon if desired – for 4 people), spread thinly, then turn in the sides and roll up like a sausage. The blintzes can be refrigerated overnight now if desired.

Heat 2 tablespoons of butter and 2 tablespoons of oil in a frying pan, and when the butter ceases to foam, add in the pancake. Cook until golden, then cook the other side. Serve hot with soured cream.

Gran's Traditional Baked Cheesecake

The Jews probably began making cheesecakes in the second century BC, when the Greeks occupied Palestine and brought the recipe with them. It has been a traditional Pentecost speciality since before the time of Christ, for the whiteness of the cheese was supposed to symbolize the purity of the Law.

For the pastry crust:
>   200g (4oz) S.R. flour (or plain with 1 tsp baking powder)
>   65g (2oz) butter or good quality margarine
>   65g (2oz) icing (confectioner's) sugar
>   1 egg yolk
>   Several drops of vanilla extract

Mix all the ingredients together and press into a loose-bottomed cake tin about 8 or 9 ins (20 or 23 cms) in diameter.

For the filling:
>   200g (¹/₂lb) curd, or sieved cottage, cheese
>   10fl oz soured cream
>   2 tbsp cornflour
>   Grated rind and juice of a lemon
>   50g (2oz) caster sugar
>   2 tsp currants, plumped for 5 minutes in boiling water,
>   then drained.
>   4 eggs separated, and the extra white, left from the pastry

Whisk the eggs and sugar until thick, then stir in all the remaining ingredients. Spoon into the cake tin, then bake at Gas No 3, 170°C for 60 minutes until golden and firm. The top may crack a little. Serve cold, sprinkled with icing sugar, with pouring cream.